T0340384

# The Economic Thought of Friedrich List

As the world grapples with increased globalization and technological change, Friedrich List's work appears more relevant than ever before. His theory of "productive powers" and his argument for protecting infant industries give us a valuable way of looking at innovation systems, winners and losers in international trade, and the current shift towards economic and political nationalism.

Comprising fifteen specially commissioned chapters from a range of international scholars, this book explores many aspects of List's economic thought, including industrial development, political economy, the economics of education, infrastructure and catching-up processes in Asian economies.

This volume will be illuminating reading for advanced students and researchers in the history of economic thought, economic history, economic policy and international trade.

**Harald Hagemann** is Professor Emeritus of Economic Theory at the University of Hohenheim, Germany.

**Stephan Seiter** is Professor of Economics and Quantitative Methods at Reutlingen University, Germany.

**Eugen Wendler** has retired from his role as Professor of International Marketing, Consumer Behaviour and Communication at Reutlingen University, Germany.

# Routledge Studies in the History of Economics

For more information about this series, please visit www.routledge.com/series/SE0341

# The Economic Thought of Friedrich List

Edited by Harald Hagemann,
Stephan Seiter and Eugen Wendler

LONDON AND NEW YORK

First published 2019
by Routledge
2 Park Square, Milton Park, Abingdon, Oxon OX14 4RN

and by Routledge
52 Vanderbilt Avenue, New York, NY 10017

First issued in paperback 2020

*Routledge is an imprint of the Taylor & Francis Group, an informa business*

*British Library Cataloguing-in-Publication Data*
A catalogue record for this book is available from the British Library

*Library of Congress Cataloging-in-Publication Data*
A catalog record has been requested for this book

ISBN 13: 978-0-367-66449-7 (pbk)
ISBN 13: 978-0-8153-7245-5 (hbk)

Typeset in Sabon
by Integra Software Services Pvt. Ltd.

# Contents

# Contributors

**Vladimir Avtonomov** is Academic Supervisor at the Faculty of Economic Sciences at the National Research University, Russia.

**Elizaveta Burina** is based at the National Research University Higher School of Economics, Russia.

**José Luís Cardoso** is Research Professor at the Institute of Social Sciences, University of Lisbon, Portugal.

**Mechthild Coustillac** is based at the Université de Toulouse-Jean Jaurès, France.

**Alexander Gerybadze** is based at the Center for International Management and Innovation at the University of Hohenheim, Stuttgart, Germany.

**Harald Hagemann** is Professor Emeritus of Economic Theory at the University of Hohenheim, Stuttgart, Germany.

**Tetsushi Harada** is Professor of Political Economy of Cultures and Societies at the School of Economics, Kwansei Gakuin University, Japan.

**Mei Junjie** is Research Professor at the Shanghai Academy of Social Sciences, PR China.

**Rainer Kattel** is Professor and Deputy Director at the Institute for Innovation and Public Purpose, University College London, United Kingdom.

**Mark Knell** is Research Professor at the Nordic Institute for Studies in Innovation, Research and Education (NIFU), Norway.

**Erik S. Reinert** is a Norwegian economist, specializing in development economics and economic history.

**Philipp Robinson Rössner** is Senior Lecturer in Early Modern History at the School of Arts, Languages and Cultures, University of Manchester, United Kingdom.

**Stephan Seiter** is Professor of Economics and Quantitative Methods at Reutlingen University, Germany.

**Dieter Senghaas** is Professor Emeritus at the University of Bremen, Germany.

**Stefano Spalletti** is based at the University of Macerata, Italy.

**Eugen Wendler** has retired from his role as Professor of International Marketing, Consumer Behaviour and Communication at Reutlingen University, Germany.

**Bernhard Wieland is** Professor Emeritus of Transport Economics at the Institute of Transport and Economics, Technische Universität Dresden, Germany.

# Introduction

*Harald Hagemann, Stephan Seiter and Eugen Wendler*

Friedrich List (born 1789 in Reutlingen, Germany, died 1846 in Kufstein, Austria) is, besides Karl Marx (1818–1883), one of the most important economists of the 19th century in Germany.

Born as the son of a white tanner Friedrich was supposed to follow his father. However, his parents realized very quickly that he should become an official. He was educated as a secretary and held the position of a *Regierungsrat* in the Ministry of Internal Affairs. In 1817 List proposed to the King of Wuerttemberg, Wilhelm I, that he found a faculty for state economy at the University of Tübingen. After gaining the approval of the king, List became a professor despite not having an academic background. About two years later, List had to resign after he wrote a critical petition favouring free trade and the integration of Germany for the *Bundesversammlung* in Frankfurt. In 1820 List was elected as member of the parliament of Württemberg. Here, he also challenged the public administration and thereby the king. He had to give up his seat in the parliament and was sentenced to ten months in prison. List left his home country to avoid the prison sentence. Nevertheless, after his return to Württemberg he was sent immediately to prison. After promising to emigrate to the USA, he was set free. In 1825 List and his family came to the United States, where List worked for the newspaper *Readinger Adler* published in German. He also founded one of the first railway companies in the United States. After becoming a US citizen, List was sent to Germany as a consul. There he fought for the construction of a German railway system. Since List was still not very popular because of his background as a former prisoner, he left Germany for Paris where he started his preliminary work on his main contribution, *The National System of Political Economy*. After several episodes of physical and mental illness he committed suicide on 30 November 1846.

Probably most modern economists know List for his idea of educational tariffs that protect infant industries from international competition and help them to become competitive before their country opens the domestic market for foreign rivals. Furthermore, List is still popular because of his contribution to establishing a railway system in the USA and Germany. However, a closer look at his work reveals that his ideas about the economic system could enrich the current theoretical and political debate on international trade and integration as well as economic growth. Especially, two major trends suggest re-reading Friedrich List's contributions:

1. Globalization
2. Technological change driven by digitalization

At the beginning of the 1990s, the failure of Soviet-type socialism was seen as the starting point of an accelerating European and global integration by focusing on free markets. Politicians relied on the findings of mainstream economics and assumed that globalization would push economic development and growth in all parts of the world, thereby reducing poverty and increasing the well-being of people. However, the financial crisis of 2007/08 and the subsequent slump of the world economy gave evidence that real markets are far away from the optimistic idea of perfectly competitive markets leading to an optimal allocation of resources. Additionally, the financial problems led to a severe economic and political crisis in the European Monetary Union and the European Union. The ongoing divergence of different members such as Greece and Germany with regard to economic growth and unemployment revealed the shortcomings of the Eurosystem. The development of productivity and labour costs as well as different sectoral structures of the European economies resulted in current account surpluses on the one side (for example in Germany) and increasing international debt on the other side (for example Greece, Spain and so on). The current frictions in the European Monetary Union show the implications of different levels of economic development for economic growth under a free trade and a single currency regime.

Besides these internal problems, the European Union is also challenged by external developments. After a long period of neglecting the economic and social disruptions in many African countries and the Near East, the European Union has had to cope with a steady inflow of refugees both due to wars such as in Syria and hopeless economic perspectives, for instance in many African states. Populism and nationalism have become more and more popular in many European countries. The British decision of 2016 to leave the European Union is probably the most obvious outcome of these movements.

From a global perspective, the election of Donald Trump in the USA and the popularity of Vladimir Putin support this impression. Slogans like "My country first, yours second!" seem to be accepted by a growing number of people. After almost seven decades of integration and internationalization, a renaissance of protectionism is taking place. Whereas ideas, such as free international trade, became dominant in the Western world after World War II, they are no longer favoured when globalization endangers jobs.

The second trend is technology. The "Internet of Things" and the digitalization of production and consumption imply a fourth industrial revolution. Like all industrial revolutions before, the current technological change offers the opportunity to substitute traditional jobs for machinery. While computers and robots represent labour-saving technology in the field of blue-collar jobs, Big Data and Artificial Intelligence open the opportunity to reduce the quantity of brainworkers. For example, robo-advisors and medical expert systems are already in use.

Consequently, academic and political debates focus on topics like technological unemployment, polarization of labour markets and an increasing inequality of income and wealth. The vision of an economy that is almost independent of the input of labour or, in the words of simplified endogenous growth theory, an economy with an AK production function, stimulates the demand for an unconditional basic income making individuals independent from being employed.

Especially the negative implications for the labour market require an economic policy that helps to generate employment growth. It is an open question whether mainstream economics offers sufficient insights and results that could be applied to a successful growth and employment strategy.

Usually, standard economic theory explains the reasons for and the implications of globalization by referring to traditional trade theory based on the approaches of Ricardo, Heckscher-Ohlin and Samuelson-Stolper and new trade theory mainly developed, for example, by Krugman and Helpman. Traditional (Solow) and endogenous growth theory (Romer, Aghion & Howitt, Grossman & Helpman) are the basic approaches to explain the implications of long-run economic growth driven by innovation and technological change.

While traditional theories assume perfect markets and constant returns to scale, more recent approaches in growth and trade theory refer to market imperfections and increasing returns to scale as drivers of growth and trade policy. However, all these theories lack factors that – following Abramovitz (1986) – could be summarized as the social capabilities of a country. This also reminds one of Kaldor's (1957, 1961) idea of technical dynamism.

When reflecting on Friedrich List's ideas on integration and trade, it becomes clear that his work contains a broad variety of insights into the benefits, but also challenges, of globalization and technological progress. For example, in his book *Das nationale System der politischen Ökonomie* (The National System of Political Economy) Friedrich List discusses the key drivers of growth and development. By challenging Adam Smith's concept of the division of labour, List refers for example to the importance of institutional settings, educational policy and the rule of law. The so-called *"produktiven Kräfte"* (productive forces) are seen as necessary determinants of growth.

List showed that free trade is not always beneficial to every trading partner. Less-developed economies need to improve their productive forces to be competitive when entering international markets. However, List was aware of the advantages of free trade and wrote a petition for the German *Bundesversammlung* (federal assembly) in Frankfurt in which he criticized the great number of tariffs and trade barriers between the different German states and showed their negative impact on economic development and growth. Therefore, he asked for an economic union that should be followed by a political union. In the end, List asserted, not only should the German states unify, but also Europe should form an economic and political union to secure peace and prosperity. List was of the opinion that such an integration process also needs a network technology, not only for the transport of goods, but for the mobility of people and their ideas. In his day, the railway offered this option. List also published a set of papers on topics such as communication technology (telegraph), aviation, agriculture and machinery, and was very optimistic with regard to their positive effects on the well-being of people.

Besides this optimism, List was aware of the potential negative implications of a free market economy. The exploitation of workers, in particular the bad working conditions for women and child labour, was one of the developments he referred to. List saw the reason for this process in the lack of laws to protect the workers from being exploited by capitalists. In contrast to Marx, who saw the solution in a complete change of the social and economic system, List expected that a civilised society would agree on rules on a national and international level to prohibit, for example, child labour. Furthermore, he expected that not only the capitalists, but also the workers would benefit from technological progress and international trade in the long run. Machines would free the workers from hard physical work and wages would allow the worker a decent living.

Friedrich List could therefore be seen as a visionary of the concept of a social market economy. In particular, his leitmotiv "Through Wealth to Freedom" is linked to the later vision of one of the godfathers of social market economy and first minister for economic affairs in post war Germany, Ludwig Erhard: "*Wohlstand für alle*" (Prosperity for Everybody). For List and Erhard, private property is the pre-condition for economic and political independence and freedom, but private property should be used in a socially responsible way.

Consequently, re-reading Friedrich List's concepts of economic development and integration gives inspiring impulses for designing an international trading system that could improve the well-being of all participants even when the assumptions of neoclassical theory do not hold. Thus, the analysis of List's oeuvre does not only make sense from a scientific, but also from a political perspective. This is the intention of the collection of papers in the volume: *The Economic Thought of Friedrich List*. The contributions give broad, but also detailed insights into the work of Friedrich List from different perspectives. In doing this, not only List's own ideas and their relevance for current economic developments are analysed, but also the intellectual influences that formed List's thinking.

A thorough analysis of the origin of List's ideas, such as the theory of productive forces, certainly has to refer to the German cameralist tradition. At the time of List at the University of Tübingen, Friedrich Carl Fulda, who also became the founding Dean of the new Faculty of State Sciences established in 1817, was the first holder of the chair in Cameralistic Sciences from 1798 to 1837 which had been created in the philosophical faculty in 1796 (see Tribe 1988, pp. 177–180).

The collection starts with a contribution by *Eugen Wendler*, who founded the Friedrich List Institute at the University of the Applied Sciences Reutlingen, List's hometown, in 1992. Wendler discusses what, according to List, were "The seven deadly sins in economics". Wendler's chapter is followed by the lecture *Dieter Senghaas*, a political scientist, gave in the townhall of Reutlingen as part of List's native city's celebrations to mark Friedrich List's 225th birthday on 8 October 2014. In his contribution "Friedrich List: looking back to the future", Senghaas, himself well known for his work on development politics, discusses the contemporary and current importance of List's ideas for development processes.

In his essay on "Growth and integration: why we should re-read Friedrich List", *Stephan Seiter* analyses the importance of List's views on growth and integration from the perspective of modern approaches to economic growth and international economics. *José Luís Cardoso* re-examines List's interpretation of the 1703 Methuen Treaty between England and Portugal from a Portuguese perspective. Cardoso also qualifies List's critique of Adam Smith's interpretation who considered that the treaty had been harmful to English interests. Furthermore, in his essay "Friedrich List and national political economy", Cardoso reflects on the importance of List's approach for the economic fate of tropical countries, in particular economic development in Latin America.

In the first half of the 19th century, the English economy was the leading one in the world and List primarily thought of the USA, France and Germany as the most important economies to catch up. List lived in the United States from 1825 until 1830 and he repeatedly stayed in France. In the US, List was strongly influenced by Alexander Hamilton and Daniel Raymond, and it was here that the ideas of productive forces and protective tariffs took shape. List's *Outlines of American Political Economy* (1827) was his first major work in economics, a precursor of his later *National System of Political Economy* (1840). *Harald Hagemann* discusses these in his essay "German, American and French influences on List's ideas of economic development". In the subsequent chapter "Friedrich List and France" *Mechthild Coustillac* discusses List's involvement with France, which represented a lifelong challenge for him. No doubt, List's treatises on economics reveal significant French influences. In particular his *Natural System of Political Economy* (1837) clearly bears the stamp of the rationalist and utopian humanism inherited from the French Enlightenment, showing obvious signs of economic liberalism. However, List's relationship with France was strained. Whereas on the one side he felt a kindred spirit to Montesquieu and to those French economists who seemed close to his own theory of productive forces and national approach to economics, and Lafayette was a great supporter of him also in the US, on the other side he disliked those economic liberals such as Jean-Baptiste Say whom he considered close to Adam Smith. As is well known, List time and again emphasized the main distinction between his "national" ideas and the "cosmopolitan" view of Adam Smith and his followers.

List's theory of productive forces is mainly directed at industrial development, in which manufacturing is strictly associated with technical progress, improved infrastructure, capabilities and so on. The production of wealth is the outcome of the interaction between mental productive powers and natural as well as material capital. Whereas in classical growth economics physical capital, or earlier land in agriculture-based economics, had played a major role, modern economics had increasingly emphasized the importance of human capital. The next chapters deal with the main factors of production. *Stefano Spalletti* discusses Friedrich List's "Economics of education". In the subsequent chapter *Philipp Robinson Rössner* discusses how "Manufacturing matters", tracing the discussion from Giovanni Botero to Friedrich List. List's enthusiasm for the construction of railways and the importance of a railway network is well known. In his chapter on "Two early views on railway regulation in Germany" *Bernhard Wieland* draws attention to a rather neglected contribution to the field of railway regulation by the banker and railway pioneer David Hansemann (1790–1864) and compares his views with the contemporary work of List.

*Erik S. Reinert* and *Rainer Kattel* in their chapter on "Friedrich List and the non-financial origins of the European crisis" argue that the ongoing current crisis in the EU can be properly understood only in the context of the dramatic de-industrialization and structural change that took place in Central and Eastern European countries after 1989. With the Eastern enlargement of the EU the previous strategy of symmetrical integration, and thereby Listian principles, were given up, thereby contributing significantly to the current problems.

As already pointed out, List originally focused on the follow-up economies of the USA, France and Germany, which were lagging behind the leading British economy. This made his ideas attractive for all countries later engaging into a catching-up process as, for example, Italy, Japan after the Meiji Revolution, Latin American countries, South Korea since the

1960s or currently China. *Tetsushi Harada*'s chapter deals with List's reception and interpretation in Japan, in particular the work of Noburu Kobayashi, a leading historian of economic thought.

When Chris Freeman (1995) engaged into the modern debate on the "National System of Innovation", following the pioneering work of Lundvall (1992), arguing that national and regional systems of innovation remain an essential domain of economic analysis whose importance derives from the networks of relationships that are necessary for any firm to innovate, he made explicit and intensive reference to the work of List. *Mark Knell*, in his chapter on "Friedrich List and the American system of innovation" takes up the key ideas of the modern discussion and applies them to the contemporary US economy where List's ideas were shaped.

*Vladimir Avtonomov* and *Elizaveta Burina* in their contribution on "List and Russia" point out that in the reception of List's ideas in Russia one has to distinguish various phases in which different aspects of his work came to the fore, although there has never been a stronger demand for his political liberalism.

*Mei Junjie* links List's work with "China's quest for development" and highlights the importance of List's work for the current and future development of the Chinese economy. He is supported by *Alexander Gerybadze* who in the last chapter on "Industrial development strategies in Asia" discusses the "Influence of Friedrich List on industrial evolution in Japan, South Korea and China". Having countries such as Indonesia, the Philippines or Vietnam in mind, Gerybadze concludes with the statement that "Friedrich List should receive much greater attention, particular in up and coming countries in Asia and in other parts of the world".

Huge infrastructure projects, such as the railway system in the case of List, help to promote growth and integration. Although List noted the deficiencies of the cosmopolitan liberal system, he clearly has to be saved from the accusation that he was a forerunner of authoritarian regimes. There can be no doubt that it was his conviction that, ultimately, liberalism should prevail.

## Further contributions on Friedrich List's life and work:

Wendler, E.: *Friedrich List (1789–1846) – ein Ökonom mit Weitblick und sozialer Verantwortung,* Wiesbaden 2013.

Wendler, E.: *Friedrich List (1789–1846) – A Visionary Economist with Social Responsibility,* Heidelberg 2015.

Wendler, E.: *Friedrich List im Zeitalter der Globalisierung – Eine Wiederentdeckung,* Wiesbaden 2014

Wendler, E.: *Friedrich List`s Exile in the United States – New Findings,* Heidelberg 2016

Wendler, E.: *Friedrich List – Die Politik der Zukunft,* Wiesbaden 2016

Wendler, E.: *Friedrich List: Politisches Mosaik*, Wiesbaden 2017.
Wendler, E.: *Friedrich List: Vordenker der Sozialen Marktwirtschaft – Im Spannungsfeld zwischen Vision und geheimdienstlicher Observierung*, Wiesbaden 2018.

## References

Abramovitz, M. (1986), "Catching Up, Forging Ahead, and Falling Behind", *Journal of Economic History*, 46(2): 385–406.

Erhard, L. (1957), *Wohlstand für Alle*. Düsseldorf: Econ.

Freeman, C. (1995), "The 'National System of Innovation' in Historical Perspective", *Cambridge Journal of Economics*, 19(1): 5–24.

Kaldor, N. (1957), "A Model of Economic Growth", *Economic Journal*, 67: 591–624.

Kaldor, N. (1961), "Capital Accumulation and Economic Growth", in F.A. Lutz and D.C. Hague (eds.), *The Theory of Capital*, London and New York: Macmillan, pp. 177–222.

Lundvall, B.-Å (ed.), (1992), *National Systems of Innovation: Towards a Theory of Innovation and Interactive Learning*. London: Pinter Publishes.

Tribe, K. (1988), *Governing Economy. The Reformation of German Economic Discourse 1750–1840*. Cambridge: Cambridge University Press.

# 1 Friedrich List's seven deadly economic sins

*Eugen Wendler*

## 1.1. The seven Christian deadly sins

Medieval Christian philosophy goes under the name of Scholasticism. One renowned Scholastic in the early Middle Ages was Petrus Lombardus (died 1164), whose work centred on the Gospel of St John and the sins that led to the loss of a state of grace, so bringing about the spiritual death of man. Whoever committed these deadly sins would without fail enter purgatory and then hell. Only those who did penance, regretted their sins, paid for an indulgence and sought to lead a life fitting to God could hope for the grace of salvation, and so enter heaven. Lombardus named seven deadly sins that he treated as unforgivable moral deviances. They were: pride, avarice, lust, wrath, gluttony, envy and sloth, or selfishness.

The most well-known medieval book was Sebastien Brant's *Ship of Fools*, first published in Basel in 1496. It was the most successful German language work right up to the end of the eighteenth century and the publication of Goethe's *Sorrows of Werther*, woodcuts illustrating the popular presentation of these and other sins. Brandt skewered the vices and stupidities of his age, representing these as fools who were wittily and candidly caricatured in 113 chapters, or shiploads (see Fig. 1.1).

I would like here to pick up this thread and name seven deadly economic sins that are contained in Friedrich List's writings. They are:

1. Bribery or corruption
2. Hard physical labour, especially excessively hard work for women and children
3. Exploitation of workers by factory owners and other employers
4. Trade in slaves and in drugs
5. Avarice and speculation
6. The destruction of nature and the environment
7. Nationalist hubris and national selfishness

Each of these deadly sins can, taken in turn, lead to severe physical and psychic damage, permanently harming human dignity; we only need to

*Figure 1.1* Allegory of the seven Christian deadly sins (owned by Eugen Wendler)

think of slave labour and drug abuse. Taken together, they involve losses great and small for humanity as a whole, and those directly affected by them: in the form of occupational diseases, an increased risk of accidents, premature incapacity, and financial losses that can lead to total ruin. Depending on their varying form and intensity, they can endanger the social fabric of a country, leading to social tensions, revolt and unrest, and in the extreme case even to revolution and the overthrow of governments, something that we can see today in Egypt, Thailand, Venezuela, the Ukraine or Brazil, to take only the most obvious examples.

## 1.2. Bribery, or corruption

In his "Thoughts on the Wuerttemberg Government", which is his earliest known text, List criticised the corruption of public officials. The salaries of civil servants should on the one hand reflect the knowledge required for their work, and on the other the level of expenses appropriate to their social standing. A judge should certainly earn more than a court official, and a director of administration more than a secretary. The salary should be set so as to enable a servant of the state to devote himself exclusively and eagerly to his office and its associated duties. If civil servants were poorly paid then their work would be like forced labour, or that of a bondsman, kept like cattle and driven to the most burdensome physical labour.

Corruption is the necessary consequence of inadequate remuneration, and nothing is more damaging to the state than the possibility of its officials being bribed. This not only leads to injustice and the concealment of misdeeds, but the subjects whom these officials are supposed to serve are met with chicanery and evasion. The harm that the people's welfare suffers from corruption is immense, and always greater than the savings that the state might hope to make from paying its officials badly.

If for instance a greedy official accepts gifts when selling fruit, or carrying out building works or other tasks, then the damage to the state or territorial authority is always far greater than the value of the gift. If by contrast the salaries of officials are set at a proper level, any such bribery should be met with court proceedings and, if necessary, summary dismissal.

It is not unusual for rewards that officials are given out of gratitude for services rendered to be tolerated. But these too should be proscribed. In the first place, this involves the official in being bribed prospectively: if in April two parties appear before an official, the first having given him a nice New Year's gift, the other not, the official will unerringly favour the former. Secondly, this would reinforce any inclination to corruption, and induce the official to make difficulties for those who had not presented him with gifts.

The scope of the cancer of corruption still abroad in the world, and its extent in individual countries, can be seen in the tables and graphs of the international corruption index. Here Scandinavian countries always come out best, and as a rule African developing states the worst.

Not long ago the EU Parliament published the CRIM Report, which addressed organised crime, money laundering and corruption in Europe. The spread of corruption was described as a "serious threat", with more than a million cases recorded annually in the public sector alone. The total cost of all this was estimated by the European Commission at 120bn. euros per year. The Report called for more determined cross-border co-operation on the part of EU member states. In addition to this, European tax havens had to be dismantled; and the buying of votes should everywhere be an offence. It can be said that in general, the more strongly corruption has a hold on a state apparatus, the more barren the corresponding economy and so the lesser the economic welfare of the country. The corruption index is a measure of the degree to which a country adheres to the rule of law, and this is in turn an important condition for business initiatives and investment, both domestic and overseas.

We all know that right across the world, in African developing countries, the Near and Middle East, Eastern Europe, in Central and Latin America, corruption is the daily bread of economic life, and is often the crucial instrument for market entry and market development.

And so today this does not simply involve the bribing of individual officials. Other professional groups, politicians, employees, physicians and professors, are by no means immune to such "special payments", as can be seen in the press almost on a daily basis. The most recent example is the financial scandal associated with the new Hamburg concert hall, or the new Berlin airport. Hamburg's *Elbphilharmonie* had cost more than ten times its original estimate because, as the investigating commission established, the politicians responsible knowingly falsified the figures in order to deceive the public. Much the same goes for the new Berlin airport, and applies to other large-scale infrastructure projects, such as Stuttgart 21.

In Turkey, short before the revolution, 350 police officers and numerous state attorneys and administrators who were investigating state corruption are serving jail terms. All over the world, in Greece, Egypt, Thailand, Brazil, the Ukraine, Tunisia, India and Spain people take to the streets to protest about corruption in the state apparatus and judiciary, and more generally about the abuse of human rights and about social injustice.

Just before the opening of the Sochi Winter Olympics it was revealed that between 25 and 35 bn. Euros had been swallowed up by corruption.

An anonymous contributor to the newspaper that List edited, *Volksfreund aus Schwaben*, wrote that officials guilty of misdeeds were seldom held to account, because they were protected by other officials. Officials could "in many instances break laws without having to worry". If it should come to a formal accusation, as a rule nothing ever came of it since the officials involved were friendly with the accused. Most lawbreaking never got this far, but was swept under the carpet. The only remedy for such circumstances was an independent judiciary. In Germany today the judiciary does have a high degree of independence, while the Federal Republic is well-regarded throughout the world. Nonetheless, infringements can happen, as became clear in the proceedings for corruption initiated against the former federal president, Christian Wulff.

## 1.3. Hard physical labour, especially excessively hard labour for women and children

In his second 1837 Parisian prize essay, "Le monde marche", List expressed his conviction that in the medium and long term new means of transport and communication would make a contribution to general welfare, improving the living standards not only of the well-off, but also of the broader mass of the population, and improving in particular the lot of the worker. The benefits of this technological revolution would be felt by 95% of the population, he wrote. In general, he anticipated that industrialisation would liberate workers from excessively hard and demanding physical labour, and replace slave labour with machinery.

This was especially the case for the work of women and children. While child labour would not be entirely forbidden, working hours should at least be limited by a maximum and rewarded with a decent wage that not only could provide for terms of sickness, but also make possible future training and education.

In the early phases of the Industrial Revolution factories favoured the employment of women and children, he wrote. This could be explained purely by the cost factor, since factory owners were not hindered from exploiting the desperate situation of the weak. In 1838 only 23% of those employed in British cotton mills were adult males. The remainder were women, children over the age of 9, and juveniles. Work in the noisy and dusty mills was broken only by very brief breaks, and sometimes extended to 17 hours per day.

For this reason, List harboured the hope that the civilised world might come to an international agreement on the prohibition of child labour, so that factory owners might be deprived of the argument that they had to employ children because of cheap foreign competition. He thought that an agreement of this kind would be one of the greatest triumphs that mankind had celebrated.

As we know, child labour is still prevalent in many countries of the Third World. According to the most recent UN statistics, the number of children involved in hard physical labour in developing countries, and who are also abused as child soldiers, is over 180 million.

## 1.4. The exploitation of workers by factory owners and other employers

Industrialisation should not make people slaves to technology, but instead contribute to making a life worth living. Working conditions in which employees are treated like slaves and exploited as such were judged by List to involve the "dishonouring", "exploitation" or "brutalisation" of the worker.

The most recent example is Qatar, where in the process of building the stadium for football World Cup within two years more than 300 workers have been killed because of the catastrophic working conditions. Just as in Sochi, in Qatar thousands of workers work in inhuman conditions, for which they are not even paid the promised pittance and then are sent home without compensation.

Even as a youth working in his parents' tannery List demanded that tiring and evil-smelling work in the tannery should be replaced with machines, a viewpoint that was treated with scorn by family and neighbours as a "brainstorm" deserving little attention.

List included as part of humane working conditions adequate pay for workers. The level of a wage should match the physical and intellectual demands of the job. The greater the physical exertion, and the more skill and talent required to learn and practice a job, the more arduous, unpleasant, dangerous and unhealthy the work was, the higher should be the remuneration. This principle is today often criminally ignored with the employment of children in Asiatic countries, the illegal employment of migrants from Eastern Europe, in firms employing people on zero hours contracts and in large enterprises across the world.

In this connection we can include, besides the issue of low pay, the pollution of the environment and the infringement of labour laws, the regular exceeding of paid working hours, the sequestration of passports and other papers held by illegal workers, together with migrant and subcontracted labour. In this context we might also assume that List would probably have supported the introduction of a general minimum wage of the kind enforced in most member states of the EU.

List thought that the wage must be high enough not only to permit the worker and his family to satisfy life's basic essentials, but also to secure him against the effects of illness and the frailties of old age, permitting a degree of independence to develop, as we would say today, a certain degree of quality of life.

Especially audacious seems his proposal to involve workers in large limited companies to become shareholders, providing them in this way with security and welfare. This idea was only put into practice one hundred years later when, after the Second World War, the first German limited companies began issuing employee shares to their workers.

## 1.5. The slave and drug trades

Serfdom and slavery were viewed by List as social evils that should be condemned and abolished throughout the world. For him, the abolition of serfdom and the prohibition of the slave trade were important elements of his theory of productive forces. They were in conflict with the respect for human rights which he emphatically demanded. He regarded slavery and the slave trade as barbaric visitations on indigenous populations. He did not limit this to the sale of adults lacking all rights, but also extended it to fathers who sired and reared offspring so that they might later be sold as goods, and that employers forced particular kinds of work on their employees, as now happens in brothels around the world. If one considers Thailand for example, a culture that has flourished for thousands of years has been irrevocably damaged within one or two generations, and quite probably destroyed for ever.

Slave labour even remains widespread in the member states of the European Union. It is estimated that there are around 880,000 slave workers, 270,000 of whom are sexually exploited. These numbers come from an International Labour Organisation report of 2012, where slave labour is defined as any form of labour that is performed under duress.

List also criticised the terrible impact of Portuguese, Spanish, French and America slave dealers in Africa, often linked to the indoctrination of indigenous peoples by Christian missionaries, especially those of the Catholic church.

He was likewise critical of the drug trade. It was a matter of indifference for the merchant whether his products were useful to his customers, or harmed them. He paid no heed to morality, nor to the welfare and power of a nation. He imported and distributed poisons as if they were patent medicines; he brought down entire nations with opium and gin. It was for him a matter of complete indifference if his goods made beggars out of people; having an eye only for the prevailing market situation, he was only interested in the bottom line, whether he was making a profit. In wartime he supplied the enemy with weapons and munitions, as is currently complained about Heckler and Koch in regard to Mexico. The merchant would even, if it were possible, sell off to foreign buyers the meadows and fields upon which he walked, and when he had sold the very last piece he would board a ship and set sail for a foreign country himself.

From this characterisation we might deduce that List probably regarded the idea of the merchant prince as a euphemistic fiction, and that he had no faith in the ethical behaviour of merchants as a whole. Nonetheless, this could be enforced by appropriate laws, and through freedom of the press, to which he ascribed great importance as an element of human rights; while he also believed in the pressure of competitors and clients in the market.

List considered strong liquor, opium and weapons as instruments abused for the purpose of "spiritual and physical murder". Here he was critical of British free trade policy, through which China was flooded with opium in the first half of the nineteenth century in order to demoralise the population. In the long run this would not end well. For "one fine day the Chinese experiment in free trade would explode like an overheated steam boiler and bring about a terrible ending".[1]

In 1773 the British East India Company had begun to establish a monopoly over the Chinese opium trade, exporting ever greater quantities of the drug from Bengal to the Middle Kingdom, until there were eventually two revolts.

Britain had in the same way flooded China with cheap textiles as a way of promoting domestic manufacturers. Both initiatives led to rebellion and unrest that have gone down in Chinese history as the Opium Wars, and which were accurately prophesied by List.

List thought that excessive consumption of liquor not only harmed the morals and customs of a people, but should also be seen as one of the great causes of poverty. For this reason he wrote a memorandum in 1846 proposing to the Prussian King Friedrich Wilhelm IV that the most important agricultural product of his country, the potato, be used not only as fodder and a raw material for schnapps, but as a source of starch, which could have a whole range of profitable industrial uses. In this way a Prussia that was otherwise short of raw materials could find a valuable export good. However, this perfectly sensible suggestion came to nothing in the Prussian bureaucracy.

Besides the drug trade, there are major problems worldwide today with internet crime, the illegal trade in human organs, and in wild animals. It is estimated that cybercrime costs the EU 290bn. euros annually, while the illegal trade in body parts and wild animals is put at 18 to 26 bn. euros.

## 1.6. Avarice and the addiction to speculation

The striving for material welfare can, according to List, be more or less strongly impaired by an "addiction to speculation" or, as we would say today, by avarice. In his last text, "Die Ackerverfassung, die Zwergwirtschaft und die Auswanderung" ("The agrarian order, dwarf holdings and emigration") of 1843, he talks for instance about the "demons of covetousness and overweening ambition", and about the "tinder of discord". This was especially applicable to speculative capital investment in shares (meaning railway shares) and other "bonds". Often these promised "one illusion through another illusion". Small investors "who can take no chances and should take no chances" were led by the promise of high returns into taking risks, as a result of which they could later lose their entire capital. One need here only mention the recent Prokon scandal and its so-called profit-participation certificates. Quite plainly this illusory procedure was invented only so that capitalists and bankers could get their hands on high premiums.

List leaves no doubt that speculation in stocks and shares was at the time only in its beginnings, and that an addiction to speculation would in the future become much more extensive. He warned that any share crisis would then not be confined to one particular European state, but would spread to others. He even feared that one day a "European Roulette Bank" would emerge in which "people could gamble away their property and welfare". Perhaps List had in mind what became the European Central Bank, or a European "bad banks".

But List was in no respect an opponent of limited companies; he supported them very strongly. He also pointed out that all economic life was based upon speculation. He did, however, distinguish between well-founded speculation, and an exaggerated addiction to speculation. To check the latter he favoured a degree of restriction in share dealing, suggesting for example that directors of a limited company could not trade in their own shares. Quite possibly he would make the same argument today, that empty trades by hedge funds should be prohibited internationally, and he probably would have had nothing in principle against the introduction of a capital transaction tax.

## 1.7. The destruction of nature and the environment

List's respect for nature and the environment was nowhere more clearly expressed than in a poem he wrote for the *Readinger Adler* of 11th May 1830[2] during his American exile. The third verse is particularly significant, where he writes:

The balsamic breath of ether's blossom,
Lilting singers of gentle melodies,
Soft vibrations on my way to worship;
And where brooks quietly wind through plains
And in the shade of woodland,
There alone is the spirit at home,
Where I silently honour there the great master.

List was convinced that nature held a surplus of everything that man needed to live, and that all that nature formed for itself was to the good. For this it had irrefutable reasons and there was nothing left for science to do other than discover these reasons and integrate them into its own system. For any infringement of natural laws would have fatal consequences for men and women.

It was only during the 1970s that the imperative of protecting the natural world and our environment began to be slowly established, 130 years after List's death. An ecological consciousness developed for which List had already made the following visionary statement[3]:

I am convinced that soon enough the British economic system [Adam Smith's doctrine of free trade] will soon meet a reckoning, from which the nations of the earth will be able to draw the important conclusion that violations of nature, whether by individuals or entire nations, will have the most terrible consequences.

(quoted in Wendler, 2014 p. 98 f.)

We need here only to refer to the catastrophic effects of forest clearances on naturally-caused forest fires in Brazil, Indonesia, Australia and in the Mediterranean countries, the overfishing of oceans, the warming of the atmosphere or the environmental pollution of water, land and air. According to the most recent estimates of the United Nations, around seven million people die annually from the effects of polluted air.

Regarding the recycling of used objects, List had already in 1834 made the following simple demand in his *Eisenbahnjournal* of 1834:

No-one should throw anything away or dispose of it without first thinking whether something that one believes to be of no use might not be used in some other way.

(quoted in Wendler, 2014 p. 99)

This clearly advocates recycling!

## 1.8. Nationalist hubris and national selfishness

Regarding patriotism, List distinguished between "national pride" and "exceptionalism". He understood the former to consist of an "inner affection and love" of citizens for the country. This also involved a preparedness, if necessary, "to shed one's last drop of blood" to defend one's liberty against foreign enemies. Exceptionalism was on the other hand a great hindrance to a country's political culture, since this was quite different from national pride. National pride was based upon the physical and spiritual advantages of a nation, while recognising the advantages of others. In contrast, exceptionalism was characterised by a blind prejudice regarding the strength of one's own nation, and was immune to all self-doubt. Not national pride, but a belief in one's own country's exceptionalism prevented the inhabitants of a country admitting the abuses and short-comings under which its people suffered.

Reason and the material interests of nations foster and demand peaceful co-operation and an international division of labour. Nations should disavow constant and increasing jealousy and ill will; it was plain that war between peoples was as foolish as it was cruel, and it was recognised that perpetual peace and free trade among all peoples would elevate all to the highest stage of wealth and power. All of this was, however, still very much undeveloped.

Even if List's vision in relation to warfare remained purely wishful, given the sorrows of the past 170 years one can but unreservedly agree with his utopian vision, and express the hope that the international arms trade and military budgets do not increase without limit, that men and women will finally come to their senses and abjure war.

In regard to the "union of the European continent" List was of the opinion that "Nothing is more inimical than the jealous and envious politics that European nations pursue and fight over, seeking to push their neighbours back into the status of nomads without a home",[4] pushing their development backwards as far as possible. For this reason he advocated the peaceful and voluntary economic and political unification of those European states that found themselves at approximately the same level of development.

In a poem entitled "John Bull's Advice to the Germans" of 1844.[5] List criticised on the one hand the selfish and cunning British adherence to free trade, and on the other the German inclination to somnolence:

Sleep little child, go to sleep,
Don't bother with factories, my little one,
From you I will buy in any number
Brooms and rags and stone.
Sleep little child, sleep on,
Aberdeen and my Peel will bring you
Any amount of sugar from Brazil
To soothe your nurse.
And my child, if you do not wake,
And feel miserable and weak,
Don't cry so!
Be friendly, happy, and laugh!

And when you grow up,
Don't go to sea, I beg;
It is so horrible at sea,
So gusty and rough.
So never leave your land,
But plant with your own busy hands
Potatoes in your thin soil.
Just feed yourself simply and honestly from your own fair land.

"Aberdeen" here is a reference to George Hamilton Gordon, 4th Earl of Aberdeen, who was the British Foreign Minister from 1841 to 1846, with Robert Peel as Prime Minister during the same period. List openly accuses the British in these verses of using their economic and political predominance to harm German duchies that failed, however, to make any suitable response, being instead lost in their own small-state politics and incapable of consistently pursuing their own interests. A contemporary cartoon in the *Punch* (Figure 1.2) shows a well-fed John Bull offering alms to those poor countries with "infant industries".

## 1.9. Conclusion

What conclusions can we draw from these seven deadly economic sins?

The Christian churches and other religions have generally failed through the ages to move men and women to adopt a pious life and to moral actions; nor will ethical economists and academic study succeed in making economic subjects into moral beings. Homo oeconomicus is far removed from the fiction of a merchant prince, whatever that may mean.

The human character harbours a predatory instinct that is insatiable, seeking juicy rewards. This is what Thomas Hobbes (1588–1679) argued. In his *Elements of Law Natural and Politic* there is an essay "On Human Nature". Here Hobbes describes the human being as selfish, concerned with his or her own advantage and seeking to possess as much material wealth as possible. In a natural state, where there is no state to establish order, there prevails a "war of all against all". This finds its empirical result in the ruinous competition of unchecked laissez-faire capitalism.

An engraving from 1720 expresses a commercial saying: "This is certain, that your efforts are bent to gathering in from neighbours what is theirs and making it yours. Deception and malice rule on sea and land, and the greater part of mankind knows it!"

We need only think here of any recent financial scandal, of the locusts and sharks of the internet. Billions are gambled on a worldwide scale, losing all contact with reality. They fritter away their short life for the sake of financial speculation; gamblers, as sick as other addicts. In so doing they make themselves no richer, rather they harm themselves and their peers. Like Croesus, they are stifled by their own worship of money.

*Figure 1.2* John Bull and the poor developing countries (Punch, c. 1850)

The other characteristic that prevents men and women from committing this sin is an unconscious belief in eternal life, that one takes the material wealth accumulated during a lifetime to the next world, just like the Pharaohs believed. They fail to grasp that the winding sheet in which they will be wrapped has no pockets.

There is an eighteenth-century engraving by Hogarth that caricatures this. It shows "The Company of Undertakers" (see Fig.1.3), a group of doctors underneath whom there is the Latin expression "Et plurima mortis imago", which can be rendered as "And many an image of death". The crossed

*Figure 1.3* The Company of Undertakers (Lithograph about 1820, owned by Eugen
Wendler)

bones at the bottom edge of the image emphasise that our life and works
have an end, departing this life with empty pockets.

Two lessons can be drawn from List's thoughts on the seven deadly
economic sins, relating to the best of all possible economic systems, and to
the way in which the individual organises his life.

Regarding economic systems, one can choose between Adam Smith, Karl
Marx and Friedrich List: capitalism, socialism or the social market economy.

Without going into details, it should be plain that both capitalism and
socialism have shown themselves inadequate. Only the social market economy provides the chance, with the assistance of politics, legislation and an
independent judiciary, of creating the framework that can keep the economic
deadly sins in check. Hence the remarks above are also directed at the global
practice of democracy, the rule of law and respect for human rights.

Regarding the way in which the individual organises his life, I refer to List's motto: "through welfare to liberty". This means that individual welfare and public welfare should create the material basis on which an individual can, according to talents and inclinations, freely choose his own fate. How this is done is a matter for the individual. But one can say that less rush, stress and obsession with profit, more decency and sense of justice, less selfishness and regardlessness, less bullying at work, more social responsibility and social mutuality, more sense of community and mutual support, especially in the family; less abuse of alcohol and drugs; less dependence on computer games and electronic media; rather less superfluity of material goods; rather more intellectual enrichment and environmental consciousness; a greater sense of humbleness in the face of creation – and we would all gain in humanity and human dignity. We have the liberty to do all that. We have reason and conscience from birth, and this enables us to use this liberty in a meaningful way, and create a life worth living for ourselves.

We need to absorb this insight, and so try to shape our lives in a humane manner!

## List of publications:

1. Wendler, E.: (2015) *Friedrich List (1789–1846) A Visionary Economist with Social Responsibility*, Heidelberg.
2. Wendler, E.:(2004) *Durch Wohlstand zur Freiheit – Neues zum Leben und Werk von Friedrich List*, Baden-Baden.
3. Wendler, E.: (2014) *Friedrich List im Zeitalter der Globalisierung*, Wiesbaden
4. Wendler, E.: (2016) *Friedrich List: Die Politik der Zukunft*, Wiesbaden.
5. Wendler, E.: (2017) *Friedrich List: Politisches Mosaik*, Wiesbaden.
6. Wendler, E.: (2018) *Friedrich List: Vordenker der Sozialen Markt-wirtschaft- Im Spannungsfeld zwischen Vision und geheimdienstlicher Observierung.*
7. Wendler, E.: (1996) *Die Vereinigung des europäischen Kontinents – Gesamteuropäische Wirkungsgeschichte von Lists ökonomischem Denken*, Stuttgart
8. List, F.: (1985): *Die Welt bewegt sich – Le monde marche*, Göttingen

## Notes

1 List, F. (1931) Daniel O'Connells Verteidigungsrede und die Handelsfreiheit in Irland und China; in: Werke VII, Berlin, p. 245.
2 Notz, W. Gedichte von Friedrich List; in: Reutlinger Geschichtsblätter, Vol. 1927 p. 7.
3 Wendler, E. (2014) Friedrich List im Zeitalter der Globalisierung; pp. 98 f.
4 Wendler, E. (2004) Durch Wohlstand zur Freiheit – Neues zum Leben und Werk von Friedrich List; Baden-Baden, pp. 227–230.
5 List, F. Poem: "John Bulls Rat" in: Schwäbischer Merkur of 29th June 1897, p. 1228.

# 2 Friedrich List

## Looking back to the future

*Dieter Senghaas*[1]

Philosophers and scientists, as well as artists and writers, become part of a classical canon if the perspectives and problems that they articulate in their own time provide a constant resource for those who, decades and centuries later, seek understanding of their own world. In many parts of the world today the state is on the retreat, and in this context thoughts turn once again to the work of Thomas Hobbes: his argument for the disarmament of citizens and the monopolisation of power by the state that at the same time secured civil rights, constructing a Leviathan formulated in a seventeenth-century England at war with itself. The relevance of Hobbes' perspective is today immediately recognisable in the context of the chronic political anarchy prevailing in the Central African Republic, South Sudan, Somalia, Iraq, Ukraine and elsewhere. And, having recalled the work of Hobbes, we could turn to another seventeenth-century classical writer: John Locke, whose conception of a social contract was intended to provide an institutional check on this monopoly of power, to promote some kind of civilising force, creating a form of political involvement as a basis for a broad legitimation of this monopoly of power, and so make unlikely the danger of any relapse into anarchy. Even today modern political theory turns on this problem, including at the same time Immanuel Kant's later contribution.

During the second half of the eighteenth century, Adam Smith put a new accent on this debate. He argued that the market functioned to promote order and welfare through the extension of the division of labour; resulting in economic differentiation within individual states, and between states in an increasingly capitalist commercial economy; he lent the state a more subsidiary function. Almost one hundred years later Karl Marx, another classical writer, provided a clear-sighted analysis of the autonomous and dynamic logic of a capitalist market that contributed to the creation of social antagonisms.

Can we talk of Friedrich List as another classical writer of the kind represented by these few examples? Did he, writing in the first half of the nineteenth century, have something to say that provided a ground-breaking revelation of contemporary developments – insights that would be relevant for decades, and which even today retain their political force and significance?[2]

## I.

Friedrich List was not the first to write about the development in his lifetime of the English Industrial Revolution. But he was the first to clearly identify the problem of increasing asymmetries that the process of industrialisation and development created between those economies that were here in the lead, and those that became at best followers, at worst left behind.[3] List argued that economies engaged in active exchange with one another, but at different levels of development, were characterised by a gap in knowledge and organisational capacity that was progressively exacerbated by the uneven diffusion of technological and organisational innovations. This created both more and less productive economies, which were distinguished by a difference of capacity that, with continuing exchange, opened up a process of cut-throat competition between, in List's terms, "more advanced" and "less-advanced" economies. The advanced economy, enjoying high levels of productivity, can easily make large quantities of goods and sell them cheaply in national and international markets, flooding the markets of less advanced economies. This overwhelms the latter, creating a decline in the motivation to innovate, the more competent leading economy having all the advantages: in production techniques, in the products themselves, as well as in the capacity for continual innovation. Cut-throat competition becomes a general phenomenon; it is not just a matter of the competitive pressure represented by cheap goods.

For List, England was the only leading economy in the first half of the nineteenth century; he thought primarily of the USA, France and Germany as economies seeking to catch up. His writing on the subject was based on his own observations, and he was a tireless agitator on behalf of these developing economies he had identified in his clear-sighted diagnosis of the problem. And there was indeed a problem: according to recent estimates, England in 1860, more than a decade after List's death, had 2% of the world's population but 40%–45% of global industrial production. In that same year, English industrial capacity was greater than that of all the next fourteen European economies combined. In 1846, the year in which List died, only 22% of the employed population in England worked in agriculture, a proportion that developing European economies such as Denmark, Sweden, Norway, and especially Finland, only reached after 1950![4] England had both a large domestic market and a dominant position in world trade, and this fostered the development of the division of labour, mass production and long production runs for both consumer and capital goods – itself the foundation for successful cut-throat competition vis-à-vis craft production and protoindustrial production both at home and abroad.

Friedrich List would have been astonished, quite possibly disgusted, by the amount and degree of division in a world that today can only be called deeply divided. According to the World Bank's World Development Report of 2012, today 1.1bn. people live in high-income countries, while 817m. live in low-income countries, a relationship of 1.4:1. However, the difference in GDP is of the order of 104:1 (assuming a purchasing power parity of 41:1). High-income countries exported goods to the value of $8689bn.; against that, low-income countries exported goods to the value of $63bn. – a relationship of 137:1. Of course, things in middle-income countries (about 5bn. people) are a lot better, but even taking account of this, international stratification cannot be ignored, and is much more marked than in List's time. For it is not only the difference between high and low that is more marked; the problems that List identified have in the last few decades become much more virulent, with deeper and accelerating interdependencies right across the world – a situation that is conceived as a process of uncontrolled globalisation.

List's own insights were directed to just one section of the world; today he would have to take account of the world as a whole.[5] He could take some satisfaction from the fact that in 35 countries, representing some 16% of the world population, there has been a more or less successful process of developmental catching-up (by the usual measures). These are the so-called OECD countries. Here, 150 years after List, what he considered as the ultimate and highly desirable aim of developmental catch-up has taken place: the dismantling of external protectionist measures and a transition to equitable commercial relations finally based upon free trade, in which the division of labour is no longer limited by borders.

List would however also see today that around 10% of the world's population lives in failing or failed states, where unending civil wars and especially ethnic conflicts rage, something that at present is especially visible in the Central African Republic and elsewhere. In these cases even the most elementary conditions for any kind of developmental advance are absent.

Interestingly, the remaining 74% of the world population falls neatly into two halves. Thirty-seven per cent of the world's population live in just two states, China and India, while 37% live in around 140 states. Among the latter, it is not clear which of them will develop more towards the characteristics of the OECD states, which of them will gradually become failing states, and which will follow a fluctuating course without there being any clear path of development. (Egypt, Thailand and other cases are typically developing countries of this last sort.) List was somewhat prejudiced, and he would not have seen all of these 140 developing countries as capable of the kind of development he had in mind. All the same, today they all face the basic problems that List diagnosed: the threat of being driven to a periphery, or being marginalised, as a consequence of the flooding of their markets with goods from more developed societies, especially those belonging to the

OECD and, more recently, from those threshold economies like China that are successful in international markets.[6]

## II.

This brings up the question of the relevance for today's questions of both List's diagnosis and his constructive developmental programme. If List's name is ever mentioned in this connection, then it is his conception of "infant industry protection", which means protectionist tariffs; but policies for external protection in order to foster the development of domestic industries involve only one dimension of his developmental scenario. And it was here, with protective measures to sustain the effort of industrialisation that List argued quite undogmatically and pragmatically: where protection was useful, then such measures should be introduced for a fixed period, and avoided where their impact did more harm than good. He treated them as auxiliary supporting measures that could secure domestic impulses towards the development of a differentiated economic system. However, and to use modern linkage terminology: the potential to link up agriculture, industry and trade and promote economic sectors within these required above all the mobilisation of *productive forces*. Among these can be counted: a stable political framework fostering development, especially in this regard legal security and efficient administration; the promotion of infrastructural development in the domains of transport, communication and finance; and in particular, the promotion of science and education, not only as a way of furthering innovation, but also as a way of overcoming prejudice and inertia, and so creating measures that should make possible the social mobilisation of those trapped in traditional relationships, fostering upward social mobility. In List's words: it was not only a matter of mobilising the "capital of nature" (raw materials, demography and so on) and the "capital of matter" (goods, foodstuffs, tools and so on), but above all the mobilisation of the "capital of mind", which in recent debate over development is called "immaterial" or "human capital".[7]

Productive forces had to be made use of according to time and place, with a view to their developmental potential in each particular case, and taking account of its specific conditions. List was quite undogmatic even in this respect, and this lack of dogmatism is something that runs through much of the argument found in his writings.

And so we have the creation of a framework that fosters development and the mobilisation of productive forces, which working together ("confederation of productive forces") make possible "autocentric development",[8] enabling an opening to the world market appropriate to the situation, without becoming the victim of cut-throat competition: this Listian perspective is still relevant, however difficult it might be to translate into the practice of development policy.[9]

## III.

The broad early history of the reception of List's historical and developmental diagnosis around the world, and of his programme for developmental policy, justifies his description as a classic writer.[10] It is true that, as already noted, much of this history began and ended with references to infant industry, hence the call for external protective measures so that domestic industry might be promoted. His more comprehensive ideas, associated with the idea of the "production of productive forces" was often overlooked in then dominant schools of economic thinking.[11]

While it is hard to understand why in the years following the Second World War List was, in the Western industrialised countries joined together in the OECD, either forgotten or marginalised as an important contributor to modern economic theory, this did reflect the fact that in these countries the problem of developmental catch-up had been fairly resolved. Ignoring the actual historical experience of these countries, representatives of business, politics and the academy in these economies as a rule supported finally free trade as a global developmental programme bearing the promise of salvation. That is especially remarkable if one considers cases such as the USA, whose modern developmental history in the second half of the nineteenth century and the first half of the twentieth was marked by very significant tariffs.[12] Even in List's time reference was made to an "American system" that was thoroughly Listian in motivation and distinct to a "British system" that was free-trade and cosmopolitan in orientation, drawing inspiration from Adam Smith. If we were to apply the terminology of modern policy, we could say that for example, US development was not based on the free trading and deregulatory principles of the "Washington consensus", but instead on one or other variants of a "Beijing consensus" that draws upon List.[13] Besides, if the US had in fact pursued the path of free trade, not only would its rapid and massive industrialisation of the second half of the nineteenth century be hindered, it could have been made impossible. Free trade could have given the southern states, using slave labour to produce cotton as an export good, an unfair advantage and so led to a lop-sided developmental process of the kind all too familiar today in those African states that export raw materials and energy resources from enclave-like zones within their territory.

If one adopts a historical perspective on European countries since the mid-nineteenth century as "developing economies" in respect of the dominant position of England, and adds to this North America and Australasia, then one can grasp the entire spectrum of possible responses to the challenge posed by the leading economy of the time.[14] The spectrum runs from successful cases of development catch-up (we think here above all of Scandinavia and Australasia, and the larger countries of Western Europe) right across to cases in which isolated regions developed an economic structure based on the export of unprocessed agricultural products and raw materials, the epitome not of a substitutive division of labour but of a complementary relationship of the kind that can be seen right up to the present day in the relationships between highly industrialised countries and African states. In Europe's more distant past this issue arose above all in the relationship of Western Europe with eastern and south-eastern societies, in which the latter experienced a phase of re-feudalisation, a "second serf-dom", while Western Europe was itself in the process of shedding feudal relationships.

Successful developmental catch-up means for List, and has meant for cases where it has occurred, the creation of a developmental process whose progress is supported in stages by the achievement of dynamic comparative advantages. It is of course possible, as outlined in the classical Ricardian model, to begin with the exchange of textiles pro-duced in England for Portuguese wine; but if Portugal sticks with this kind of exchange it will get into the difficulties of peripherisation, some-thing that Portugal is still today trying to overcome, even if at a higher level of development.

Following on from the example of Scandinavian economies over the last one hundred years, recently the East Asian states, especially Taiwan and South Korea but also Singapore and Hong Kong, have skilfully pursued a developmental strategy employing dynamic comparative advantages that have, in an extraordinarily short time, made it possible for them to effect a breakthrough to high-level industrialisation. The strategy was thoroughly Listian, using the state to enable a massive but selective connection with the world market that was at the same time combined with a selective uncou-pling from the world market to create the free space considered necessary for the promotion of domestic social and economic productive forces. This was not something that was confined to developmental practice; academics rediscovered the idea of a "developmental state", so reaffirming a frame-work for successful developmental catch-up that from a Listian perspective would be self-evident.[15]

The productive role of a developmental state could also have been seen at work in the example of Japanese development in the final decades of the nineteenth century, and also with the attempt to foster developmental catch-up in the Soviet Union after 1917 and then elsewhere after 1945 in a socialist mode. But these last examples, and their collapse over the period 1989–1992 dramatically highlighted the inevitability of setbacks, and ulti-mately the failure of a developmental project that failed to engage in the overdue transformation of state and non-state institutions, and to foster the formation of new social groups with their own interests and identities.[16] This was something that was obviously recognised in China three decades ago in connection with the economy, a problem that this country, the largest in the world, confronted and with which it successfully began experimenting. China set out on a path of deliberate economic change, seeking to introduce and build dynamic comparative advantages, without blocking the emergence of new social groups with their own interests and identities but instead controlling them, bridging tradition and modernity and at the same time guaranteeing political stability. This was all done in a country at the scale of China's geography, ecology and population; a Listian project representing an incomparable challenge whose success up to this point is very impressive, but which cannot simply be extended unproblematically into the future given that there are a number of increasingly tense domestic issues to deal with (about which there is much discussion in China), and also that China has yet to find its own place, appropriate to its size and status, in a multipolar world structure.[17]

The problems of other threshold countries are in principle not different to those of China: everywhere, following a more or less successful process of economic development and the resulting upheaval of social structure, there emerges a need for the reform of political institutions that has to be successfully dealt with if economic development is not to be manoeuvred into a cul de sac.[18] Here again we can see the experiences of recent European developmental history repeated, across the range from gradual processes of adaptation to situations of uncontrollable upheaval that result from the failure of a collective learning process. The dramatic developments with which we are confronted are in this respect much more accentuated than in List's time, for List's social context was for the most part very traditional: in his time, most people still lived in and off the countryside; the drive for universal literacy was still in its early stages; decades after List political participation was in many countries still restricted by class-based franchises and other measures. These limitations are not any more typical of many developing countries, and so they are experiencing a broadly effective process of politicisation: a process that, as can be seen worldwide, becomes even more marked where economic and political development is thwarted.

## IV.

The experience of development over the last 150 years, and especially the last few decades after the Second World War, also make plain the conditions under which Listian developmental catch-up is either improbable or, conversely, possible. If a developing country, whether within Europe or not, takes the Ricardian path of complementary division of labour because they have agricultural goods, raw materials and energy sources that can easily be marketed, then all experience indicates that there is a very good chance they will achieve 'growth without development'. Local political elites will treat this as a profitable line of business for themselves and their clients, at any rate, more profitable than investment in Listian development projects. List would argue that the static comparative advantages arising out of trading these resources should be linked to investment in productive powers that are capable of extending local processing and manufacturing, and so contribute to a broad-based differentiation of the economic structure, resulting in a general upgrading of the country's economic profile. But this kind of qualitative structural re-profiling, resulting in emerging dynamic comparative advantages, is precisely what often does not happen, leading those observing international economic development to talk of the "curse of plenty".[19]

The situation is not different with respect to the emergence of international value-creation chains, where multinational businesses outsource the more labour-intensive parts of a production process to countries with cheap labour, which in turn creates the same kind of organised enclave for economic activity in the latter economies that mostly has few significant spillover effects for the broadly undifferentiated economic structure of the developing country. If the local conditions for investment change, then there is a probability that a decision will be made to relocate production to another country, leaving behind only the ruins of a former investment. The leading example of this was and is the constant relocation of the labour-intensive textile and clothing industries.[20]

Regarding the situation today and in the foreseeable future, we also need to ask ourselves whether the processes of globalisation, or even hyperglobalisation, have undermined the principles upon which List's developmental project was based. The turnover of the world's financial markets eclipses in a few days the annual volume of world trade (currently around $13,000bn.), and is annually ten-times total annual global GDP. An autonomous and uncontrollable dynamism has been unleashed that makes the prospect of guiding developmental processes at best difficult, at worst impossible. In this situation it is understandable that some call for deglobalisation, a cry for help in the face of the steamroller of international economic transactions that originate in the highly developed industrial societies, and increasingly in the developing threshold states.[21]

Quite possibly we will hear this call from the central economies too (consider France today!): when threshold countries move beyond the production of labour-intensive goods, and are able to impose the constraints of cut-throat competition in the domain of advanced, technologically intensive products on these central economies. China's sale of high-speed trains and aircraft are only the tip of an iceberg forming an ever-growing menu of products that threshold economies can supply. The key term here is dependency reversal, whether in particular economic segments, or on a broader front: structural dependency would then become very much sharper not as hitherto in relationships running from north to south, but increasingly from south to north.

List's ideas were formed 150 years ago in a relatively limited empirical context, and it has been assumed that within the advanced industrial countries these issues of uneven development have largely been dealt with. But given open markets, this issue could see a renaissance. The question becomes: what external economic measures are needed, and what kind of productive forces have to be created to enable the current centres of the world economy to confront in a constructive and long-term manner an issue that can quite possibly become more significant? Discussion of the problems of development will once more be on the agenda, and will apply to these highly industrialised economies themselves. This discussion originated some 150 to 200 years ago in the work of Friedrich List, who presented to his contemporaries a far-sighted diagnosis of the time and of the future. In a globalised world we will need, both here and elsewhere, many such Lists, so that List's original problematic, so evident across the world in developing economies, but also potentially accentuated in the centres of the world economy, can be constructively dealt with.

## Notes

1 This text is based on my lecture presented in the Reutlingen Rathaus as part of the city's celebrations to mark Friedrich List's 225th birthday, 8 October 2014, with additional remarks.
2 On Friedrich List see the comprehensive biography by Eugen Wendler, *Friedrich List (1798–1846). Ein Ökonom mit Weitblick und sozialer Verantwortung*, Wiesbaden 2013.
3 See the recent republication of List's principal text, first published in 1841: *Das nationale System der politischen Ökonomie*, edited by Eugen Wendler, Baden Baden 2008 (Monographien der List Gesellschaft NF Bd. 25).
4 See Senghaas (1985), ch. 1.
5 For the following data see Senghaas (2012).
6 See Bourguignon (2015).
7 The concepts can be found in Friedrich List (1996), *Outlines of American Political Economy. Grundriss der amerikanischen politischen Ökonomie, in Twelve Letters to Charles J. Ingersoll*, edited by Michael Liebig and with an epilogue by Lyndon H. LaRouche Jr., Wiesbaden 1996 (first published in English 1827).
8 See Amin (1976).
9 The surprisingly contemporary socio-political dimension of List's programme is dealt with in Wendler (2014), Chs. VII and IX.
10 See here Wendler (2014), Ch. V.5, and other writings by Wendler.
11 See Sai-Wing Ho (2005), who takes issue with this common limitation of the reception literature.
12 See Chang (2002) and also Mei (2014).
13 See Ramo (2004), Breslin, 2011, Lin (2009a), Deckers (1994; finally Reinert (2007).
14 See Senghaas (1985) for empirical material.
15 See on this Lin (2009b) and on this the interesting exchange between Lin and Ha-Joon Chang concerning the differing extent of integration in the world market and uncoupling from it, and also of the role of the developmental state, in Lin, Chang (2009).
16 See Senghaas (1985) for an early diagnosis relating to this, with many references to related discussion that had already taken place in the 1960s and 1970s.
17 On China, besides many monographic studies see the issue of *Aus Politik und Zeitgeschichte* devoted to China APuZ (2010).
18 See on this Nölke (2014) as well as the APuZ (2013).

19  On the situation on African countries see Oesterdieckhoff (2013). On the problematic efforts on the part of progressive Latin American governments to finance welfare from the extension of the production of raw materials, without altering the traditional developmental model, see Brand, Dietz (2014), Agostino, Dübgen (2014) and Acosta (2013).
20  See Dörre (2014),
21  May (2013) discusses the positive (!) outcomes for threshold countries arising from the financial sector.

## References

Acosta, A. (2013), "Vom guten Leben. Der Ausweg aus der Entwicklungsideologie", in: *Blätter für deutsche und internationale Politik*, 58, pp. 91–97.

Agostino, A., Dübgen, F. (2014), "Die Politik des guten Lebens. Zwischen (Neo-) Extraktivismus und dem Schutz der 'Mutter Erde' - Konfliktlinien und Potentiale lateinamerikanischer Traditionsmodelle", in: *Leviathan*, 42, pp. 267–291.

Amin, S. (1976), *Unequal Development: An Essay on the Social Formations of Peripheral Capitalism*, New York: Monthly Review Press.

APuZ (2010), "China", in: *Aus Politik und Zeitgeschichte*, Heft 39.

APuZ (2013), "BRICS", in: *Aus Politik und Zeitgeschichte*, Heft 50/51.

Bourguignon, F. (2015), *The Globalization of Inequality*, Princeton, NJ: Princeton University Press.

Brand, U., Dietz, K. (2014), "(Neo-) Extraktivismus als Entwicklungsoption? Zu den aktuellen Dynamiken und Widersprüchen rohstoffbasierter Entwicklung in Latein-amerika", in: *Politische Vierteljahresschrift*, Sonderheft (special issue) 48, pp. 128–165.

Breslin, S. (2011), "The 'China Model' and the Global Crisis – From Friedrich List to a Chinese Mode of Governance?" in: *International Affairs*, 87, pp. 1323–1343.

Chang, H.-J. (2002), *Kicking Away the Ladder. Development Strategy in Historical Perspective*, London: Anthem Press.

Deckers, W. (1994), "Mao Zedong and Friedrich List on De-Linking," in: *Journal of Contemporary Asia*, 24, pp. 217–226.

Dörre, K. (2014), "Unternehmen in transnationalen Wertschöpfungsketten", in: *Aus Politik und Zeitgeschichte*, Heft 1–3, pp. 28–34.

Lin, J. Y. (2009a), *On China's Economy – Der chinesische Weg zur Wirtschaftsmacht*, Heidelberg: ABC Verlag.

Lin, J. Y. (2009b), *Economic Development and Tradition. Thought, Strategy, and Viability*, Cambridge: Cambridge University Press.

Lin, J. Y., Chang, H. J. (2009), "Should Industrial Policy in Developing Countries Conform to Comparative Advantage or Defy It? A Debate between Justin Yifu Lin and Ha-Joon Chang", in: *Development Policy Review*, 27, pp. 483–502.

List, F. (1996), Outlines of American Political Economy. Grundriss der amerikanischen politischen Ökonomie, in: *Twelve Letters to Charles J. Ingersoll*, edited by Michael Liebig and with an epilogue by Lyndon H. LaRouche Jr., Wiesbaden: Dr. Bottiger Verlags-GmbH (first published in English 1827).

List, F. (2008), Das nationale System der politischen Ökonomie, in: *Monographien der List Gesellschaft e.V., N.F. 25*, (edited by) Wendler, E., Baden-Baden: Nomos.

May, C. (2013), "Die Dissoziation der BRICSs im finanzialisierten Kapitalismus", in: *Peripherie*, 33, pp. 264–286.

Mei, J. (2014), *The Myth of Free Trade*, Beijing (in Chinese, with an English summary pp. 339–342).

Nölke; A. (ed.) (2014), *Die großen Schwellenländer*, Wiesbaden: Springer.

Oesterdieckhoff, P. (2013), "Defizite des wirtschaftlichen Wachstums in Africa", in: *Neue Gesellschaft/Frankfurter Hefte*, 12, pp. 37–43.

Ramo, J. C. (2004), *The Beijing Consensus*, London: Foreign Policy Centre.

Reinert, E. S. (2007), *How Rich Countries Got Rich and Why Poor Countries Stay Poor*, London: Public Affairs.

Sai-Wing Ho, P. (2005), "Distortions in the Trade Policy for Development Debate. A Re-examination of Friedrich List", in: *Cambridge Journal of Economics*, 29, pp. 729–745.

Senghaas, D. (1985), *The European Experience. A Historical Critique of Development Theory*, Leamington Spa and Dover.

Senghaas, D. (2012), *Weltordnung in einer zerklüfteten Welt*, Berlin: Suhrkamp.

Wendler, E. (2013), *Friedrich List (1798–1846). Ein Ökonom mit Weitblick und soziale Verantwortung*, Wiesbaden: Springer.

Wendler, E. (2014), *Friedrich List im Zeitalter der Globalisierung*, Wiesbaden: Springer.

# 3 Growth and integration
## Why we should re-read Friedrich List

*Stephan Seiter*

## 3.1. Introduction

The financial crisis of 2008 and the resulting world economic crisis led to an intensive discussion on the relevance of mainstream economics. Since the 1970s neoclassical theory dominated economic debates. Not only students were left with the puzzling impression that economic theory not only became more and more an application of mathematical tools und methods, but also was less and less able to contribute to the explanation of and solutions for real life economic challenges. Consequently, heterodox approaches experienced a renaissance. Robert Skidelsky's book on *Keynes: The Return of the Master* (Skidelsky 2009) is probably one of the most famous examples for this development. Behavioural economics gained increasing popularity not only in scientific, but also in general public discussion. For example, the founding of the Institute of New Economic Thinking (INET 2018) is an outflow of this development. Thus, the understanding and explanation of the imperfectness of markets and seemingly irrational behaviour came more to the centre of economic analysis.

Furthermore, the interest in economic governance, especially in the characteristics of a social market economy, grew. How should a society design the legal framework of an economy to avoid severe economic crises in the future? How much market is possible and how much regulation is necessary for reducing the instability of markets, in particular of financial markets? In addition, ethics and morality found their way on the agenda and into the curriculum of economic education and research.

The new interest in long-neglected approaches also leads to the work of Friedrich List (born 1789 in Reutlingen, Germany, died 1846 in Kufstein, Austria) who is besides Karl Marx (1818–1883) one of the most important economists of the 19th century in Germany. List is mainly known for his idea of educational tariffs to protect infant industries from international competition. However, a closer look at his work reveals that his ideas of the economic system could enrich the current theoretical and political debate on international trade and integration as well as economic growth. Especially, two major trends suggest re-reading Friedrich List's contributions: globalization and technological change driven by digitalization.

Friedrich List's ideas on integration and trade deal with the different aspects of globalization and the ongoing technological progress. He offers a comprehensive insight into the benefits, but also challenges of these developments. In his famous book *Das nationale System der politischen Ökonomie* (The National System of Political Economy), Friedrich List analyses the key determinants of growth and development (List 2008). Being very critical towards Adam Smith's concept of the division of labour, List shows beside other variables the relevance of institutional settings, educational policy and the rule of law. The so-called 'produktiven Kräfte' (productive forces) are seen as necessary determinants of growth.

He also explained that not every country involved in a free trade system would benefit from this openness. If an economy lacked the productive forces that are necessary for being competitive in international markets, it would end in a low growth path. Nevertheless, List was aware of the advantages of free trade. In a memorandum he wrote to the newly founded German Association for Trade and Commerce that was forwarded to the 'Bundesversammlung' (federal assembly) in Frankfurt, he complained about the great number of tariffs and trade barriers between the different German states and showed their negative impact on economic development and growth (List 1927–1935: Vol. 1 (2)). For him, the solution was an economic union that should be part of a political union. After a unification of the German states, List was of the opinion that Europe should form an economic and political union to secure peace and prosperity. Such an integration required, in List's opinion, the establishment of network technologies, transport goods, people and ideas. While in List's time the railway provided the economy with this service, he was very optimistic that new technologies such as communication technology, aviation, agriculture and machinery would contribute to the integration of markets and countries (nations) and improve the well-being of people.[1]

The paper analyses the importance of List's views on growth and integration from the perspective of modern approaches to economic growth and international economics. Furthermore, some ideas will be presented on how List's ideas could help to explain and understand current economic developments, such as the crisis of the European Union or the new form of isolationism of the United States of America. Hereby, the discussion focuses on his most comprehensive contribution, the *National System of Political Economy*. Section 2 focuses on the concept of productive forces and its link to modern growth theories, Section 3 will deal with List's ideas on integration and lessons for the European Union. In Section 4 some light will be shed on the question of whether so-called *Trumponomics* is linked with List's approaches. Section 5 contains conclusions.

## 3.2. The productive forces from a modern perspective

In his book *Das nationale System der politischen Ökonomie* (The National System of Political Economy) Friedrich List (2008) develops an alternative explanation of growth and development by challenging Adam Smith's concept of wealth. For List, the power to create wealth is decisive, not the amount of wealth. Wealth allows an individual or a nation to consume, but it is more important to possess the ability to create new wealth and to replace used goods (List 2008: 192).

List does not reject the idea that the division of labour is important for the creation of wealth. Furthermore, he also accepts the statement that the productivity of labour depends on the skills and intelligence of the workers. Smith's explanation that the degree of the division of labour and its positive implications on labour productivity is also accepted. However, List misses the analysis of the drivers behind this process. For him, the materialistic theory of value requires a complement: the theory of productive forces. The latter stressing the influence of immaterial factors, such as traditions, institutions, education or religion (List 2008: 195).

List illustrates the difference between these two theories he has in mind by comparing the raising of pigs with teaching in school. Pork is sold in the food market. The willingness-to-pay expresses the value of pork to the buyer. The higher it is the more productive is the farmer. When there is (or at least was in List's days) no market for education, the teacher does not create value. She is, according to the theory of value, unproductive. According to the theory of productive forces, the teacher is more productive than the farmer is, since she enables the next generation to produce more due to being better educated (List 2008: 198). List calls professions like teachers, scientists and physicians, *producers of productive forces* (List 2008: 200).

List's had the idea that intellectual capital is one of the key productive forces. The intellectual capital of a society is the result of the accumulation of knowledge in the past (List 2008: 196). It is the ability to use the knowledge of former generations as a starting point for the creation of new knowledge, skills and abilities, i.e. the creation of more productive forces.

Based on these findings, the question arises of what coordinates the production of productive forces and their producers. Accepting List's distinction between the two theories leads to the insight that the market will not work as a coordination and selection mechanism for the supply of and the demand for productive forces and producers of them. If the individuals put no value on these forces or services or do not see their value, then there will be no prices for them. Therefore, the government and other institutions become important. The creation of wealth depends for List not only on the endowment with labour, capital and resources, but on the type of government, the rule of law and liberty, too.

Moreover, List stresses that the creation of productive forces requires giving up material wealth. In this context, he does not only refer to the investment and saving but also to the benefits of free trade. In the short run, opening an economy allows access to a greater variety of products. In general, the leading economy is able to produce at lower costs. Therefore, the short run opportunity costs are low for the less developed country. Nevertheless, since it does not develop its own productive forces it will give up more benefits in the end. This is another reason for List to levy tariffs on the imports from more advanced countries until the process of development is successful (List 2008: 201). The development of a manufacturing sector will then create the potential for more productive forces. Pure agricultural economies would possess less productive forces and a lower potential for creating them than an economy with a strong manufacturing sector besides the agricultural. The reason for this lies in the fact that manufacturing requires more qualification and more freedom. List sees manufacturing as a reason and a result of a free civic society (List 2008: 197, 204–212).

Nevertheless, the fact that List postulates an active role for the government does not imply a socialistic system. Rather, he demands a restriction of free markets as long as it is beneficial for the nation as whole. Free competition should be restricted, if it was bad for the nation's wealth and productive forces (List 2008: 216–220).

Reflecting on List's concept of productive forces and its relevance for economic growth and development, comparing it to modern approaches in growth theory is obvious. Many statements remind of theories presented in the 1950s and later. The idea of productive forces could be interpreted as another expression for Kaldor's concept of technological dynamism that he introduced in his models to explain endogenous growth by applying the concept of a technical progress function. Technical dynamism gives a vague idea of the willingness and ability of a society to create and to apply new technologies. In other words, how innovative a society is (see for example Kaldor 1957, 1961; Kaldor, Mirrlees 1962).

Furthermore, endogenous growth theory stands in the tradition of List, too. His idea of productive forces stresses many of the determinants of long-run growth that were later the focus of growth models presented in the 1980s and later. One of the drivers in the set of productive forces is human capital. As mentioned above, List saw especially the education of young people as an important aspect in creating productive forces. The relevance of human capital for economic growth was analysed by Lucas (1988) and Romer (1990). Human capital and its creation are prominent drivers of growth in endogenous growth theory, because both induce external effects. Working and studying in a group of better-educated individuals increases the productivity of the group's members. In addition, there is an intertemporal externality. Future generations benefit from the human capital their ancestors acquired in the past. Here, Lucas (1988) gives a good example for this idea. Arrow (1962) already showed the relevance of such intertemporal effects when analysing the effects of capital accumulation and learning by doing on productivity. The case of the West German economy after World War II gives evidence to this idea. German workers gained human capital and knowhow while working in factories during the war. Then in the 1950s, their knowhow, for example on mechanics, engineering or production process, was not lost such as parts of the physical capital stock. Therefore, intertemporal effects can be assumed to be even more relevant when general knowledge is analysed. The latter is non-rival in its application. Knowledge can be applied at different places at the same time. Furthermore, knowledge shows non-excludability when it is made available to the public. Romer (1986) triggered this idea in his seminal paper. With regard to the contribution and relevance of human capital and knowledge, Becker, Murphy and Tamura (1990) as well as Azariadis and Drazen (1990) give interesting insights into the relevance of human capital and its rate of return to economic growth. Individuals will invest in human capital, if the rate of return is higher than the ones of other forms of investment, such as physical capital or children. Therefore, an economy requires a minimum of human capital to make investment in one's human capital attractive. List was aware of this phenomenon when, for example, stressing the relevance of traditions.

Another link between endogenous growth theory and List's productive forces is the role of entrepreneurship for innovation and development. The development of new products as the outflow of the inventor spirit needs incentives. The businessperson will take the risk to invest in research and development, if a patent law will protect his knowledge, so that he can gain at least temporarily extra profits as a monopolist. Due to this opportunity, an inventor without monetary means will find a (venture) capitalist willing to support him (see, for example List 2008: 311). This reminds indeed of Schumpeter's idea of the innovative entrepreneur and the process of creative destruction (see Schumpeter 1912, 1942).

In endogenous growth theory, this idea can be found in the models by Aghion, Howitt (1992a, 1992b, 2009) or Grossman, Helpman (1991). Here, the authors show the influence of extra profits as a determinant for investment in research and development as well as its indirect influence on the knowledge base of an economy. Innovative entrepreneurs increase the product variety or product quality leading to more knowledge on which future generations could build. In this context, the question arises of how much patent laws should protect innovations. If a patent lasts for a very long time, then the incentive for research and development for potential competitors decreases. Less innovations and less growth will be the outcome.

Another important productive force is the transport and communication system of an economy. List realised that a complex economic system based on specialization and division of labour needs an infrastructure enabling the exchange of goods, labour and ideas (List 1838: 1, 1985). For List, the infrastructural system included primarily the railway system that linked towns and thereby market places, so goods and information could flow fast from one place to another. This allowed for a better integration of markets resulting in more productive ways to produce, since knowledge could be used widely in the economy. List also saw the future relevance of telegraphy and its relevance for growth and development. In modern times, information and communication technologies could be seen as the new 'railway'. In the information society of the 21st century, data are the immaterial goods that are traded. The fast flow of data necessary for the introduction of new technologies, such as autonomous driving, requires high investment in the fibre cable network. If List had to write a report on the current growth potential of Germany, he would probably complain about the poor shape of the telecommunication network compared to other economies. Maybe, he would write a new petition to the government stressing the negative implications of the lack of investment on the productive forces of Germany that reduces the growth potential of the country. Somehow, List anticipated network economics by having an idea of network externalities as discussed, for example, by Economides (1996, 2008) or Shapiro, Varian (1999).

The concept of productive forces offers a comprehensive system of factors determining the growth potential of an economy. List also stressed that the productive forces are important on the national level. For him, a nation was more than the sum of the individuals being the citizens of this nation (List 2008: 214–221). In Lists view, a nation's institutions, traditions, legal system and informal relations between its citizens contribute to the productive forces and enable an economy to grow. Part of this system is also the social capital in the meaning of Putnam (1995).[2] Furthermore, productive forces remind of Abramovitz's (1986) concept of social capabilities, as will be shown below.

### 3.3. List on integration – lessons for Europe?

One of Friedrich List's most famous contributions to the discussion on free trade is the petition he wrote in 1819, which he addressed to the Bundesversammlung (federal assembly in Frankfurt). Here, List criticized the huge number of trade barriers, especially tariffs, in Germany (List 1927–1935: Vol. 1 (2)). The existence of more than 30 frontiers within Germany would increase the prices of goods and thereby lower the incentive to trade goods. Consequently, German goods were not competitive with the ones produced and exported by England or France. This critique seems to be a contradiction of his idea of tariffs to protect infant industries against international competition.

In his book, *The National System of Political Economy*, List elaborates this idea in more detail when he deals with the implications of free trade. He saw the political integration/union as a precondition for the introduction of free trade (List 2008: 187–188). Only then, nations can benefit from the participation in an economic union. If the economic union is established before the political union, the less developed economies will depend more and more on the leading economy. Thus, the former will not be able to catch up. List refers here to the example of the United States of America to illustrate the implications of such a confederation. If a region/state is characterized by a surplus of labour, captial, talents and skills, then this will lead to a movement of these resources to the less developed regions/ state as predicted by international trade theory. Since all regions/states are member of the same confederation, they share the same institutional set-tings, such as the legal system. Furthermore, a confederation like the United States has a common interest that somehow unifies the regions/states. In List's words, they would share a national interest (List 2008: 190).

In contrast to this positive scenario, List claimed that economic reality of the first half of the 19th century does not meet this precondition. In particular, different nations were following different national strategies and interests. The self-interest of a nation that is not in accordance with the collective interest of all nations will make the technologically most advanced and most productive economy, for List England, to focus on manufacturing in the domestic economy and all countries closely related to this leading country. Any country that is not a member of this 'club' will not be attractive to capital investment from England (List 2008: 190–191). Thus, these countries will not benefit from the technology of the leading nation. Divergence and not convergence will be the outcome.

Thus, List could be seen as a predecessor of the catching-up-hypothesis that was made popular mainly by Abramovitz's article of 1986 on 'Catching-up, Forging Ahead, Falling Behind' (Abramovitz 1986). According to this approach, a successful catching-up process requires not only the interaction between the technologically leading country (such as England), but also a sufficient level of so-called social capabilities. In other words, institutions, such as the knowledge and skills of the working force, the legal system and political stability are important. Foreign direct investment is a necessary condition for catching up, but it must take place in a setting that allows the adoption of the new technology. One of these capabilities seems for List the sharing of the same interests in develop-ment. If this is not the case, the dominance of the leading economy could be challenged by protecting the infant industries from international competition. Domestic firms are then able to develop competitiveness by becoming more productive.

List's line of reasoning can help to explain the current situation of the European Union. The European project started with the intention to achieve peace and political integration in Europe by an increased economic integra-tion between the member countries. According to List's ideas in the *National System of Political Economy*, such an economic union could not result in an integration process that leads to better economic situations in the less developed European economies, if there was not a common interest and a common institutional setting.

The challenges the European (Monetary) Union faces due to the Euro crisis give evidence to List's view, too. Due to its highly productive manufacturing sector and its competitiveness, Germany can be seen as the leading economy within the Union that achieves high surpluses in trade with less competitive trading partners. For example, the position of the IMF (2015) claims that Germany's big trade surplus does not only reflect the advantages in competitiveness with regard to prices and quality, but also the focus of national economic policy on export-led growth. Higher wages in Germany could lower trade surpluses by fewer exports and higher imports of the German economy. However, according to List this would not be the strategy to expect because Germany would give up comparative advantages and thereby national interest.

The European Union abolished international trade barriers, such as tariffs, and established the common market. The goal was that all member countries would benefit from free trade in the integrated markets. Capital, labour and goods are completely mobile to reach the optimal allocation of resources. Thereby, countries lagging in competitiveness, but offering, for example, lower labour costs, will be attractive for foreign direct investment. Tools such as the European Cohesion Fund offer support in achieving convergence. This could be seen as one of List's proposals for rules enabling countries to attain a higher level of knowledge as a precondition for economic development. The idea of a unified Europe providing common institutions could be understood as a universal union in the sense meant by List. The positive economic development as well as the long period of peace also gives reason to this strategy.

However, the European Monetary Union and the growing number of member countries caused by the accession of Eastern European countries put the union under stress. First, the single currency, in other words the loss of monetary sovereignty, terminated the opportunity to use the exchange rate to steer competitiveness with regard to prices and thereby exports and imports. Thus, these economies became completely open. Depreciation as a form of protectionary policy ended. Furthermore, the European Growth and Stability Pact reflects the fear that the members will use fiscal policy to achieve their national interests and undermine collective goals, such as price stability. Since the rules of this contract were not consequently applied and sanctions not imposed, the common interest was not achieved; governments prefer their own national goals to the European ones. Following List, this could be read as a lack of a common institutional setting that is binding for all members.

Second, the growth of the European Union due to the accession of Eastern European countries increased the variety and heterogeneity of national interests. Thus, finding a widely shared European position becomes more difficult. List therefore shows us the need for a European vision that unifies the different national interests.

### 3.4. Trumponomics – an application of List's ideas

Since the election of Donald Trump as the 45th president of the United States, the US position with regard to free trade and globalization changed. By stopping, for example, the negotiations on Transatlantic Trade and Investment Partnership (TTIP) and Trans-Pacific Partnership (TPP), the new US administration gave evidence that the US will focus more on their domestic market and is willing to protect their producers. Imports from Europe or China should be liable to higher customs duty to increase the prices of imported goods in the US market. Trump promised that this policy would help to regain jobs for US workers, since relatively lower prices would give an incentive for American buyers to prefer domestic products. Furthermore, Trump appeals to the American sense of honour. His slogan *Make America Great Again* expresses for him and his supporters the national interest in protectionism to save jobs and attract investment in the US manufacturing industry. Tax cuts and more rigorous immigration laws shall complete the economic policy. The negative implications of globalization and technological change for the US economy shall be turned back.[3]

At first glance, this strategy seems to be backed by List's ideas of protecting the domestic economy from international competition to develop infant industries. However, List did probably not have in mind an isolationist policy such as Donald Trump's. Rather, the protection system should be temporarily applied while the medium- and long-run goal was to integrate the economy into the world market to benefit from the gains of free trade. According to List's view, the US economy of the early 21st century is probably not an economy he had in mind when delivering his ideas on infant industries in low developed countries. The US was already integrated in the world economy and was the key driving force of globalization and technological progress. However, an increasing number of countries, in List's terms nations, are challenging the position of the US as the leading economy. Nations, formerly hosting the work benches of the US enterprises, caught up and are on their way to become technological leaders at least in some industries. This change is also driven by disruptive technological change. On the one hand, digitalization and the internet will imply labour saving ways to produce. Not only physical, but also brain work is expected to be substituted by robots and artificial intelligence. On the other hand, ecological requirements ask for new types of mobility and energy production.

Based on List's approach, the US economy was able to develop their set of productive forces necessary and sufficient to be successful in the late 19th and the 20th century. For example, the ongoing inflow of immigrants and the size of the domestic market combined with the availability of natural resources and food were pre-conditions for the successful development process of the US economy in the age of industrialization and mass production. However, the set of productive forces did not match the requirements of the information age to guarantee jobs and in particular raising incomes for a majority. Somehow, the US is characterized by an imbalance between the human capital-intensive information technology (IT) sector, represented by Silicon Valley, and the physical labour intensive manufacturing sector. The workers who lost their jobs in manufacturing, such as in the automotive industry, were not able to find new positions in the IT sector, since the educational system did not provide them with the qualifications necessary for working in IT, and the latter does not require the input of many workers, but is characterized by a higher (human) capital-labour ratio. Here, we are back to List's example of raising swine and educating young people. The public educational system in the US failed to deliver the qualifications crucial for a successful participation in the gains due to growth and globalization. For example, teachers in state schools earned less than jailers, making it less attractive for skilled students to become teachers. In List's view, this expresses the problem that teachers in state schools are not seen as productive, since there is no market price for their services.

Thus, List's approach should not be misused to justify Trumponomics. Rather, it helps to understand the conditions that must be met for staying successful in a globalized world. Governments should focus on the productive forces of their country, and in the age of fast technological change and international competition, this is primarily the educational system.[4]

## 3.5. Conclusions

List's ideas on the determinants of economic growth and development that he expressed comprehensively in his *National System of Political Economy* in 1841, or before in 1838 in *Et la patrie, et l'humanité*, which was later translated and published under the title *Das Natürliche System der Politischen Ökonomie (The Natural System of Political Economy)*, are still relevant. List not only enriched the theoretical and political debate in the 19th century, but gave insights into the growth determinants of a more and more internationally integrated market economy. The modern debates on the advantages and disadvantages of free trade could benefit from his contributions, since they help to understand why some countries oppose globalization and prefer protectionism to develop their competitiveness. Furthermore, they could be a starting point to reflect the challenges the European Union faces at its current stage: the tension between the common European interest (goals) and the member nations' interests and goals.

Probably, List was not a theorist according to rigorous rules of science. However, he was able to draw lessons from the experience he made for himself as an emigrant, railway pioneer and intellectual.[5] Based on his knowledge of history and literature, as well as the developments he witnessed, he created an understanding of the determinants and implications of industrialization and its challenges for a society, in his words, a nation. In more modern terms, he put stress on the innovation system within an economy. Far from being a nationalist, and despite of his critique of Smith's view, List had a deep interest in the integration of Germany and Europe to secure peace, freedom and wealth.

List was many-faceted: as a practitioner, he was able to reflect empirics and draw consistent conclusions; as an applied scientist he held a firm grip on reality and followed his common sense. In particular, the latter makes his work so worth reading today.

## Notes

1 For an overview of List's contribution to the economics of globalization, see especially Wendler (2013).
2 See also Schechler (2002).
3 For a comprehensive discussion on Trumponomics see e.g. Fulbrook, Morgan (2017).
4 A comprehensive overview of List's ideas on the long run development of Europe and the world economy is given in Wendler (2016).
5 Tribe (1995) shows the important influence of American authors and American politics on List's perception of the economic system and his writings.

## References

Abramovitz, M. (1986), 'Catching Up, Forging Ahead and Falling Behind', *Journal of Economic History*, 46 (2): 385–406.

Aghion, Ph., Howitt, P. (1992a), 'A Model of Economic Growth through Creative Destruction', *Econometrica*, 60 (2): 323–351.

Aghion, Ph., Howitt, P. (1992b), 'The Schumpeterian Approach to Technical Change and Growth', in: Siebert, H. (ed.), *Economic Growth in the World Economy*, Tübingen: Mohr Siebeck.

Aghion, Ph., Howitt, P. (2009), *Economics of Growth*, Cambridge, MA: MIT Press.

Arrow, K. (1962), 'The Economic Implications of Learning by Doing', *Review of Economic Studies*, 29: 155–173.

Azariadis, C., Drazen, A. (1990), 'Treshold Externalities in Economic Development', *Quarterly Journal of Economics*, 105: 501–526.

Becker, G.S., Murpha, K.M., Tamura, R. (1990), 'Human Capital, Fertility, and Economic Growth', *Journal of Political Economy*, 98 (5): S12–S37.

Economides, N. (1996), 'The Economics of Networks', *International Journal of Industrial Organization*, 14: 673–699.

Economides, N. (2008), *The Economics of the Internet*, NYU Working Paper No. 2451/26031.

Fullbrook, E., Morgan, J. (eds.) (2017), *Trumponomics – Causes and Consequences*, World Economics Association Books, London: College Publications.

Grossman, G.M., Helpman, E. (1991), *Innovation and Growth in the Global Economy*, Cambridge, MA: MIT Press.

IMF. (2015), *Germany. Selected Issues*, IMF Country Report 15/188, Washington, DC: IMF.

INET. (2018), *Institute of New Economic Thinking*, www.ineteconomics.org.

Kaldor, N. (1957), 'A Model of Economic Growth', *Economic Journal*, 67: 591–624.

Kaldor, N. (1961), 'Capital Accumulation and Economic Growth', in: Lutz, F.H., Hague, D.C. (eds.), *The Theory of Capital*, London and New York: reprinted in: Targetti, Thirlwall, A.P. (eds.) (1989), *The Essential Kaldor*, London: Holmes & Meier Pub: 282–310.

Kaldor, N., Mirrlees, J.A. (1962), 'A New Model of Economic Growth', *Review of Economic Studies*, 29: 174–192.

List, F. (1838), *Das deutsche National-Transport-System in volks- und staatswirtschaftlicher Beziehung*, Altona und Leipzig: Hammerich.

List, F. (1927–1935), *Schriften/Reden/Briefe*, von Beckerath, E., Goeser, K., von Sonntag, W.H., Lenz, F., Salin, E. et al. (eds.), Vols. 1–10, Berlin: Reimar Hobbing.

List, F. (1985), *Die Welt bewegt sich: über die Auswirkungen der Dampfkraft und der neuen Transportmittel auf die Wirtschaft, das bürgerliche Leben, das soziale Gefüge und die Macht der Nationen (Pariser Preisschrift)/nach der franz.* Handschrift übersetzt u. kommentiert von Eugen Wendler (based on the hand written manuscript in French, translated and annotated by Eugen Wendler, Göttingen: Vandenhoeck & Ruprecht.

List, F. (2008), *Das nationale System der politischen Ökonomie*, Wendler, E. (ed.), Monographien der List Gesellschaft e.V., N.F. 25, Baden-Baden: Nomos.

Lucas, R.E., Jr. (1988), 'On the Mechanics of Economic Development', *Journal of Monetary Economics*, 22 (1): 3–42.

Putnam, K. (1995), 'Bowling Alone. America's Declining Social Capital', *Journal of Democracy*, 6 (1): 65–78.

Romer, P.M. (1986), 'Increasing Returns and Long-Run Growth', *Journal of Political Economy*, 94 (5): 1002–1037.

Romer, P.M. (1990), 'Endogenous Technological Change', *Journal of Political Economy*, 98 (5): S71–S102.

Schechler, J. (2002), *Sozialkapital und Netzwerkökonomik, Hohenheimer volkswirtschaftliche Schriften*, Vol. 41, Frankfurt am Main: Lang.

Schumpeter, J.A. (1912), *Theorie der wirtschaftlichen Entwicklung*, Leipzig: Duncker&Humblot.

Schumpeter, J.A. (1942), *The Theory of Economic Development*, Cambridge, MA: Harvard University Press.

Shapiro, C., Varian, H.A. (1999), *Information Rules: A Strategic Guide to the Network Economy*, Boston, MA: Harvard Business School Press.

Skidelsky, R. (2009), *Keynes: The Return of the Master*, London: Allen Lane.

Tribe, K. (1995), *Strategies of Economic Order. German Economic Discourse, 1750–1950*, Cambridge and New York: Cambridge University Press.

Wendler, E. (2013), *Friedrich List im Zeitalter der Globalisierung. Eine Wiederentdeckung*, Heidelberg: Springer.

Wendler, E. (2016), *Friedrich List: Die Politik der Zukunft*, Heidelberg: Springer.

# 4 Friedrich List and national political economy

## Ideas for economic development

*José Luís Cardoso*

## 4.1. Introduction

The life and work of Friedrich List provide many good reasons and pretexts for further exploring the richness of his legacy. We may dispute whether or not List made any substantial contributions to the development of theoretical economic analysis. Nevertheless, if we avoid adopting a merely internalist and positivist view of the development of a scientific discipline, it is more than obvious that the inputs of supposedly "minor" economists are relevant and important elements for understanding the historical nature of doctrinal and policy-oriented contributions. Even those economists whose views were superseded by the theoretical relevance of their contemporaries should be rescued from oblivion when our approach to the writing of the history of economic thought implies looking at the context and the processes involved in the production, dissemination and appropriation of economic knowledge. This is certainly the case with List, since his work had so many implications for the development of political economy on a worldwide scale, throughout the second half of the nineteenth and the twentieth century (see Tribe 1988, 1995).

My approach does not attempt to provide any new insights into List's works or to elaborate on the usual topics selected by List's scholars. My aim is instead to show that the relevance of List can also be assessed through a close look at the contributions made by other authors or at the research subjects for which List's writings are worth revisiting, either because List paid them the utmost attention or because they serve to challenge the conventional interpretation put forward by canonical scholarship.

I will focus on three different historical moments or episodes, selected from my previous research into the history of economic thought in Portugal and Brazil, whose interpretation and contextualization benefited from a consideration of List's legacy and historiography. These encounters with List are related to the following topics: 1) the Methuen Treaty signed between Portugal and Britain in 1703; 2) the influence of American protectionist economic literature on early nineteenth-century Portuguese authors; and 3) the protectionist arguments put forward by the economists of the United Nations Economic Commission for Latin America – ECLA (CEPAL)

I shall deal separately with each of these issues and try to channel my arguments in order to explain how they serve to illustrate List's notions and ideas on economic development.

## 4.2. The Methuen Treaty

List's interpretation of the meaning of the Methuen Treaty (as presented in Chapter 5 of Book I of *The National System of Political Economy*) follows some basic assumptions commonly accepted by nineteenth-century authors concerned with the conditions offered by, and the constraints imposed on, national economies.

According to the conventional reading, Portuguese manufacturing experienced a considerable increase throughout the last decades of the seventeenth century, largely due to the policies fostered by the minister Ericeira, influenced by Duarte Ribeiro de Macedo, the Portuguese ambassador in Paris and a man who was well acquainted with Colbert's industrial protectionist policies. By that time, Portuguese industry was already very prosperous and the country was able to ban imports of foreign clothes, as acknowledged by contemporary English writers. However, in 1703, the signing of the Methuen Treaty put an end to the previous successful measures: England permitted the importation of Portuguese wines at a duty that was one third less than the duty imposed on the wine imported from other countries, while, in return, Portugal allowed the importation of English woollen clothes at the reduced duty charged before Ericeira's policies.

In List's own words: "Directly after the conclusion of this treaty Portugal was deluged with English manufactures, and the first result of this inundation was the sudden and complete ruin of the Portuguese manufactories" (List 1885 [1841], 61).

List considered that the treaty deserved the acclaim that it had received from merchants and politicians in England, with the exception of Adam Smith. And a large part of Chapter 5 of Book I of the *National System of Political Economy* was devoted to arguing against the interpretation made by Smith, who considered that the treaty had been harmful to English interests.

List disclaims the evidence offered by Smith in his attempt to demonstrate the inefficiency of trade agreements based on preference relations of a monopolistic nature. And he concludes that:

> Certainly this treaty conferred a privilege upon Portugal, but only in name; whereas it conferred a privilege upon the English in its actual operation and effects. A like tendency underlies all subsequent treaties of commerce negotiated by the English.
>
> In short, but for the Methuen Treaty, the manufactures, the trade, and the shipping of the English could never have reached such a degree of expansion as they have attained to.
>
> (List 1885 [1841], 65)

One should not dismiss the relevance of List's interpretation for understanding the development of the Portuguese historiography of the treaty.

List's position could be easily accepted by those who later shared with him a nationalist blueprint, and who nourished the accusation against the English control over Portuguese economic development (especially during the mid-nineteenth century). This was a common view in other European circles, whenever the fight against the English economic hegemony called for a rejection of their policy instruments.

However, the rationale put forward by eighteenth-century Portuguese politicians (Luis da Cunha and the Marquis of Pombal) shows that there was a clear awareness of the political and diplomatic conditions that made the signing of the treaty necessary: the War of the Spanish Succession and the Portuguese choice of the best solution for preventing a new Iberian union (such as the one that had prevailed between 1580 and 1640). Therefore, the Methuen Treaty was the political price to be paid. Just as the treaty of 1810, signed in the context of the Napoleonic wars, had also been, albeit, in that case, with much more severe consequences.

Recent developments in Portuguese historiography also show that the economic consequences of the treaty were not as negative as the nationalist economic literature has painted them. The substantial increase in wine exports, and the fact that the special conditions of entry were limited to woolen clothes and did not prevent other industrial sectors from developing, must be taken into account.

The interpretation of the Methuen Treaty as the main factor preventing a Portuguese economic takeover in the eighteenth century is no longer accepted (cf. Cardoso 2017). It is not necessary here to dispute whether or not List was right about the consequences of the treaty. The important thing is to understand that List uses the example of the Methuen Treaty to argue that we should look with some suspicion at the treaties of commerce negotiated by the English, and to demonstrate that Smith's doctrine of trade based on laissez faire principles should be disputed.

However, List's interpretation was based on facts that could not be historically confirmed, and it makes us think about Viner's warning:

> List is entitled to praise as a pioneer of the historical point of view in economics. But his actual use of historical material is not worthy of praise. His sources are meager and second-hand, he selects and paraphrases therefrom with flagrant bias, and he uses them to fit the course of economic development into a neat and simple pattern of economic stages which, providentially, always and in every detail supports his argument.
>
> (Viner 1929, 365)

According to Viner, List's references to Smith are unfair and merely amount to a caricature that he developed for propaganda purposes.

## 4.3. American protectionist literature and the critique of cosmopolitan political economy

My second encounter with List occurred as a consequence of my interest in the American political and economic literature of the late-eighteenth and early-nineteenth centuries. According to List, it is the nation, and not the individual, that serves as the starting point for economic enquiry.

This notion implies the rejection of the abstract, and allegedly universal, principles applied to any circumstances of time and place. The realm of economic policies is particularly sensitive to the specificities imposed by such circumstances.

It is the historical account and experience of nations considered individually that provides us with the basis for interpreting the process of development and the economic policies required to achieve it. Economies need to be seen in their political context if one wishes to consider and understand their relative successes and failures (cf. Winch 1998).

The infant industry argument presented by List as the focus of his nationalist endeavor was strongly influenced by ideas originally put forward in the United States by Alexander Hamilton in 1791 and Mathew Carey in the early 1820s (Tribe 1988, 23). However, it is usually taken for granted that it was List who made a serious attempt to formulate this political argument as an alternative to the classical theory of international trade. List's justification of infant industry was that industrialization could contribute to the development of the civilizing attributes of an urbanized society (which could not be achieved by all countries) offering a broader interpretation of the contribution that infant industry protection made to the development of the productive powers, which included "political, administrative, and social institutions, natural and human resources, industrial establishments, and public works" (Henderson 1983, 159–160).

The relevance of this American influence notwithstanding, it is nevertheless important to mention that List was not the only European economist-journalist to travel to the United States in that period and to be in close contact with American protectionist writers.

The same thing happened with Francisco Solano Constâncio, a Portuguese polymath (doctor, journalist, politician, linguist, economist, and diplomat).

In May 1822, two years after the liberal revolution that occurred in Portugal, Constâncio was appointed as the ambassador of Portugal to the United States. Due to the political instability of the new liberal regime in Portugal, Constâncio was dismissed one year later and then moved from Philadelphia to New York, where he was offered a fresh opportunity to practice medicine and to follow the activities of American scientific associations, up to 1826 (cf. Cardoso 2009).

This American interlude in Constâncio's life was quite relevant for the formation of his economic thought. Indeed, this brought him into close contact with the American protectionist literature and caused him to develop a special esteem for the writings of Benjamin Franklin, Alexander Hamilton, and Mathew Carey. These influences were paramount, and proved to have a most lasting effect on Constâncio's permanent concern with the national element in economic reasoning.

However, in previous articles published in the first journal he edited in Paris, between 1818–1822, entitled *Anais das Ciências, das Artes e das Letras*, Constâncio left us in no doubt about what he found to be wrong in the mainstream political economy of the time, which can be summarized as both the ignorance and the dismissal of the peculiarities of national economic realities. This is precisely what explains the need for "exceptions and modifications" to the main tenets of the science of political economy, namely when he argues in favor of state intervention to protect infant industry.

The same line of thought is explained in a lengthy review of Chaptal's work on the French industry, in which Constâncio claims that:

> As far as customs are concerned there are no general principles and all resolutions have to be taken according to the comparative state of the industry, the needs of the consumer, the particular circumstances characterizing each nation, the degree of prosperity that has been reached by its manufactures, and the likelihood of its future progress.
>
> (Constâncio 1819, 144)

Constâncio's main contention, presented in a variety of reviews published in the *Anais* between 1818 and 1822, is that, notwithstanding its instrumental and temporary nature, protection is a necessary step to enable a less developed country to reach the level of wealth and prosperity needed to establish open trade relations with its partners. Free trade could not be harmful to a nation wishing to open up its economy. Free trade would be a necessary consequence of a successful process of strengthening the pillars of a national economy.

The appeal to take into account the distinctive nature of national realities is a permanent feature of his critique of the abstract principles of political economy. Constâncio was not motivated by a nationalist approach, nor was he interested in promoting the conceptual principles of national identity. Yet he tried to point out that there is an obvious interaction between ideas related to the functioning of economic life and the very nature of the institutions and social arrangements that shape national realities and their distinctiveness. In other words, he could not overlook the specific environment to which general assumptions and principles about both the interpretation of economic phenomena and the implementation of economic policies could be applied.

Constâncio's enduring motto, expressed in his own words, was "to verify the truth of the principles of political economy and to know the modifications that, due to their practical implementation, are required in each country" (Constâncio 1819, 106).

This does not mean that Constâncio was opposed to theoretical approaches to political economy. His translations into French of Ricardo's *Principles of Political Economy and Taxation* and Malthus' *Principles of Political Economy*, as well as his articles on the Malthus-Say debate on the *loi des débouchés*, provide robust evidence of both his keen interest and firm knowledge of the theoretical tool-box of the science he was dealing with. However, it was precisely this activity as a translator and reviewer that made it possible for Constâncio to develop a new awareness of the limits to the application of the general abstract principles of political economy. In this sense, Constâncio's methodological position on the limitations of scientific discourse could even be validated through an approval of Malthus' considerations on the scope and shortcomings of political economy:

> His [Malthus'] purpose is to show that those wishing to use science in a practical way should never adopt any general rules without consulting the relevant experience, nor should they use these rules without taking into account the particular circumstances of the case in mind. All his work is an attempt to prove that political economy is a science of proportions, and that it does not embody absolute truths.
>
> (Constâncio 1820, 152)

The gradual withdrawal of Francisco Solano Constâncio from the abstract, allegedly universal, principles of political economy, and his consequent acceptance of political economy as a "science of proportions", was considerably reinforced during his stay in the United States between 1823 and 1826. In fact, his close contact with the American economic literature of this period – as well as the opportunity to follow economic policy debates on the system of tariffs, incentives and protection for industry, taxes and contributions, public debt, and economic development – acted as an essential tonic to stimulate Constâncio's vision of the instruments and conditions that the government should deal with in order to promote the progress of the nation and the development of the national economy.

Constâncio acknowledged and paid tribute to the intellectual legacy he had received from Franklin, Hamilton, and Carey, namely in the articles that he published after his return to Europe (Constâncio 1838).

The historical reconstruction of these influences on Constâncio's thought allows for the acknowledgement of an interesting similarity between the Portuguese author and Friedrich List, who also spent a few years of his life on American soil, between 1825 and 1832. Besides their similar journeys, both authors explicitly demonstrated their debt to the American protectionist literature in the formation of their system of thought, especially with regard to the development of arguments in favor of industrial protection.

While List's work enjoyed a widespread dissemination and influence in many European circles (and List was able to build up a coherent argument explaining the rationale of protection as a means of achieving national development), there is no doubt that Constâncio was the first to draw attention to the same issues that were to establish List's position as a central figure in the critical appraisal of the shortcomings of classical political economy.

I am not suggesting that Constâncio, instead of List, should be considered as the pioneer of the national approach to the system of political economy. What is shown by these similar and independent influences, simultaneously captured from American doctrines and policies, is the universal nature of the processes involved in the dissemination, appropriation, and adaptation of ideas that can be used in the service of the development of economic nations.

To sum up: List was not alone in his crusade supporting the development of the national system of political economy.

## 4.4. Economic development in the tropics

My third and last encounter with List was a consequence of my research interest in the approach to economic development adopted by the United Nations Economic Commission for Latin America (ECLA/CEPAL) in the postwar period.

The concern with economic development has been present at various moments in the history of economic thought, although it is only since the mid-twentieth century that it has become a prominent feature in the agenda of economists. One of the pioneering approaches was built up by Paul Rosenstein-Rodan (1943), who began by presenting the idea that the process of economic modernization would require a "big push" in order to solve the vicious circle of economic backwardness. Such a process implied the creation of industrialization programs fostered by the state, which could only be made feasible through public investment and foreign aid. Planning and investment were the keywords in this approach to economic development, taking into account the situation in Eastern and South Eastern European countries, where the effectiveness of the market mechanism was called into question during that period.

However, it was in a different geographical setting that the literature on economic development would soon increase dramatically, in the context of the United Nations' general concern with the ever greater differences between developed, developing and underdeveloped countries. The awareness of the causes of, and solutions for, economic backwardness was clearly revealed by Hans Singer (1949) and Raul Prebisch (1962 [1949]), the latter being unanimously considered as the founding father of the structuralist doctrine of development associated with the mission and work undertaken by the United Nations Economic Commission for Latin America (ECLA).

Many economists from Argentina, Brazil, and other Latin American countries joined in the efforts of ECLA, which was to become a fundamental institution dealing with the implementation of economic policy measures designed to overcome economic underdevelopment.

The basic intuition of the economists working under the auspices of ECLA was to note an unequal and asymmetric relationship between the industrialized core and the periphery supplying raw materials, a relationship that is, in every respect, identical to the typical form of relationship between the old imperial metropolises and their colonies.

According to this analysis, it was essential to initiate an industrialization process in the peripheral countries through the import substitution of products that could be manufactured internally without worsening the relationship of technological dependence. In this process, it fell to the state to play an essential role in the creation of a protective environment that would make use of the customary instruments of economic policy (infant industry and protective tariffs) needed to encourage the take-off and consolidation of the industrial sector. The Latin American structuralist school did not invent such instruments, but contemplated the opportunity of their being used in order to lessen the inequalities in the levels and rhythms of development between the countries at the core and those on the periphery.

Contradicting the presuppositions and developments of the Ricardian theory of comparative advantages, Prebisch and his followers tried to show that the constant and progressive deterioration of the terms of trade in the peripheral countries made it impossible to maintain the illusion that all countries could simultaneously benefit from the expansion of trade at an international level. This is also a very peculiar and distinctive feature of Latin American structuralism, when compared to other forms of structuralism, namely the analysis put forward by François Perroux or Albert Hirschman, for whom there was no need to fight against the arguments of the classical and neoclassical theories of international trade and specialization. According to Prebisch, the assumptions of both the perfect mobility of the factors of production and the advantages of free trade were not confirmed. The international environment was therefore one further structural determinant of the difficult situation experienced by Latin American economies, which needed to be faced with different theoretical means and policy instruments. The central message was that international trade and specialization could no longer be only for the benefits of industrialized, developed countries.

Many of these arguments and analytical efforts were supported by references to List's work. However, List was opposed to the adoption of protectionism in countries that had not reached the minimum level of cultural, institutional, political, and economic development.

In this regard, it is curious to see how List was a victim of the irony of destiny: although not considering the application of his stages theory to tropical areas, but considering that "a country of the torrid-zone would make a very fatal mistake, should it try to become a manufacturing country" (List 1885 [1841], 75), it was precisely in Latin American countries that List's theories and policies became popular (cf. Boianovsky 2013).

In fact, List's ideas on the role of the nation-state in channeling the allocation of productive powers to foster a process of economic development made him a popular mentor within the intellectual circles of development theories and doctrines of the postwar period, both in Europe and in the Hispanic-American world.

List's colonialist prejudices concerning the cultural, institutional and climatic conditions that could prevent a country from developing a manufacturing sector, hence causing any policy of protection to be counterproductive, were overcome by those who saw List's work as an invitation to believe in sustainable and balanced development on a global scale.

## 4.5. Conclusion: in search of a new notion of economic development

The three encounters with List referred to above enable us to identify a set of components featuring a notion of economic development to which List has certainly contributed. The concept of development in List implies the consideration of the elements summarized below.

**Objective and purpose**: catching up and emulation, how to attain other countries' levels and standards, how to deal with the conditions needed to overcome economic backwardness. Against the policies implemented by the dominant countries or nation-states (especially Great Britain), which prevented the autonomous development of a nation's potential.

However, it was important to understand how England had reached its supremacy and economic power, and to identify the main English achievements in building up a commercial society. This was an approach that went back to the Enlightenment's ideas about the merits of a commercial society. It implicitly claimed that any other nation could follow the same steps and emulate England on its way to progress and growth. Such a process did not imply the expansion of borders or the conquest of other territories. Commerce was a key element, but it was not the only way to catch up. It was also necessary to create industrial power and to reinforce the means for facing economic competition on an international scale.

**Stages**: the transition to high levels of development and the successive incorporation and integration of economic sectors (agriculture, industry, and commerce) is a gradual process that passes through several stages (savage stage; pastoral stage; agricultural stage; agricultural and manufacturing stage; agricultural, manufacturing, and commercial stage).

**Protection vs. free trade**: industrial development in economically weak countries requires protectionist policy measures for infant industry and trade tariffs. And it requires state intervention through public investment and budgetary deficit policies. List was more concerned about the dangers of laissez faire than he was about the dangers of protectionism. However, protection is not an end in itself and some of the arguments defending free trade can be accepted and accommodated. List took a pragmatic attitude towards protection. (cf. Harlen 1999 and Palacio 2014). As far as agriculture was concerned, he was resolutely opposed to any type of protection. And, whenever a country has reached a comfortable stage of industrial development – overcoming the natural and artificial advantages of other countries, namely England – protective instruments should be gradually reduced and the country should benefit from the good effects of competition at an international level (cf. Maneschi 1998, 92–103).

List believed that some protectionism was needed, since free trade would not bring about equality among different countries. If a nation that was capable of industrializing had not yet reached that stage of development, it was in its own interest, but also in the interest of others, that the government of that nation should implement public aid to industrialization (cf. Gomes 1987). His basic reasoning can be summed up as follows:

> List simply advocated temporary protective measures in countries passing through a certain type of development to ensure that they could trade on an equal footing with more advanced countries in producing manufactured goods.
>
> (Irwin, 1996, 127)

**Internal market**: protectionism applied to industry produces inductive effects in the economy as a whole, fostering domestic demand and a balanced growth strategy.

> A nation which exchanges agricultural products for foreign manufactured goods is an individual with *one* arm, which is supported by a foreign arm … an agricultural-manufacturing nation is an individual who has *two* arms of *his own* at his disposal.
>
> (List 1885 [1841], 180)

> The whole social state of a nation will be chiefly determined by the principle of the variety and division of occupations and the co-operation of its productive powers. Therefore, each country or nation-state should not promote specialization, but rather seek "the balance or the harmony of the productive powers.
>
> (List 1885 [1841], 159–160)

**Infrastructures**: there is no economic growth without investment in modern economic infrastructures, especially in the transport sector.

**Human capital**: there is a hierarchical order of the various types of capital (natural, material, and mental/intellectual). Education is a basic condition of economic development, through the application of science, skills, and knowledge to increase economic performance (cf. Levi-Faur 1997). As Freeman puts it: "List did anticipate these essential features of current work on national systems of innovation" (Freeman 1995, 6).

**Institutions**: the role of social and institutional arrangements that shape national realities and their distinctiveness. The special role of educational institutions to build capacities and competences.

**Economic nationalism**: the relevance of individuals, not as producers and consumers, but as citizens and members of nations, conceived as collective communities. The role of national culture and identities (cf. Helleiner 2002).

We may certainly find all these ingredients in List's writings, thus proving his comprehensive and wide-ranging approach to development. List did not consider protectionism as the central motive of differentiation from classical political economy. The dispute was not about a mere policy issue, but instead concerned a conceptual divide about the crucial relevance of nations in economic analysis. Throughout his public career, List gave us a testimony of his personal commitment and intellectual engagement in pursuing the endeavor of economic development, through protection, when needed, but especially – as the motto highlights – "through wealth to freedom".

## References

Boianovsky, M. (2013), Friedrich List and the economic fate of tropical countries, *History of Political Economy*, 45:4, 647–691.

Cardoso, J. L. (2009), F. Solano Constâncio on political economy: A "science of proportions", *History of European Ideas*, 35:2, 227–235.

Cardoso, J. L. (2017), The Anglo-Portuguese Methuen Treaty of 1703: Opportunities and Constraints of Economic Development. In Alimento, A. and Stapelbroek, K. (eds.), *The Politics of Commercial Treaties in the Eighteenth Century. Balance of Power, Balance of Trade*. Cham, Switzerland: Palgrave Macmillan, 105–124.

Constâncio, F. S. (1819), Review of "De l'industrie française par M. Le Comte Chaptal". In *Anais das Ciências, das Artes e das Letras*, Vol. 5, Part I, 116–137 [reprinted in Constâncio, Francisco S., *Leituras e Ensaios de Economia Política*. Lisboa: Banco de Portugal, 1995 (Series of Portuguese Economic Classics, edited with an Introduction by J.L. Cardoso)].

Constâncio, F. S. (1820), Reflexões acerca de algumas questões relativas à economia política, e sobre a obra recente de M. Malthus. *Anais das Ciências, das Artes e das Letras*, Vol. 10, Part I, 72–88 [reprinted in Constâncio, Francisco S., *Leituras e Ensaios de Economia Política*. Lisboa: Banco de Portugal, 1995 (Series of Portuguese Economic Classics, edited with an Introduction by J.L. Cardoso)].

Constâncio, F.S. (1838), *Armazém de Conhecimentos Úteis, nas Artes e Ofícios*. Paris: J.-P. Aillaud.

Freeman, C. (1995), The 'National System of Innovation' in historical perspective, *Cambridge Journal of Economics*, 19:1, 5–24.

Gomes, L. (1987), *Foreign Trade and the National Economy. Mercantilist and Classical Perspectives*. London: Macmillan.

Harlen, C. M. (1999), A reappraisal of classical economic nationalism and economic liberalism, *International Studies Quarterly*, 43:4, 733–744.

Helleiner, E. (2002), Economic nationalism as a challenge to economic liberalism? Lessons from the 19th century, *International Studies Quarterly*, 46:4, 307–329.

Henderson, W. O. (1983), *Friedrich List: Economist and Visionary, 1789–1846*. London: Frank Cass.

Irwin, D. A. (1996), *Against the Tide. An Intellectual History of Free Trade*. Princeton: Princeton University Press.

Levi-Faur, D. (1997), Friedrich List and the political economy of the nation-state, *Review of International Political Economy*, 4:1, 154–178.

List, F. (1885 [1841]), *The National System of Political Economy*. London: Longmans, Green and Co (translated by Sampson S. Lloyd).

Maneschi, A. (1998), *Comparative Advantage in International Trade. A Historical Perspective*. Cheltenham: Edward Elgar.

Palacio, J. F. (2014), Reconsidering protectionism in Friedrich List's economic theory. In Cardoso, J. L., Marcuzzo, M. C. and Sotelo, M. E. R. (eds.), *Economic Development and Global Crisis: The Latin American Economy in Historical Perspective*. London: Routledge, 53–64.

Prebisch, R. (1962 [1949]), The economic development of Latin America and its principal problems, *Economic Bulletin for Latin America*, 7, 1–22.

Rosenstein-Rodan, P. N. (1943), Problems of industrialisation of Eastern and South-Eastern Europe, *The Economic Journal*, 53: 210/211, 202–211.

Singer, H. (1949), The distribution of gains between investing and borrowing countries, *American Economic Review*, 40:2, 473–485.

Tribe, K. (1988), Friedrich List and the critique of "cosmopolitical economy", *Manchester School*, 56:1, 17–36.

Tribe, K. (1995), *Strategies of Economic Order. German Economic Discourse, 1750–1950*. Cambridge: Cambridge University Press (Chapter 2: Die Vernunft des List. National economy and the critique of cosmopolitical economy).

Viner, J. (1929), Review of Friedrich List, Schriften, Reden, Briefe. Band IV, eds Salin, E and Sommer, A. *Journal of Political Economy*, 37:2, 364–366.

Winch, C. (1998), Listian political economy: Social capitalism conceptualized? *New Political Economy*, 3:2, 301–316.

# 5 German, American and French influences on List's ideas of economic development

*Harald Hagemann*

## 5.1. Introduction

Friedrich List (1789–1846) is probably, besides Karl Marx (1818–1883), Germany's most famous economist of the 19th century, although both were not professional academics. "What is the value of a science which does not illuminate the way practice should walk?" was a statement List made repeatedly.[1] According to his self-estimation List was an independent and original thinker who appropriately could be called a "theorizing practitioner". Life and work were strongly intertwined, and the combination of theory and practical application was characteristic of List throughout his life. List was active successively as a civil servant, short-time professor of administrative practice at the newly founded faculty for state economy at the University of Tübingen in 1817–1819, journalist, railway promoter and American Consul to Leipzig, restlessly agitating public opinion with his reformist spirit in favor of industrial development. As expressed in his formula "Through Wealth to Freedom", economic progress for List was inseparably linked with his liberal convictions.

List lived in Germany, from 1825–1832 in the United States, and repeatedly for longer periods in France at a time when England was the leading economy in the world or "dominant nation" (List [1837] (1983), ch. VI). He considered France and the USA as the first followers; the French economy without doubt the first contemporary follower, but the US economy, as sometimes predicted by List, had enormous potential to forge ahead of the British economy in the long run, a prediction which materialized about half-a-century after List's death. List wanted to promote Germany to a leading industrial nation but considered her only as a contemporary manufacturing power of third order, which intends and is capable of advancing to one of second order (List [1837] (1983), ch. V).[2]

List's three more elaborated treatises of political economy, his *Outlines of American Political Economy* ([1827] 1965), *The Natural System of Political Economy* ([1837] 1983) and *The National System of Political Economy* ([1841] 1885) were published in the three countries where he spent most of his life, being influenced by contemporary economic developments, authors and policy debates. Despite these influences, which affected the elaboration of his ideas, there exist convincing arguments that the origin of List's national-economic theorems, which culminated in the *National System* ([1841] 1885), is already contained in the memorandum on tariff arguments that he presented in April 1819 to the merchants assembled at the Bundestag in Frankfurt.[3]

At that time, when Germany still consisted of a conglomerate of 39 individual states, the democratic movement was characterized by the fact that liberal and national ideas were almost inseparably linked, somehow expressing also the experiences of the Napoleonic period. Accordingly, we find List as a liberal and democrat who emphasized that respect for human rights and civil liberties should accompany industrial development, and as an author and activist in whose conceptions there is a sharp accentuation of the nation as the decisive economic unit in between individualism and cosmopolitanism.

In the following I first trace German, American and French influences in List's writings and ideas in *Section 5.2*. These influences were formed in economically ascendant nations which had entered into a catching up-process towards the leading British economy at List's time and after. Germany in particular lagged behind before an enormous catching up-process, which would have impressed List, took place between national unification at the end of the French-German war in 1871 and 1914. Core elements of List's approach are discussed with the theory of productive forces in *Section 5.3*, his stages theory of economic development in *Section 5.4* and the infant industry argument in *Section 5.5* before some conclusions are drawn in the final *Section 5.6*.

## 5.2. German, American and French influences

From a history of economic thought perspective List's work is not easy to classify because he sits on a fence between different "schools". In his early period he was certainly strongly influenced by Mercantilism and German Cameralism, as represented by his Dean Friedrich Carl Fulda at the Tübingen Faculty, and less so by romanticism. List distanced himself from British classical political economics, in particular Adam Smith, and later from rising socialism, although in the wake of the July Revolution 1830 in Paris he had been influenced by early French socialists, especially by the Saint Simonians. List did not only fight against the dominance of England as the leading economy but also against British hegemony in political economics. However, as Waentig (1910, p. X) has already stated in his Preface to the republication of the *National System*, "although reluctantly" List "was not for nothing apprenticed to Adam Smith". A main mediator and driver of the diffusion process of Smithian ideas in Germany had been Georg Sartorius (1765–1828) at the University of Göttingen who also dealt with Lauderdale's objections against Smith's distinction between private wealth and the wealth of nations and a too passive role of the state.[4] As Keith Tribe has rightly emphasized in his insightful treatise on German economic discourse, Sartorius, despite his allegiance to Smithian principles, had already pointed out the necessary modification of general economic principles, such as the theory of value, with respect to nations, customs, climate, etcetera and thereby stated "his adherence to an 'empiricist' approach to economic analysis that was quite consistent with the arguments put forward by Friedrich List" (Tribe 1995, p. 167).

List's work has often been classified in the mercantilist tradition as, for example, Werner Sombart has done in his *Modern Capitalism* (II/2, p. 919). Surely, his ideas and conceptions were conditioned by the afterglow of mercantilist and cameralist doctrines and the economic and political situation in Germany after the end of the Napoleonic wars. The work of the Scotsman, Sir James Steuart's *An Inquiry into the Principles of Political Economy* ([1767] 1966), a leading contribution of late Mercantilism, was not only well known in Germany (and even commented on by the famous philosopher Hegel) but also for a greater part written in his exile years in Tübingen from 1757–1761. Steuart's work, which is characterized by a broader historical and sociological perspective, was later appreciated by the members of the younger historical school. His belief that the government has an important role to play in the management of economic development also fits well with List's conceptions.

The notion and emphasis on productive forces had a long tradition in Germany and also took central stage in the work of Adam Müller (1779–1829), the leading representative of the German Romanticist school of economic thought, even more hostile to Smithian ideas than List and a personal enemy of List. Eisermann (1990, p. 38) rightly points out that List and Müller have to be considered as the "Janushead", in other words the double-sided nature of the same transforming historical-sociological movement. Whereas Müller embodied the backward-looking feudal-conservative viewpoint and characteristically became a close associate of Metternich (List's most influential lifelong enemy[5]), List conceived the forward-looking perspective of the rising industrial bourgeoisie, one not equal to the dominant British competitors at an early stage of industrial development.[6] Although Müller had been trained as an Anglophile by Friedrich Gentz in his younger years, he never was impressed, as List was, by the British role model of industrial development and political liberalism, but shaped his reactionary views in opposition to the French Revolution and Napoleon.

After his release from prison List had to emigrate and arrived in the USA on 10 June 1825. There he was primarily engaged in the industrial development of Pennsylvania in the following six years and ran directly into the contemporary American tariff controversy, which was at its peak. Whereas the cotton or tobacco producers in the southern states did not suffer from England's dominance as the world industrial leader and the related "free trade imperialism", representatives of the northern states, such as Pennsylvania, were convinced that industrial development could not take place successfully under the conditions of free trade and therefore opted for protective tariffs. The Pennsylvania Society for the Encouragement of Manufactures and the Mechanic Arts, which had its headquarters in Philadelphia, became the spearhead of the protective tariff movement or the so-called "American System", a conception originating with Alexander Hamilton as early as 1787, and later elaborated in a series of state papers such as his 1791 *Report on Manufactures*. There Hamilton energetically proposed to promote economic development, in particular manufacture, and he favored an active role of the government to strengthen this process. Hamilton, who died in a duel in 1804, surely had a strong influence on economic writers such as Mathew Carey, Daniel Raymond and Friedrich List.

Earlier in Germany, List had primarily fought for the abolition of internal duties at the borderline of the 39 states and for the introduction of a customs union. In America emphasis shifted to the requirement of levying high import tariffs for the protection of young industries. The infant industry argument, which originated with Alexander Hamilton, certainly belonged to List's "American heritage". Immediately after his arrival in America List had joined Lafayette on his second American tour. In the course of the next three months List became acquainted with the most prominent American politicians and leading northern industrialists. After a short period as a farmer he mainly worked as a journalist, as the editor of the *Readinger Adler*, a German-language newspaper in Pennsylvania.[7] This gave him ample time to write his *Outlines of American Political Economy* ([1827] 1965). These comprise a series of twelve public letters to Charles J. Ingersoll, the Vice Chairman of the Pennsylvania Society, which first appeared in the *National Gazette* of Philadelphia under the title "The American System", soon after published as a pamphlet (without letter XII). In these *Outlines* ([1827] 1965), his most important American publication, List points out the fundamental distinction between political and cosmopolitical principles. As a strong and enthusiastic advocate of the "American System" and with his common patriotic spirit, he soon became a leading representative of the protective tariffs movement in public opinion, attacking the cosmopolitan system of free trade as upheld by Adam Smith and Jean-Baptiste Say.[8]

List's *Outlines of American Political Economy* were also inspired by Daniel Raymond (1786–1849) and his *Thoughts on Political Economy. A Theory of Productive Power* ([1820] 2019) was the first systematic treatise of economics in the USA, as forcefully argued by Erik Reinert (2015) recently,[9] thus supporting Tribe's earlier statement that "the similarity of the arguments is evident" (Tribe 1988, p. 24).[10] As the subtitle suggests, Raymond in 1820 elaborated a theory of economic development based on productive power. He also attributed a key role to state and governmental intervention to promote economic development. Furthermore, as Hamilton, Raymond argues in favor of an adequate balance of agriculture and manufacture for a harmonious development. Like List, Raymond rejects the arguments of Smith and his followers as focusing exclusively on the individual and private wealth and thereby neglecting the nation as an organic entity. Political economy should place the nation and not the individual into the center. Raymond and List alike confront the theory of productive power with the theory of value, and they both reject Smith's classification of productive and unproductive labor.

In his *Report on Manufactures* Hamilton ([1791] 1966) had pointed out that manufacture should take the lead in the development process. A nation could only increase its wealth on the basis of a prospering manufacturing sector, because productivity increases are more likely and higher than in agriculture. Whereas Hamilton ([1791] 1966, pp. 247–9) in this argumentation followed Smith's reasoning against the Physiocrats, he departed from Smith in favoring a system of protective tariffs to shelter the young American manufacturing companies against the dominant European, i.e. mainly English and French, competitors in their infant stage. A free international trade system would victimize them and prevent the building up of a manufacturing industry that confined America to agriculture.

These arguments had a stronger influence on List, who certainly had studied Hamilton. List's *Outlines* deserve "a place of honor in American economic literature" (Notz 1926, p. 261). Accordingly, Paul A. Samuelson (1960, p. 34) "would add the name of Friedrich List to the array of important American economists". The strong impulses List received in America are also reflected in his later main works, the *Natural System* and the *National System* whose "author was as much American as German" (Tribe 1988, p. 23). Furthermore, "America was to him a great practical school of experience" (Notz 1926, p. 261), and List transferred the knowledge he had acquired as a railway pioneer in Pennsylvania and co-founder of the Little Schuylkill Navigation Railroad and Coal Company to his subsequent activities in Germany.

List lived in Paris from October 1837 to May 1840, after being urged aside as a railway pioneer in Saxony and failed attempts for a political rehabilitation in Wuerttemberg. List had been in France quite often before as, for example, in 1824 when he became friends with Marquis de Lafayette, or after the July Revolution in 1830 in which Lafayette also played an important role. Furthermore, as a young man he was deeply inspired by the ideas of the French enlightenment. In particular List, a lifelong liberal, considered Montesquieu as a kindred spirit whose articulation of the theory of separation of powers, the executive, the legislative and the judicial, which also had a deep impact on the fathers of the American constitution, remained a powerful influence on List. On the other side, List felt deep animosities against French centralism whose negative consequences he experienced during the Napoleonic occupation when his hometown Reutlingen lost its status as a free city.

List's second main treatise *Le Système Naturel d'Économie Politique* ([1837] 1983) was his contribution to the first of two prize competitions announced by the Académie des Sciences Morales et Politiques.[11] The *Natural System* was rather hastily written, since List had less than two months to meet the deadline of 31 December 1837. "Natural" was intended in the sense of the French enlightenment as the "rational" or "reasonable". List gave his essay the leitmotiv "*Et la patrie, et l'humanité*", a motto which he took over from the freemasons and which reflects that patriotism should be embedded in humanism, in other words a clear statement against aggressive nationalism.

The question raised by the French academy reads: "What circumstances must a nation consider if it intends to proceed to free trade or to modify her customs legislation to balance the interests of the national producers with those of the masses of consumers in the fairest manner?" List's answer links up with his *Outlines* but also contains new elements and aspects. For the first time there is an explicit although short chapter (3) on the "Theory of Productive Powers", later extended in the *National System* (List, [1841] 1885). The most novel element is that the *Natural System* is characterized by List's stages theory of development in an extensive way. French influences show up in the rationalist and cosmopolitan flavor of the argument which, as in *Outlines*, from the perspective of an advanced catching up-economy is directed against England as the dominant nation.

List was already at the age of 48 and his decisive economic and political views were shaped long before. In the elaboration of these views French influences were not as strong as German or American ones. Nevertheless, they existed in line with List's empiricist-historical approach. Among French authors who exerted a greater influence on List are Jean Antoine Chaptal (1756–1832) and Charles Dupin (1784–1873), who had both been supporters of Napoleon's economic policy and were leading French protectionists.[12] List certainly had read Chaptal's study on French industry (1819), because he referred to it in an 1820 memorandum to Metternich. Chaptal, a professional chemist and co-founder of the École Polytechnique in Paris in 1794, served Napoleon as a Minister of the Interior and advisor. As a kind of modern Colbert, he pursued the administration of industry, enhanced also by urgent French needs in the period of the continental blockade, by stimulating the installation of new machines, the introduction of new production processes by dissemination of scientific discoveries via industrial exhibitions and the *Société d'encouragement pour l'industrie national* which was founded in 1801. In Letter III of his *Outlines* List ([1827] 1965, p. 177) praised Chantal for having done "more for the promotion of the industry of France than ever one man did in any other country".

Dupin, who was a leading French protectionist, was just five years older than List. His main work was published parallel to List's *Outlines* and focused on the recovery of the French economy in the decade after the end of the Napoleonic wars (Dupin 1827). List considered Dupin as congenial in advocating for France the same kind of economic policy List recommended Germany to adopt, in other words to promote the productive forces for economic development. List referred to Dupin several times in his *Natural System* as, for example, in Chapter 12 on "The Productive Powers of Industry" which begins with the statement: "Industry is the mother and father of science, literature, the arts, enlightenment, freedom, useful institutions, and national power and independence" (List [1837] 1983, p. 66). List did not plagiarize Dupin but he took him mainly as supporting his own views, not least because Dupin played a key role in drafting the more detailed questions of the prize competition of the French Academy of Moral and Political Sciences. In the end, the prize was not awarded, which disappointed List, but his contribution was among the three out of 27 submissions that were classified as "*ouvrage remarquable*". It took four more years before the subsequent *Das nationale System der politischen Ökonomie,* written in Paris in 1839/40 but published in Germany in 1841, brought List the success and recognition he had been desperately looking for.[13]

## 5.3. The theory of productive forces

From the beginning List pitched his theory of productive forces, which in its most elaborated form is contained in Chapter 12 of the *National System*, against Adam Smith's theory of value, which he considered to be too static in character. Thus, we read on the first page of his chapter: "*The causes of wealth* are something totally different from *wealth itself* ... The *power of producing wealth* is therefore infinitely more important than *wealth itself*".[14] The prosperity or wealth of a nation, according to List, does not depend on the accumulation of exchange values or riches but on the development of her productive forces. List illustrates his case with the comparison of England, but also the recovery processes of post-Napoleonic France, of the United States after the Civil War and of Germany after many devastating wars with the "rich and mighty but despot- and priest-ridden Spain" (ibid., p. 133) which "has sunk deeper into poverty and misery" due to a lack of productive forces.

List held an evolutionary view of economic development. Focus therefore is on central elements which are important for the *creation* of wealth in the long run. With his theory of productive forces, he attempted to comprehend the preconditions of economic growth, but he was unable to transform his vision of economic dynamics into a theoretical model. However, List was not interested in theory for its own sake but in the application of his theory of productive forces for economic policy, and this purpose was served rather well.

If one looks at the core elements of List's category "productive forces" one cannot avoid the impression that it has a lot in common with the notion of "social capability" in Abramovitz's classic paper (1986), which initially was strongly criticized as a "catch-all variable" which is empirically almost impossible to measure. Numerous attempts in the last three decades to measure the key factors that constitute social capability as a requirement for a successful catching-up process of initially backward economies, allowing for the efficient use of the modern production technologies available in the advanced nations, have identified that, besides real capital, human capital and institutional factors such as the rule of law play an important role.

List provides on the one hand a long mix of factors, on the other hand, however, he emphasizes time and again three core elements: mental or intellectual capital – today's human capital – the role of institutions and the importance of railway networks for the integration of larger economic areas.

List could observe that with the foundation of the University of Berlin in 1810, with Wilhelm von Humboldt as the key architect, an enormous amount of intellectual capital was mobilized after the losses of material capital in Prussia's defeat against Napoleon. List does not talk yet of "human capital", but in his American period he had already coined the notion "capital of mind".[15] The role of human capital for List is important in his critique of Adam Smith's distinction between productive and unproductive labor as well as in his early emphasis on services in contrast to material goods. List's metaphor that the upbringing of pigs would be productive, whereas the education of humans by teachers or professors would be as unproductive as the doctor who saves his patient is famous, as is the extended critique against McCulloch that a Newton, Watt or Kepler would be less productive than a donkey, horse or plough animal.[16] Thus intellectual capital is decisive for long-run development:

> The present state of the nations is the result of the accumulation of all discoveries, inventions, improvements, perfections and exertions of all generations which have lived before us: they form the intellectual capital of the present human race, and every separate nation is productive only in the proportion in which it has known how to appropriate those attainments of former generations and to increase them by its own acquirements.
>
> (List [1841] 1885, p. 142)

In his "The 'National System of Innovation' in historical perspective" Chris Freeman ascribes to List a "clear recognition of the interdependence of tangible and intangible investment" but also asserts that

> [i]t was thanks to the advocacy of List and like-minded economists, as well as to the long-established Prussian system, that Germany developed one of the best technical education and training systems in the world ... one of the main factors in Germany overtaking Britain in the latter half

of the nineteenth century, but to this day is the foundation for the superior skills and higher productivity of the German labour force in many industries.

(Freeman 1995, p. 6)

List's early emphasis on the crucial role of institutions is remarkable. He clearly illustrates this in the confrontation between the long-run political and economic developments of Spain and England. The parliamentary system, the rule of law, public control of governmental administration, freedom of press and a kind of subsidiarity principle on the level of the communes are major components of List's explanation of the much better performance of the English economy. It is clear that in his considerations on institutional factors List has a more macroeconomic perspective with an emphasis on nations. He therefore could not be regarded as a precursor of the "New Institutional Economics" which is linked to neoclassical equilibrium concepts. But List clearly was a fore-runner of the German Historical School or American Institutionalism of the Veblen-Commons type.

List was advocating the generation and application of technical progress as a key source of economic development. Productivity increases are a decisive means for the growth of the wealth of nations. List's ideas of development are characterized by an organic systems approach with the nation in the center. Without having yet a clear theoretical conception of economies of scale, emphasis on communication and transport networks as a rich source of productive power without doubt make List a precursor of modern network economics (Shapiro, Varian 1999). As a railway pioneer List perceived that the construction of a German railway network would foster a prospering domestic market and German industrial development, and thereby induce a successful catching-up process to the leading British economy. List, who had already been a pioneer American railway builder, after his return to Germany became the driving force of the railway construction between Dresden and Leipzig, an important traffic junction, which opened in 1837.

It is List's early emphasis on a railway and communications network linking the major centers of economic activities as an efficient driver for the creation of strong national economies for which his work stands out against other contemporary works. Thus he points out: "The needs of industry and communication will compel the railway systems of the larger Continental nations to assume the form of a *network,* concentrating on the interior principal points and radiating from the center to the frontiers" (my italics).[17] In his reflections on why England acquired the position of the leading nation, List repeatedly pointed out how much productive power had been increased due to an extensive street and canal system.[18] A century later, interestingly, it was Joseph Schumpeter who frequently emphasized the impor-tant role of railways for economic development, as stated by his student

Wolfgang Stolper (1988, p. 17): "Railroads ... opened new territories and markets and thus led to new possibilities throughout the economy."

## 5.4. Stages theory of economic development

In his *Natural System* List had elaborated a scheme of economic development as a sequence of stages of agricultural, manufacturing and commercial activity, which he also applied in the *National System*. In the second of List's three main stages (following the earlier primitive and pastoral stages) the establishment of manufacturers contributes decisively to the development of agriculture, whereas in the third stage, which according to List only fully developed in England during his time, in the agricultural-manufacturing-commercial period, industrial production reaches its most advanced state and internal and external trade dominate.

List elaborated his stages "theory" of economic development mainly to be applied in the context of economic policy. As a young man he had observed in Wuerttemberg, in France and elsewhere the flourishing of new industries during the Continental blockade and their subsequent collapse after the end of the Napoleonic period when cheaper exports from the dominant British industry with their economies-of-scale effect were flooding the market. List's stages theory of economic development is strongly linked to his trade policy and infant industry argument, as is his theory of productive forces. Thus in his *Outlines* List had already referred to the positive effects of free trade among nations on the same stage of economic development.

List's stages theory of economic development did not only fit the interests of the bourgeoisie in the catching-up countries, but with his observation that nations pass through different stages of economic development and with his scheme he also became the "father" of the stages doctrine, which is a common characteristic of the German Historical School from Roscher to Schmoller, Karl Bücher and Sombart's *Modern Capitalism* (1916).

List criticized classical economics for not having shown how the prospering nations have reached their higher stage of development, or for what reasons other nations were falling behind. Roscher (1874, p. 978) attested that List already had a "first-rate historical mind", but that his historical erudition was not always drawn from literary sources, which explains some theoretical lacunae. List often declared that for a long period he had been "a very faithful disciple" of Adam Smith and "that the fundamental principles of the science could only be discovered by his researches in the economy of individuals and of mankind".[19] However, it then has to be pointed out that Books III and IV of *Wealth of Nations* already contain a stages theory of economic development in which Adam Smith ([1776] 1976) formulates an embryonic model in which an economy develops through a series of stages from agriculture to manufacture and commerce. As Landesmann (1991) has shown in his critical assessment, there is a certain ambiguity in Smith's approach. Smith's model of unbalanced growth focuses on employment productiveness, in other words a development strategy that advocates the creation of maximum employment for productive workers as quickly as possible. There exists, however, a certain ambiguity because a development strategy that focuses on output productiveness, as in Smith's discussion in Book I whereby productivity growth in manufacture is due to an increasing division of labor, may lead to different results if the ranking of sectors changes in the course of the development process.

It might be added that the conception of stages of economic development can be found also in the writings of James Steuart ([1767] 1966), whose work was known to List. Steuart's sequence resembled that of Smith: from a hunting stage via a pastoral stage to a commercial stage in which the subsistence economy finally is superseded by an exchange economy. Cities grow and a national market emerges. The difference is that governmental intervention plays a greater role in Steuart's view in the evolution of commercialization and industrialization than in Smith's, where this development is more a spontaneous process. With emphasis on a more active government, List's ideas are closer to Steuart's than to Smith's.

## 5.5. The "infant-industry" argument

In his April 1819 memorandum to the newly founded German Association for Trade and Commerce, List made a strong plea for the abolition of barriers to trade and for the generation of free trade within Germany. He considered the abolition of internal tariffs also as a precondition for German (economic) unification. On an international level List favored free trade only among nations on the same stage of economic development. His proposals to protect the building up of infant industries are clearly part of his American heritage and date back to Hamilton. He also applied these to France and Germany as the other main followers of the dominant English economy, which later made List's argument attractive to other nations entering into a catching-up process, for instance China in recent decades.

As a liberal List always considered free trade and economic freedom as highly desirable for an international civil society (and a final world economy of economic equals), but a valuable ideal in historical time only appropriate to and for a group of nations with some degree of equality in their stage of development. If this condition was not met, some form of protectionism aimed at the optimal development of national productive forces was necessary: the infant-industry argument.

List favored temporary but not permanent protective tariffs, and he explicitly excluded agriculture from protection. For him it was not a departure from liberal principles but a tool to shape society by fostering its development potential. He might have underestimated the problem that tariffs once introduced as a temporary protection have a tendency to become permanent due to vested interests acting in the political sphere. A careful reading of his *National Economy* shows that List was by no means a narrow-minded nationalist or chauvinist. If the author would have been an Englishman, List candidly declares, he would hardly have called into question the basic principle of Adam Smith's theory.[20] It is therefore completely misleading to denounce List as a professional protectionist or even autarkist, or to refer to him as backing these policies in a general way.

List did not witness the final abolition of the corn duties in Britain in the year of his death. Two years later, in the Paulskirchen parliament of 1848, the trade debate was one of the most controversial. The followers of List, mainly from southern Germany, finally got a majority for the levying of tariffs to protect domestic industries, whereas the *Zollverein*, the customs union that had been established under Prussian leadership in 1834, initially favored free trade ideas. It can only be speculated what List's position would have been three decades later when, in 1878/79, unified Germany completely re-orientated her policy from free trade towards protective tariffs. This caused heavy controversies at the 1879 meeting of the *Verein für Sozialpolitik* in Frankfurt. Due to an unusually high attendance of industrialists and agricultural protectionists, the liberals lost the final vote in the general assembly. Schmoller, who in his younger years had favored a liberal trade policy, now followed Bismarck in his re-orientation of trade policy towards protective tariffs. List, in his plea for an accelerated diffusion process of industrial capitalism, probably would have favored a lower level of protective tariffs, since Germany was not a backward manufacturing country of third order anymore, but had not yet reached the same stage of development as England or the rising US economy. No doubt exists, however, that half-a-century later List's name was misused in Nazi Germany and Imperial Japan. "I am far away to assert that hatred and envy against other nations should be preached to the nation", List[21] had stated a century before.

## 5.6. Conclusion

List aimed at a synthesis of liberalism and nationalism, but he was neither a libertarian nor a nationalist. Despite his critique of Smith and Jean-Baptiste Say as cosmopolitical economists, List considered himself as a cosmopolitan, as a citizen of the world, "but our cosmopolitanism rests on a sound basis, on nationality ... We are citizens of a nation before we are citizens of the world".[22] He wanted to "serve especially to benefit my German Fatherland",[23] as he said in the Preface to his *National Economy*. For that purpose List became a prophet of industrialization, advocating policies designed to direct the German economy to the highest stage of economic development, the agricultural-manufacturing-commercial stage, which had been attained by England as the dominant nation.

As List stated himself, he had "studied the book of life". Scientifically he was an *autodidakt*, a self-educated person with a grand vision of a national situation, which Schumpeter (1954, p. 504) compares with the vision of

Keynes a century later. List "was a great patriot, a brilliant journalist with definite purpose, and an able economist who coordinated well whatever seemed useful for implementing his vision" (ibid., p. 505). List was unable to transform his vision into a theoretical model. His audience was the informed public opinion. As he states, his *National Economy* "offers the means of placing theory in accord with practice and makes political economy comprehensible by every educated mind".[24]

As a theorizing practitioner List was successful. In his history of economics in Germany, Roscher had already stated that "the great theoretical importance of Friedrich List can only be understood on the strength of his even much greater practical importance" (Roscher 1874, pp. 970–1). In a similar direction Schumpeter argues eight decades later when he comes to the assessment: "List made no original contribution to the analytic apparatus of economics. But he used pieces of the existing analytic apparatus judiciously and correctly. And this, too, spells *scientific* merit".[25]

## Notes

1  See, e.g., List (1927–1936, vol. VI, p. 40).
2  List's assessment of the ranking of the leading industrial economies is widely confirmed by the list of 160 major innovations from the early 19th century to the 1970s in van Duijn (1983, pp. 176–9).
3  See Eisermann (1990, pp. 20–1).
4  See Hagemann (2018, pp. 125–6).
5  See Wendler (2014).
6  For an excellent early comparison of List with Müller see Roscher (1874, pp. 975–8), who elaborates that despite some important similarities, including also emphasis on the nation, differences prevail. List and Müller criticize Smith from completely different viewpoints.
7  On List in America see Notz (1925, 1926), Schafmeister (1995) and Wendler (2015) for greater details.
8  On "Friedrich List and the Critique of 'Cosmopolitical Economy'" see also Tribe (1988).
9  Reinert ([1820] 2019) also edited and introduced a new edition of Raymond's classic work.
10  See Reinert (2015, pp. 523–31) for a direct confrontation of excerpts from List and Raymond documenting this similarity.
11  On the second prize competition, which focused on the diffusion process of steam power and the new means of transport and their effect on the economy, social life and the power of nations see Wendler (2014, p. 9), who had also discovered List's essay "Le Monde Marche" in the Institut de France in Paris in 1983.
12  For a more detailed discussion see Henderson (1982). Henderson also argues convincingly that F.L.A. Ferrier was much less an inspiration for List's doctrines than stated by Marx. See also Eisermann (1990, pp.53 ff.).
13  The *Natural System,* which had been re-discovered by Artur Sommer in the archive of the Institut de France, was first published only as late as 1927.
14  List ([1841] 1885, p. 133; italics in original). Characteristically Chapter 12 is entitled "The Theory of the Powers of Production and the Theory of Value". For some more recent assessments of List's theory of productive forces, written

in the bicentennial year of his birth, see Werner and Mauch (1989) and Schmidt (1990).

15 See vol. II, p. 117 of List (1927–1936).
16 List ([1841] 1885, p. 142).
17 List (1927–1936, vol. 3.1, p. 264). Vol. 3 of *Schriften, Reden, Briefe* contains List's contributions on railways as, for example, the essay "Das Deutsche Eisenbahnsystem zur Vervollkommnung der Deutschen Industrie" (The German railway system for the perfection of German industry, pp. 347–77). The transport system of every country or space is considered by List as an organized whole with main branches, side arms, etcetera, which only as a clearly structured entity increases the productive forces of a nation substantially. "An isolated canal is like a single railway line – a stump without arm and fingers" (Ibid, p. 391).

See also Henderson (1983, part 3) for a summary of List's activities as a railway pioneer. Henderson (p. 278) also reproduces List's map of the development of the Central European rail network until 1855.
18 See, for example, List ([1837] 1983, ch. 27).
19 List (1927–1936, vol. 2, pp. 109 and 102).
20 See Ibid, vol. 6, p.47.
21 Ibid, vol. 9, p.115.
22 List (1927–1936, vol. 4, p. 396). See also List ([1837] 1983, p. 122).
23 List ([1841] 1885, p. XXXI).
24 Ibid, p. XXIX.
25 Schumpeter (1954, p. 517; emphasis in the original).

# References

Abramovitz, M. (1986), "Catching Up, Forging Ahead and Falling Behind", *Journal of Economic History*, 46(2): 385–406.

Chaptal, J.A. (1819), *De l'industrie fFrancoise*, 2 Vols, Paris: Renouard.

Dupin, C. (1827), *Forces productives et commerciales de la France*, 2 Vols, Paris: Bachelier.

Eisermann, G. (1990), "Friedrich Lists Lebenswerk", in B. Schefold (ed.), *Studien zur Geschichte der deutschsprachigen Ökonomie*, Vol. 10, Berlin: Duncker&Humblot, pp. 11–62.

Freeman, C. (1995), "The 'National System of Innovation' in Historical Perspective", *Cambridge Journal of Economics*, 19(1): 5–24.

Hagemann, H. (2018), "German Editions of Adam Smith's *Wealth of Nations*", in J.L. Cardoso, H.D. Kurz and P. Steiner (eds.), *Economic Analyses in Historical Perspective. Festschrift in Honour of Gilbert Faccarello*, London: Routledge, pp. 123–132.

Hamilton, A. ([1791] 1966), *The Report on the Subject of Manufactures, Papers of Alexander Hamilton*, Vol. 10, New York: Columbia University Press.

Henderson, W.O. (1982), "Friedrich List and the French Protectionists", *Journal of Institutional and Theoretical Economics*, 138(2): 262–275.

Henderson, W.O. (1983), *Friedrich List: Economist and Visionary, 1789–1846*, London: Frank Cass.

Landesmann, M.A. (1991), "Adam Smith's Stages Theory of Economic Development and the Problem of the Relative Productiveness of Different Economic Sectors", in *Ökonomie und Gesellschaft*, Yearbook 9: Adam Smiths Beitrag zur Gesellschaftswissenschaft, Frankfurt/New York: Campus, pp. 224–243.

List, F. ([1841] 1885), *The National System of Political Economy*, translated by S.S. Lloyd, London: Longmans, Green and Co.

List, F. (1927–1936), *Schriften, Reden, Briefe*, E. Von Beckerath, K. Goeser, F. Lenz, W. Notz, E. Salin, and A. Sommer (eds.), 10 Vols, Berlin: Reimar Hobbing.

List, F. ([1827] 1965), *Outlines of American Political Economy*, reprinted in *Life of Friedrich List and Selections from his Writings*, edited by M. Hirst [1909] with an Introduction by Joseph Dorfman and the Addition of Letter XII to Outlines of American Political Economy, New York: Augustus M. Kelley.

List, F. ([1837] 1983), *The Natural System of Political Economy*, translated and edited by W.O. Henderson, London: Frank Cass.

Notz, W. (1925), "Friedrich List in Amerika", *Weltwirtschaftliches Archiv*, 21(2): 199–265.

Notz, W. (1926), "Frederick List in America", *American Economic Review*, 16(2): 249–265.

Raymond, D. ([1820] 2019), *Thoughts on Political Economy: A Theory of Productive Power*, edited and with a foreword by E.S. Reinert, London: Anthem Press.

Reinert, E.S. (2015), "Daniel Raymond (1820): A US Economist Who Inspired Friedrich List, With Notes of Other Forerunners of List from the English-Speaking Periphery", in H. Peukert (ed.), *Taking Up the Challenge. Festschrift for Jürgen Backhaus*, Marburg: Metropolis, pp. 517–536.

Roscher, W. (1874), *Geschichte der National-Oekonomik in Deutschland*, Munich: Oldenbourg.

Samuelson, P.A. (1960), "American Economics", in R.E. Freeman (ed.), *Postwar Economic Trends in the United States*, New York: Harper & Brothers, pp. 31–50.

Schafmeister, K. (1995), *Entstehung und Entwicklung des Systems der Politischen Ökonomie bei Friedrich List*, St. Katharinen: Scripta Mercaturae.

Schmidt, K.-H. (1990), "Lists Theorie der produktiven Kräfte", in B. Schefold (ed.), *Studien zur Geschichte der deutschsprachigen Ökonomie*, Vol. 10, Berlin: Duncker&Humblot, pp. 77–102.

Schumpeter, J.A. (1954), *History of Economic Analysis*, London: George Allen&Unwin.

Shapiro, C. and Varian, H.A. (1999), *Information Rules: A Strategic Guide to the Network Economy*, Boston, MA: Harvard Business School Press.

Smith, A. ([1776] 1976), *An Inquiry into the Nature and Causes of the Wealth of Nations*, Glasgow edition, Vol. II, R.H. Campbell, A.S. Skinne and W.B. Todd (eds.), Oxford: Oxford University Press.

Sombart, W. (1916), *Der moderne Kapitalismus*, Vol. II/2, Munich and Leipzig: Duncker&Humblot.

Steuart, J. ([1767] 1966), *An Inquiry into the Principles of Political Oeconomy*, 2 Vols, edited and introduced by A.S. Skinner for the Scottish Economic Society, Edinburgh and London: Oliver & Boyd.

Stolper, W.F. (1988), "Development. Theory and Empirical Evidence", in H. Hanusch (ed.), *Evolutionary Economics. Applications of Schumpeter's Ideas*, Cambridge: Cambridge University Press.

Tribe, K. (1988), "Friedrich List and the Critique of 'Cosmopolitical Economy'", *Manchester School*, 56(1): 17–36.

Tribe, K. (1995), *Strategies of Economic Order. German Economic Discourse, 1750–1950*, Cambridge and New York: Cambridge University Press.

Van Duijn, J.J. (1983), *The Long Wave in Economic Life*, London: George Allen&Unwin.

Waentig, H. (1910), "Introduction to the Republication of the 2nd ed. of Friedrich List", in H. Waentig (ed.), *Das nationale System der politischen Ökonomie*, Jena: Gustav Fischer.

Wendler, E. (2014), *Friedrich List (1789–1846). A Visionary Economist with Social Responsibility*, Berlin: Springer.

Wendler, E. (2015), *Friedrich List's Exile in the United States. New Findings*, Heidelberg and New York: Springer.

Werner, J. and Mauch, G. (1989), "Friedrich List und die Lehre von den produktiven Kräften", *Jahrbücher für Nationalökonomie und Statistik*, 206(6): 533–545.

# 6 Friedrich List and France

## The history of a lifelong engagement

*Mechthild Coustillac*

## 6.1. Introduction

I wish to begin by stating a conclusion that I have come to following intensive study of Friedrich List's life and work: France had a strong and lasting impact upon List unlike that of any other country. He was born in the year of the French Revolution, and grew up in the German southwest, a region over which Revolutionary and Napoleonic France had such great influence. Not only did List make repeated attempts to settle in France and make his living there, from his early years he turned to French authors and politicians for answers to the political, economic and philosophic questions that preoccupied him. Here I will examine these influences, and will demonstrate that List's relationship to France, French thought and French politics was thoroughly ambivalent, filled with tension, even conflicted, such that in his final years it turned into mistrust and rejection.

Chronology offers the best approach to these issues. I will begin with his early years in Württemberg, where we can detect, in his basic thinking and its liberal political orientation, an engagement with the French model. Following this, I will deal with the development of List's system of political economy during the 1820s and 1830s, and its particular relationship to France and French thought. The third part shows how, and for what reasons, List turned his back on France geographically and emotionally, but also politically and philosophically; although this turn away from France did not alter the many ways in which the country had left its mark on him.

## 6.2. 1789–1820: the Württemberg years

The ambivalence of List's relationship to France was developed from some of his earliest experiences. List was a modern thinker, friend to the Enlightenment and liberty, and for him France was the cradle of political liberalism in Continental Europe, the motor of a historical progress understood by him to involve the overcoming of older prejudices by the power of reason. As he wrote in 1818,

Thoughts are free to travel, and no Chinese Wall or military cordon can stop them crossing frontiers. Great minds sent the fruit of their thinking to us; philosophy shined a light into the thick gloom and the doctrine of the state began to be founded upon principles of reason.[1]

(List 1927–1935, Vol. 1, p. 285)

Like Karl von Rotteck and Carl Theodor Welcker, List belonged to that generation of southwest German early liberals whose thinking was stimulated, in many direct and indirect ways, by France; but which also had reason to distance itself from France – from the Terror and the authoritarian centralism of the Jacobins to Napoleon, in 1806 feted as the herald of a new era but also disliked for his Caesarist methods of rule and his trampling upon the rights of national self-determination.

From 1805 to 1813, Württemberg was an ally of Napoleon and a member of the Rhine Federation; in 1806 it became a kingdom and was then ruled in the French, centralised manner, something of which the young List was critical. Throughout his life, France remained for him the country of centralism. In a lecture on the Württemberg Constitution in 1818 he stated that "Tyrants and revolutionaries have here followed the same path, and in this way true civil liberty has been destroyed in the French Republic as surely as it was in Roman despotism."[2] This was a model that he often compared with a lifeless mechanism[3] contrasted with an organically constructed state he considered rooted in German traditions,[4] a model whose introduction into France he recommended. As he said in his critique of the 1817 draft constitution for the Württemberg Estates Assembly,

I further believe that France, enlightened as it is, cannot remain in this monstrous condition and that it will only find rest if it returns to its natural state as a progressively ascending social organisation, if therefore provinces are organised in the same way as are Departments.[5]

(List 1927–1935, Vol. 1, p. 208)

In a liberal and organically constituted state of this kind civil liberty would be a source of energy moving beyond the dispersed and local organisations of society to the state, lending the commonwealth health and strength.[6] This figure of the creation and circulation of strength and energy lays the foundation for his later theory of productive forces, at least in outline.

Another point of his criticism concerned the methods of political action. He thought that the French tended to impulsive action which lacked all forethought, hence to revolution, whereas the more thoughtful Germans would favour more cautious reforms. In 1816 he wrote that:

The German holds on to an institution long after it has become fragile, tirelessly patching it up. Only when he sees that the patchwork will no longer hold does he calmly investigate the causes, coldly calculates what can be retained of the old, and how something new could work better; then he gets down to work. The Frenchman slams his carriage together before he has looked into why it will not move.[7]

(List 1927–1935, Vol. 1, p. 90)

List did think the Germans too cautious and bound up with tradition, but left no doubt that, for him, the only path was that of reform; although this did not stop him lauding the impulse to modernisation that the French Revolution had given Germany, an act of providence that "recognises no *jus quaesitum*, that brings down the old so that from this material a new organic whole can be made."[8]

During these years List turned mainly to French authors for an answer to this question of what the new whole should look like, treating them as the vanguard of modernity. It might be assumed that Rousseau was behind his belief in the perfectibility of man and of human societies, together with his idea that history must lead into a universal union; however, this dimension of List's thinking, drawn from utopian Enlightenment ideas, ultimately failed to withstand historical reality.

More enduring was the influence of Montesquieu, with whom he felt a real intellectual affinity, upon whom he drew as a source of caution more frequently than all other authors. Like Montesquieu in *The Spirit of the Laws* (1748), List is searching for the laws that the development of human societies follow, but above all as an empiricist, observing the special forms assumed by these laws, and the way in which human beings deviate from them. In his book of 1841, *Das nationale System der politischen Oekonomie*, List wrote that Montesquieu, like no other before or after, understood that "history can teach lessons to legislators and politicians."[9] In List's view, this enabled him to see that the free trade theory of the physiocrats was erroneous, and to understand that backward countries could only achieve wealth and liberty through, as he put it, "the development of domestic manufacturing powers".[10]

Like Montesquieu, List sought the means to bring ideal and reality together in the service of the common good. The principle of moderation to which he adhered all his life was also based upon Montesquieu's model of the division of political powers, in which antagonistic forces held each other in check. Modelling himself upon Montesquieu, List always sought a middle path between the general and the particular, the universal and the local, norm and reality, ideal and positive laws, and between rationalism and empiricism.

In addition, List could find in Montesquieu a political myth that had gained great resonance in Germany: according to Tacitus, the English political system, a system that the French philosopher considered exemplary, had Germanic origins.[11]

During his early years in Württemberg List was also a keen reader of French political economy, to which we now turn.

## 6.3. 1820–1840: Three nations and three versions of the system of political economy

List was often on the move in the 1820s and 1830s, during the formation and maturing of his system of political economy. The first version, in English, was his *Outlines of American Political Economy*, written in the USA where he went into exile following his conflict with the Württemberg government. The second version, in French, was his prize essay "Système naturel d'économie politique". The third version, in German, was *Das nationale System der politischen Oekonomie*, written in Paris during 1839–1840, and published in 1841 in Germany, to which he had finally returned.

Characteristic of these writings is List's attempt to mediate between two poles, his political and economic thinking seeking a delicate and unstable balance between nationalist and cosmopolitan dimensions. While the concerns of the nations and their advancement are at the core of his thinking, he treats the nationalist approach as part of a larger system that will, after a phase of national competition, revert to an international equilibrium that includes free trade;[12] so that he had here, just as much as in the political writings of the Württemberg period, the welfare of mankind in view.

In his first American text this perspective at first seems unclear. In a polemical defence of American protectionism List aims above all at the teachings of Adam Smith, which, as he wrote, served the British as a theoretical weapon in seeking to convince rising nations of the benefits of free trade, with the ulterior purpose of smothering their industrial development at birth by the import of British goods. In List's view, which certainly has to be critically scrutinized, Adam Smith's thinking, drawing as it does on the universalism of the eighteenth century, only took account of the individual and mankind, while abstracting from the existence of the nation. List regarded Smith's value theory as purely materialist, static, and mechanical, incapable of assisting a country seeking to attain welfare and power. Underlying these views was what List considered to be the core rebuttal of classical economic liberalism: his theory of productive forces, a dynamic theory of the creation, circulation, and interaction of material and immaterial powers. As he emphasised, in an organically functioning whole these material and immaterial forces would generate wealth and power whilst industry had the task of creating a virtuous circle. List also demonstrated that the development of economic power in such a "rising nation" required protection from foreign, especially British competitors, advocating a flexible tariff system.

List claimed the theory of productive forces as his own invention, but he did cite a number of writers whom he saw in one way or another as forerunners of his dynamic nationalist approach, and with whom he felt some intellectual affinity. It is striking that most of these are French writers.

Of course, we need to be careful in simply taking List at his word, and his statements often say more about his general regard for French sources, or about the particular context in which he cites any one writer – more than about any actual influence on his own thinking.

First among these sources was an economic history of France written by the chemist and politician Jean-Antoine Chaptal.[13] List read this in 1819–1820 when it was first published, and he highly praised it. He also probably drew upon Jean-Baptiste Say's *Traité d'économie politique.*[14] In *Outlines of American Political Economy* List would, however, name Say as an antagonist in the same breath as Smith. There are some indications that List had read the original 1803 edition of Say's *Traité* while a student at Tübingen;[15] in 1819 he did recommend to German merchants that they obtain copies of the 1807 German translation.[16] Just like List, Say was an empiricist who understood political economy to be a "science of observation"; but unlike List, he considered that Adam Smith was the founder of the inductive and experimental method of political economy.[17] Given that Say presented himself as a student of Smith, and was the leading economic liberal on the European continent, List argued that he gave too little attention to the importance of the national perspective, and included him in his crusade against "Smith & Co.", as he put it in *Outlines*. It can, however, be stated with some degree of certainty that List found many ideas in Say that he employed in his own critique of Smith.[18]

This distinction between those French authors List thought of positively, and those about whom he was negative, reflects List's divided relationship to France. He was only positive about those writers who adopted a clear nationalist position within an economically liberal perspective, and who were pragmatic when it came to economic policy. He was full of admiration for French statesmen who, from Colbert through Napoleon to the July Monarchy, instinctively did the right thing and disregarded the influence of the liberal school.

During these years List was convinced that France was in the vanguard of political liberalism, and was as such called upon to be the motor of progress in Europe and the rest of the world. After being sentenced to imprisonment in 1822 he fled and sought political exile abroad, finding his way to Strasbourg, although this ended, after five months of agitation on the part of the Württemberg government, with his expulsion from France. During brief visits to Paris in 1824 he had met the Marquis de Lafayette and formed a lasting friendship with him. He hoped that, with the support of this hero of the American War of Independence and participant in the French Revolution, he might in France be recognised as a persecuted liberal. As he wrote in 1826 in a draft letter to Lafayette, he considered France to be

the only country on the Continent where public opinion exists, where one might, without prompting individual persecution, express support for someone who had been unjustly persecuted, where the free press is allowed to discuss affairs such as my own.[19]

(List 1927–1935, Vol. 8, p. 341)

Following the July Revolution in 1830 List broke off his residence in the USA so that he might, like many liberal and democratically-minded Germans, hurry to Paris. He remained there from December 1830 to October 1831, socialising with the poet Heinrich Heine and with Ludwig Börne, a writer and publicist. He promoted the idea of constructing a railway network centred upon Paris and agitated for the intensification of trade with America, without however any success. In letters to his wife Karoline he expressed his dislike of the country and its inhabitants, writing in January 1831 that "The French are not especially to my taste" and "They are a heartless, superficial people."[20] List admired France and in some respects treated it as a model, but with few exceptions, he had little fellow-feeling with the French.

Following the failure of an attempt after 1834 to establish himself in Germany as a railway pioneer, List moved in 1837 once again to Paris with the intention of participating in railway schemes. Instead, however, he quickly became interested in submitting essays for two prize competitions announced by the Académie des sciences morales et politiques that involved his two special interests, political economy and railway construction. The more important of these two essays was the "Natural System of Political Economy", in which he for the first time presented a fully developed economic argument. The way in which this text diverges from *Outlines* is very much due to the context in which it was composed. The "Natural System" was written as a scholarly treatise, its addressees being the Academy judges for the essay competition. List thought that these judges were mostly inclined towards economic liberalism in a country not needing to establish itself as an economic power, but which could improve its position with respect to Britain. While he did not hide his criticisms of Smith or his claim that he had founded a new system, he emphasised that this system should be understood as part of a wider liberal project whose eventual aim was the establishment of free trade in a world of equally developed countries. The essay came with an epigraph that List had borrowed from a French freemasons' lodge – "Et la patrie et l'humanité"[21] – indicating List's intention of mediating humanity and nation. New in this essay was List's theory of economic stages, a sequence of ideal-typical national stages for each of which there was an appropriate tariff policy. The highest stage corresponded to the position at which Britain had already arrived. The rationalist and cosmopolitan elements of List's system are here more marked than in either his previous *Outlines*, or the later *National System*.

Here we can say a few words about List's other prize essay, entitled "Le monde marche", which is devoted to the diffusion of steam-driven transport and its economic, social, and political effects. This text had been lost, and was only found in the archives of the Institut de France in 1983 by Eugen Wendler, who then translated it into German.[22] The fact that List never again mentioned this second, comparatively brief prize essay could suggest that he later had no especial desire to draw attention to it. This text has a particular significance, since it reflects some acquaintance with the arguments of early French socialists, and especially with those of the Saint-Simonians. Following the dissolution of the sect in 1832 several Saint-Simonians became active as railway promoters, linking their railway projects with a utopian vision of the future in which liberty, equality, and fraternity could become a reality. List was personally acquainted with one of these, Michel Chevalier, becoming one of his admirers. In "Le Monde marche" List also enthused over the spectacular acceleration of progress that railway communication would bring about. The intensification of the circulation of people and material values would lead to the perfection of humanity, bringing people closer together; war would finally become impossible; well-being would spread around the whole world; social differences would disappear. This essay is strikingly similar to contemporary Saint-Simonian writings on steam-driven transport[23] and reflects the most extreme version of List's rationalist and universalist speculations that were ended with the realism of the *National System*.

### 6.4. 1840–1846: List in Germany – from the *National System of Political Economy* to the break with France

As already mentioned, List wrote the *National System of Political Economy* in Paris about two years after the prize essay, but in German and with German developments in view. This text was continuous with *Outlines* insofar as it sought to rouse the public and demonstrate to an economically underdeveloped country that the path to economic growth lay through his theory of productive forces and protective tariffs. The mutual dependence of economy and politics, of national wealth and national power were also here once more at the centre of his argument. Added to this was the issue of national unity; in the case of the USA this already existed, while List was of the view that in Germany this could be brought about through the Zollverein and with Prussian leadership. From the "Natural System" he took a watered-down version of his stages theory, placing his national perspective within the framework of a universalist project. New in this text was the systematic role that he gave to history within political economy, describing it as a mediator between philosophy and politics.[24]

List returned to Germany a disappointed man, neither of his two essays having been awarded a prize, and dismayed at France's claims to the Rhineland, leading in 1840 to the outbreak of the "Rhine crisis". The *National System* included a settling of accounts with France, seeking to arrive at a balanced judgement and render to Caesar what is Caesar's. It has to be emphasised here that List was not among those who adopted a tone of open hostility to France in the context of the Rhine crisis – both in tone and actual judgement he remained moderate.

He never had before cited so many French writers. He is unsparing in his criticisms of the Academy's prize essay judges, accusing them all of having "watered down" the teachings of Adam Smith and Jean-Baptiste Say; they had no understanding of the real world with the exception of Charles Dupin, the jury president, whom he considered occupying a position close to his own, even though he accused him of being an opponent of all theory.[25]

As far as his political thinking went, in spite of all the reservations that List had regarding France, he remained convinced that the only way to successfully resist British competition was through a Franco-German partnership, this being the only way that the European continent could come together in the future. Long years of Franco-German belligerence of course separate List's hopes and their realisation in the second half of the twentieth century, but it may not be concealed that List's *National System* in some respects bears the seeds of these conflicts to come. List is not, in the context of the Rhine crisis, here merely rehearsing criticisms of France's expansionary ambitions with respect to Germany and expressing doubts about France's peaceful intentions;[26] he is also clearly registering German claims to territory and power that are hard to reconcile with French interests. In the *National System* he employs for the first time the concept of the "normalised nation" (*normalmäßige Nation*) and a theory of natural frontiers in order to present Germany as an incomplete national entity, so that he might then legitimate claims to territorial expansion which, in particular, involved the annexation of the Netherlands.[27] There is also in the *National System* the beginnings of an idea that he would subsequently develop, involving the creation of an economic space from the North Sea to the Black Sea under German hegemony. Later this gave rise to the idea of Central Europe (*Mitteleuropa*) during the First World War. While in his 1837 essay List had still presented France as a leading power in the continental alliance that he favoured, by the 1840s the focus had shifted to Germany, whose central position and federal traditions, as he thought, made it the natural mediator between east and west, north and south.[28]

All of which suggests that List, as a pragmatist and realist, could not under these circumstances long sustain his belief in peaceful co-operation between France and a united, and so strengthened, Germany. The rupture and radical reorientation of his political plans was completed by 1845 at the latest.

This was not only related to the Franco-German relationship, but to the anticipated development of human history that List's practised eye saw progressing in a direction that ran counter to the cosmopolitan utopia which he had formerly foreseen and embraced. He now thought that in an era of colonialism the emergence of a small number of autarchic powers was to be expected, a development that would destroy any hope for ascendant nations like Germany of achieving the highest possible stage of development. The prospect of the formation of a universal union in a

peaceful world of equal nations now vanished entirely. Having once predicted the rise of the USA to the position of leading economic power, more
recent developments seemed to indicate that Britain was well on the way to
maintaining and extending its position as the leading imperial nation. In
1846 he expressed the fear that France would not hesitate for long "to slake
its burning thirst for martial glory, to appease those ardent aspirations to be
an unrivalled national power which the French nation has always been bent
on", and which he saw to be rooted in French national character. In the
long or the short term the French would seek, he went on, "to compensate
for France's misfortunes at sea and overseas through continental
conquest."[29] He thought that France could ally itself with Russia and
threaten Germany militarily. These passages are taken from a memorandum
that List presented during the summer of 1846 to members of the British
government, and in particular the then prime minister, Sir Robert Peel. The
memorandum sought to win over the British government to the idea of an
alliance with Germany, a political plan that derived from the recognition
that Germany had, as he wrote elsewhere, "missed the opportunity to
become a great manufacturing and trading nation like Britain, a destiny
that is not in its nature",[30] so that it was as a consequence in Germany's
interest to secure its development through an alliance with Britain. The
memorandum did not only address its arguments to British political interests, but also to the relationship between the German and the British
peoples, both of whom were part of the Germano-Teutonic "race", something that set themselves apart from France and the "Latin races",[31] the use
of the term "race" here not yet implying a strong biological sense. During
this period he expressed repeatedly his sympathy for Britain,[32] and the
feeling of cultural and intellectual affinity that he had never had for
France, a country that had always remained somewhat alien to him.

This new perspective could be reconciled with List's belief that the
eventual triumph of liberty, something which as a liberal he never relin-
quished, would, so he thought, be secured by the fact that Britain as a
colonial power, predestined to rule the world, was also thereby predestined
to diffuse European culture and liberal ideas through the world, and so fulfil
its work of cultivation for the good of humanity.[33]

## 6.5. Concluding remarks

List's relationship to France was most ambivalent. I would propose that this
ambivalence was primarily a consequence of the differing developmental
phasing of Germany and France during the first half of the nineteenth
century. France had a distinct advantage over Germany in both economic
and political respects, and could in many areas present itself as a model that
Germany could seek to emulate. A number of factors nonetheless combined
to increase List's irritation with France leading, after 1840, to a turn away
from France and to Britain. There was much that he found to dislike in

France, or to find alien – its traditional centralisation, or what he called its national character. However, none of this is I think decisive. He could have loathed Napoleon as the occupier of Germany and the representative of French centralism, but instead List admired Napoleon for his genius when it came to economic policy, as evidenced by the continental system, which steered economic policy in the direction of France's interests. But I think something else was decisive: the competitive relationship between Germany and France, or, more properly, the question of the power relationship as it took shape around 1840. The rupture came when List had to admit that, in the medium term, there was no realistic prospect for a Franco-German partnership in the context of a developing German national state, together with the economic and political ambitions that List had for Germany. When it came to Germany's future, List's thinking was shaped by *Realpolitik*. When at the beginnings of the 1840s he saw the dawning of an imperial era and the waning prospects for a continental alliance between France and Germany, he turned to an alliance with Britain.

He did make use of arguments in support of this new political orientation that we might today find questionable, and this is a matter for regret. List was, however, a skilled observer of historical developments, and he thought that he had to move with them – not as a matter of personal opportunism – but from a deep sense of conviction that one could in these historical developments read the designs of providence. It was List's tragedy, I think, that as he stood on the threshold of a new era he was led to doubt what he had wanted to retain from his *National System*: the toleration by France of Germany's development into a nation state, and the coming together of the European continent around a Franco-German partnership.

From the distance of more than 170 years we should today clearly grasp what is valuable in the legacy of Friedrich List: his political liberalism, his contribution to development theory and, not least, his long and enduring hope of Franco-German co-operation in the uniting of the European continent.

## Notes

1   Friedrich List (1927–1935), "Die Staatskunde und die Staatspraxis Württembergs im Grundriß" in *Schriften/Reden/Briefe* Vol. 1.1 p. 285. In the following I will cite List's writings from the ten volume edition edited by Erwin von Beckerath, Karl Goeser, Wilhelm Hans von Sonntag, Friedrich Lenz, Edgar Salin et al., Reimar Hobbing, Berlin 1927–1935.
2   "Über die Württembergische Verfassung (1818)", in: List (1927–1935) Vol. 1.1, p. 381.
3   See for example "Kritik des Verfassungsentwurfs der Württembergischen Ständeversammlung (1817)", in: List (1927–1935), Vol. 1.1 p. 208.
4   The young List seemed to be of the view that the republican system was not a French achievement of the eighteenth century, but was rooted in the free imperial cities of the Holy Roman Empire, and so were anchored in the German tradition – see List (1927–1935), Vol. 8 p. 10.
5   "Kritik des Verfassungsentwurfs", in: List (1927–1935), Vol. 1.1, p. 208.

6  "Über die Württembergische Verfassung (1818)", in: List (1927–1935) Vol. 1.1, p. 366.
7  "Gedanken über die württembergische Staatsregierung (1816)", in: List (1927–1935) Vol. 1.1, p. 90f.
8  "Kritik des Verfassungsentwurfs", in: List (1927–1935), Vol. 1.1, p. 227.
9  *Das nationale System der politischen Oekonomie*, in: List (1927–1935), Vol. 6, p. 245.
10 List (1927–1935), Vol. 6, p. 245f.
11 Montesquieu (1950), Book XI ch. VI, p. 221.
12 List (1927–1935), Vol. 6, p. 167f.
13 Comte De Chaptal (1819).
14 Say (1803).
15 Tagebücher, in: List (1927–1935), Vol. 8, p. 9.
16 List (1927–1935), Vol. 1.1 "Einleitung" p. 48 – see Say (1807).
17 J.-B. Say (1803), p. 25, 28
18 See Coustillac (2009), p. 206.
19 Letter to Lafayette 1 March 1826, in: List (1927–1935), Vol. 8, p. 341.
20 Letter to Karoline List, 18 January 1831, in: List (1927–1935), Vol. 2, p. 44 (Introduction).
21 Salin (1972), p. 350.
22 See List (1985).
23 There are for example many parallels between "Le monde marche" and the prize essay written by List's competitor Constantin Pecqueur – *Économie sociale: Des intérêts du commerce de l'industrie et de l'agriculture, et de la civilisation en général, sous l'influence des applications de la vapeur: machines fixes, chemins de fer, bateaux à vapeur*, 2 vols., Desessart, Paris 1839. During the 1830s Pecqueur was first a Saint-Simonian, then a Fourierist, and very much under the influence of early socialist ideas.
24 List (1927–1935), Vol. 6, p. 41.
25 List (1927–1935), Vol. 6, p. 20.
26 List (1927–1935), Vol. 6, p. 408f., 416.
27 List (1927–1935), Vol. 6, p. 210f.
28 List (1927–1935), Vol. 6, pp. 409f.
29 "On the Advantages and Conditions of an Intimate Alliance between Great Britain and Germany (1846)", German: Über den Wert und die Bedingungen einer Allianz zwischen Großbritannien und Deutschland ("Allianzdenkschrift"), in: List (1927–1935), Vol. 7, p. 277.
30 "Die politisch-ökonomische Nationaleinheit der Deutschen IV (1846)", in: List (1927–1935), Vol. 7, p. 475.
31 "On the Advantages and Conditions" in: List (1927–1935), Vol. 7, p. 275.
32 See for example "Die englische Allianz und die deutsche Industrie (1843)", in: List (1927–1935), Vol. 7, p. 250: "The British are a great and reputable nation which Germans among all the nations appreciate most, and with which they are most in sympathy …".
33 "Bülow-Cummerow und die deutsche Nationalökonomie (1843)", in: List (1927–1935), Vol. 7, p. 120.

# References

Comte de Chaptal, A.-J. (1819), *De l'industrie françoise*, Paris: Renouard.
Coustillac, M. (2009), "Friedrich List (1789–1846): la construction d'un système d'économie politique entre libéralisme et nationalisme", in: Alcouffe,

A., Diebolt, C. (eds.), *La pensée économie allemande*, Paris: Economica, pp. 201–226.

List, F. (1927–1935), *Schriften/Reden/Briefe*, Von Beckerath, E., Goeser, K., von Sonntag, W.H., Lenz, F., Salin, E., et al. (eds.), Vol. 1–10, Berlin: Reimar Hobbing.

List, F. (1985), *Die Welt bewegt sich. Über die Auswirkungen der Dampfkraft und der neuen Transportmittel auf die Wirtschaft, das bürgerliche Leben, das soziale Gefüge und die Macht der Nationen*, (Pariser Preisschrift 1837), trans. and ed. Eugen Wendler, Göttingen: Vandenhoeck & Ruprecht.

Montesquieu. (1950), *De l'esprit des lois, Œuvres complètes de Montesquieu*, Masson, A. (eds.), Paris: Nagel.

Pecqueur, C. (1839), *Économie sociale: Des intérêts du commerce de l'industrie et de l'agriculture, et de la civilisation en général, sous l'influence des applications de la vapeur: machines fixes, chemins de fer, bateaux à vapeur*, Vol. 2. Paris: Desessart.

Salin, E. (1972), "Nachwort zum Neudruck der Werke Friedrich Lists", *Mitteilungen der List Gesellschaft*, No. 14, pp. 345–350.

Say, J.-B. (1803), *Traité d'economie politique ou simple exposition de la manière dont se forment, se distribuent ou se consomment les richesses*, Paris: Crapelet.

Say, J.-B. (1807), *Abhandlung über die National-Oekonomie oder einfache Darstellung der Art und Weise, wie die Reichthümer entstehen, vertheilt und verzehrt werden*, Halle: Ruffsche Verlagshandlung.

# 7 Friedrich List's 'economics of education'

*Stefano Spalletti*

For centuries, various judgments and some allegations of plagiarism have surrounded the issue of the sources of Friedrich List's thought. Going back to the sources of the idea of 'productive force' – as the *primum movens* of List's economics of education and human capital approach – the question becomes a problem within a problem.

Obviously, one can recall that several German works in the economic and juridical fields, connected with the goal to increase national human capital (*Geistiges Capital*), were presented early on (for example, in C.D. Voss's *Staatswirtschaftslehre. Erste Abtheilung. Zweyter Abschnitt* (*State Administration. First division. Second section*, 1798) (Ganilh 1812: 4). According to Turunen (2016: 185–7), it is also possible to find interesting references in Christian von Schlözer's *Anfangsgründe der Staatswirtschaft* (*The Beginnings of the State Economy*, 1805), Friedrich Buchholz's *Untersuchungen über den Geburtsadel und die Möglichkeit seiner Fortdauer im neunzehnten Jahrhundert* (*Studies on the Hereditary Nobility and the Possibility of its Continuation in the Nineteenth Century* 1807) and Johann Paul Harl's *Vollständiges Handbuch der Staatswirtschafts- und Finanz-Wissenschafthen* (*Complete Handbook of Economics and Finance*, 1811). List himself wrote of the physical and intellectual powers of the nation in *Gedanken über die württembergische Staatsregierung* (*Thoughts on the State Government of Wurttemberg*, 1816) very early (List [1816] 1971) and also referred to the 'forces intellectuelles et productives' in *Idées sur les Réformes Économiques, Commerciale et Financières Applicables à la France* (Ideas on Economic, Trade and Financial Reforms Applicable to France, 1831) (List 1831).

In other words, the main root of the economic concept of productive power as human capital in German literature is not easy to find, and this essay does not aim to solve this historiographic impasse. However, from the perspective of the international transmission of economic ideas, the literature on human capital has been correctly related to German economic culture owing in particular to three leading economists: Adam Müller, Johann Heinrich von Thünen and, obviously, List.[1] In particular, there are noteworthy similarities between Müller's *Elemente der Staatskunst* (*Elements of State Art*, 1809) and Friedrich List's *Nationales System der politischen*

*Ökonomie (The National System of Political Economy,* 1841). Müller orients his old-style nation toward a romanticised and organic community, but both authors attribute the growth of nations to productive forces. Schumpeter calls them an 'educational device' and 'a label for an unsolved problem' (Schumpeter 2006: 480). However, the 'visionary' List (Henderson 1983; Wendler 2014) perceives the German nation as moving towards an ideal future characterised by technical maturity in industry, with special emphasis on education, institutions and infrastructure. In order to reach this objective, he drafts a simple stage theory of economic growth, leading from hunting societies all the way to a developed economic state (Hutter 1994: 295–8).

List is not only interested in the total value of the output of his nation, but also in how rapidly or how slowly its economy is growing. He conceives of economic growth as an improvement in the ways and means of producing output, whether or not through technological advances. Of all the technological advances in history, none was more seminal and far-reaching than the development of agriculture. Especially where agriculture is the principal economic activity, people follow old practices for centuries before modern agricultural improvements begin to appear. Moreover, advances in manufacture and technology are more important in some nations of the world than in others, and greater during some periods of history than in others. Looking at historical and technological progress from a national point of view, List becomes an economist with a deep 'political' dimension to his economic thinking.

Nonetheless, List is not a major economic theoretician. Mark Blaug – also one of the 'masters' of the history of economic thought – reviewing Henderson's 1983 translation of the *Système Naturel D'Économie Politique (The Natural System of Political Economy,* 1837) recalls the frequent translations of the *National System* and he does not see the analytical aspects of List's arguments as very strong (Blaug 1984: 369). Nevertheless, Blaug both underlines the virtually unlimited economic powers of the government in List's approach and credits the prosperity of any country almost exclusively to the economic policies of the state. This is a useful political starting point to examine the theory of the economic stages from the perspective of List's national education. In doing so, it is important to review the relationship between Smith and List in light of the interpretation of education as human capital. The differences between the two authors clarify List's educational approach as macroeconomic in nature. Moreover, in taking to a retrospective approach to the economics of education, it is possible to recall a debate about List's aims both in the 'National Innovation System' of today and in the 'Economic Planning by Education'.[2]

With his experience in American economic growth and the related debate on protectionism and industrialisation, together with Alexander Hamilton List recognises economic development as the result of the working of economic forces on an international scale, although they are divided into heterogeneous national entities (Tribe 1988: 29). In this framework, political economy is

> that science which limits its teaching to the inquiry about how a given nation can obtain (under the existing conditions of the world) prosperity, civilisation, and power, by means of agriculture, industry, and commerce.
>
> (List [1841] 1904: 97)

The essence of national economics is that it 'teaches' how to regulate the economy of individuals to increase productive powers within the nation. List's emphasis upon innovation and a national system of education both reflects the role of the national organism and forecasts the focus on positive spillovers in relation to growth theory (Bronk 2009: 156–207). Political economy, therefore, assumes the character of economic policy (economics as art). List's success lies in the transformative power of his message, thanks to a working life dedicated to journalism, a major form of political activity (Greenfeld 2001: 204). The policy of national development needs to follow a specific road map where the influence of education, cultural traditions and national institutions can help shape the trajectory of the nation. In particular, the state can help the nation by increasing its productive powers. Their development historically takes place through a sequence of growth stages: (a) the savage stage, (b) the pastoral stage, (c) the agricultural stage, (d) the agricultural and manufacturing stage and (e) the agricultural, manufacturing, and commercial stage, which teaches how the entire human race can attain prosperity. The transition from the agricultural stage to the agricultural and manufacturing stage is key, characterised by the makeover of a developed agricultural state into one where the productive powers are finally able to introduce industry. Industry can be considered the mother of all sciences, literature, arts and other useful institutions, while a pure agrarian society consists of 'primitive peasants [...] without culture, knowledge or any competitive spirit', without 'mental powers [...] adequately used or properly developed' (List [1837] 1983: 53). The secular idea of the civilising mission is an imperative notion: List's transition from the agricultural to the manufacturing stage represents both a correct route to material development in the national economy and a seminal step toward the fulfilment of a civilising process (Ince 2013: 13). In the transition, the state cannot act as a public notary of abstract values. Development means change in the economic stage, and the passage from state (c) to (d) can be mainly the result of interventions by a state that protects and enlarges the national productive powers.

## Productive powers and human capital

Over the past several decades, forms of intangible wealth such as knowledge, innovation, technological change and technological learning have been identified as engines of progress. In this sense, National Intellectual Capital (NIC) can be seen as consisting of five components, each with its own measurement methods: human capital, market capital, process capital, renewal capital and financial capital (Yeh-Yun Lin, Edvinsson 2010: 4). Let us start from a definition of productive powers as a first component of NIC, keeping in mind the historical evolution of the notion of human capital and its relation to the economics of education (formerly Becker 1964). While economics and history of economic thought tend to see human capital as a 'driver' useful for making education more productive in income and wealth augmentation (Hartog 2000), List establishes that the power to produce wealth is infinitely more important than wealth itself. Firstly,

> a person may produce wealth, that is, exchangeable value; if, however, he cannot produce goods of a higher value than the ones he consumes, he will become poorer. A person may be poor; if, however, he can produce a larger quantity of goods than he consumes he will become rich.
>
> (List [1841] 1904: 108)

Secondly, capital is not a common stock with a substitute effect. Capital has three different components: the 'capital of nature', the 'capital of mind' and the 'capital of productive matter' (List [1827] 1909: 188). Also, the productive forces are not confined to a set of material goods, but include a diverse set of intellectual forces. According to List, for example, sources of productive forces are the invention of the press, the postal system, money, standard weights and measures, the calendar, watches, the police and new means of transport, as well as the introduction of property rights in agriculture (List [1841] 1904: 113). The productivity of the 'capital of productive matter' depends upon the 'capital of nature' and the 'capital of mind'. Intelligence and the social conditions of a nation, indeed, are linked to advances in science and technology, the legal-institutional framework and the educational system. Therefore, the powers of production are instruments to increase wealth.

The Scottish economist Joseph Shield Nicholson (1850–1927), in his introduction to the English translation of List's *National System*, points out that the productive powers look like 'the result of the accumulation of all discoveries, inventions, improvements, perfections, and exertions of all generations which have lived before us; they form the mental capital of the present human race' (List [1841] 1904: xviii). List himself explains that every nation is productive to the extent to which it has known how to appropriate the attainments of former generations and increase them by its own acquirements. In conclusion, according to several scholars, we can agree that in List's thought, education is a kind of mental power (or mental capital).

Productive powers are linked to education and human capital formation by education itself. This is exemplified by the father of a family who employs his savings in educating his five sons (as landowners or traders), in accord with the theory of productive powers (List [1841] 1904: 112). Another useful quotation in enlightening the power of production of the education is:

> The private renter himself, as the father of a family [...] must at least expend on the education of his heirs as much value of exchange as will enable them to administer the property which is some day to fall to their lot.
>
> (List [1841] 1904: 184)

There are no doubts about List's awareness of the cost-benefit analysis in education and human capital formation. In the same place, indeed, List acknowledges that 'books and newspapers act on the mental and material production by giving information' and that their acquisition is subject to market costs. He is worried about the difficulties of investment in the education of youth ('what great exertions do parents make to obtain the means of giving their children a good education!') However, he thinks that 'the enjoyment which they afford is also an inducement to material production'.

In modern terminology, we may conclude that List emphasises the importance of human capital in economics, a topic formally absent from mainstream economic theory until 1960 (Kiker 1968). Starting at the end of the 1950s, a growing body of academic work has addressed the concept of human capital as investment in human beings. The theory shows individualistic results in terms of market equilibria between demand and supply of education. With the concept of human capital, education assumes the notion of rate of return; the approach calculates its private costs, estimates the discounted private benefits of education itself and compares the two. Costs and benefits are a stream of expenditures or returns spread over the life of an individual during and after his education, when he is working as a contributor to the economy.

Human capital theory is a micro result and an issue internal to market theory. Surely List finds the roots of his human capital theory among the pages of Adam Smith's *Wealth of Nations*. As scholar and as historian of economic thought, he is able to emphasise the productivity of the human being in the work of past economists. List understands that, in Smith's theory, the skills and the intellect with which economic activities are carried out cannot be ignored. The Scottish economist belongs to that group of classical economists who elaborate the definition of skill to work as capital, but do not go beyond this. He groups the costs of education into four typologies: the directly requested list of rates by the master; the costs borne by the family of the apprentice for his upkeep; the cost of not having at his disposal the products of his work that nevertheless belong to the master; and the opportunity cost not being used to do other income-producing work without specialisation. Smith does not proceed to measure the amount of wealth originating from the human being and rejects the idea of applying an empirical measurement to any concrete activity (Kiker 1968: 29).

Even if he had proceeded, he would have found List as an adversary in such a procedure. In fact, the German economist criticises the 'emphasis on material things' given – for example – by the American economist Thomas Cooper in the evaluation of 'human beings by the money spent on their education. Thus he declares that a lawyer is worth 3,000 or 4,000 dollars' (List [1837] 1983: 34). This measure would be a correct application of the Chicago individual approach to human capital theory, but it is not an adequate procedure in List's framework. Therefore, List underlines the carelessness of Smith in defining the productivity of human resources. The investigations of the Scottish economist are limited to human activity which creates material values, while List's idea of human capital assigns value to a series of workers that, according to Smith, are unproductive in nature: teachers, physicians and other mental-capital-based occupations. On the contrary, according to List,

> each individual can concentrate his efforts on the occupation for which he is best fitted by his physical and *intellectual qualities*, by his education, by his experience, and by the natural resources at his disposal. In this way the output of each individual reaches the maximum that his abilities permit and *the surplus goods* that he makes can be exchanged for the greatest quantity of goods produced by others.
>
> (List [1837] 1983: 25, italics added)

Smith's individualistic interpretation does not do justice to the important role of the nation in political economy, nor does it permit a mass development of education as it is possible in the national powers of production or in the NIC. In classical economic theory, many single producers 'can be taken into consideration so far as their services are rewarded by values of exchange' (List [1841] 1904: 116), but List wants to escape from the microeconomic feature of human capital. This is also proved by his criticism of the French economist Jean Baptiste Say. It is not enough to avoid the definition of unproductive mental (immaterial) labourers, and the French author has not remedied this defect in the doctrine of Smith by his fiction of immaterial goods or products. The mental producers are not merely productive because they produce things of exchangeable values, but Say doesn't see that they produce productive powers in the national perspective.

> The prosperity of a nation is not, as Say believes, greater in the proportion in which it has amassed more wealth (i.e. values of

exchange), but in the proportion in which it has more developed its
powers of production.

(List [1841] 1904: 117)

As can be seen by examining List's economic policy, the German author
uses the concept of 'macroeconomic activism' as one strand of his nationalist analysis (Helleiner 2002). No traditional economic operators like
'instructors of youths and of adults, virtuosos, musicians, physicians,
judges and administrators, are productive in a much higher degree' (List
[1841] 1904: 116). In fact, whenever emphasis is given to the macro level of
the analysis, those workers produce further productive powers:

> some by enabling the future generation to become producers, others by
> furthering the morality and religious character of the present genera-
> tion, a third by ennobling and raising the powers of the human mind, a
> fourth by preserving the productive powers of his patients, a fifth by
> rendering human rights and justice secure, a sixth by constituting and
> protecting public security, a seventh by his art and by the enjoyment
> which it occasions fitting men the better to produce values of exchange.
>
> (List [1841] 1904: 116)

Thanks to improvements in both mental and material production, List
develops a vision of an advanced German nation. His analysis of the
productive powers connects government, educational policies and macro
human capital with the desired outcome in economic development. He
works toward an economic nationalism that increases mental capital for
the creation of new knowledge where the human capital appears to be close
to the aims of the nation-state. The boundaries of the political economy
themselves disappear, and the topic is better approached from the perspective of a wider social and political science; it is not exclusively a question of
natural resources, population, agriculture, manufacture and commerce. In
the advanced nation-state,

> arts and sciences, educational establishments, and universal cultivation
> must stand in it on an equal footing with material production. Its
> constitution, laws, and institutions must afford to those who belong to
> it a high degree of security and liberty, and must promote religion,
> morality, and prosperity; in a word, must have the well-being of its
> citizens as their object.
>
> (List [1841] 1904: 142)

From this wider perspective, List's mental capital appears to be a set of
skills, training, enterprises, industry and government. Together with natural
and material capital, mental capital and government contribute to the
wealth of a nation by improving its productive powers. In so doing, as

Levi-Faur notes, mental capital becomes the most important driver of development; the government is responsible for the education of its citizens and the augmentation of human capital. Therefore, at the most primitive stages of an economy, mental capital is limited, while in the higher stages of development its constraints are removed (Levi-Faur 1997: 160).

In List's thought, education and productive powers are strictly linked to the economic performance of a nation and to its economic policy. In general, the creation of a skilled workforce and managerial cadre is central to the production of higher value goods (Selwyn 2009: 160). Moreover, a nation should tune its educational system in relation to the level of its international commerce, and the measures the government should take, mainly during the period of transition from a system of prohibitions to a policy of protection, include:

> the extension of technical education to the best of its ability. Technical and agricultural schools and colleges should be established not only in the capital of a country but throughout the provinces. The cost of building these schools should be defrayed by the provincial authorities. They should be run under the supervision of provincial chambers of commerce and agriculture and competition between them should be encouraged. The Ministry of Education should exercise only a general oversight over technical and agricultural schools.
>
> (List [1837] 1983: 118–19)

## From human capital to the National Innovation System

Thanks to education, human beings will find that their technical skill and their zeal for work will increase as time goes by and consequently their output will increase. They should possess 'a good knowledge of science as well as high standards of technical skill'. This aspect of the notion of productive powers is so important that List concludes that 'there must be a good system of education' (List [1837] 1983: 184–5). In his political economy, the sphere of education and its notion of mental capital reflect the economic status of a nation. List's focus on mental power is completed by an analysis of the state's role in coordinating different economic sectors in order to enhance a country's education and productive power. Quoting the *Outlines of American Political Economy*, Levi-Faur recalls that a nation should be evaluated not by its self-sufficiency, nor by its trade balance, but by the degree to which its industry is independent and its productive powers are developed (Levi-Faur 1997: 167; List [1827] 1909: 189). Finally, Henderson in his introduction to the English translation of the *Natural System* points out that in List's doctrine, the skills of the people should be fostered by elementary education, adequate training facilities at universities and technical colleges for the more gifted (List [1837] 1983: 6–7).

However, we owe to Chris Freeman and Christopher Winch two innovative and broader explanations of List's educational thought. A 1995 article by Freeman puts external international connections and the influence of the national education system side by side. In Freeman's view, industrial, technical and scientific relations, the role of government and cultural traditions are institutions forming a 'National Innovation System' (NIS) (Freeman 1995). Identifying the best practices for the knowledge-based economy, the NIS is a focal point of the Organisation for Economic Cooperation and Development (OECD) work in the field of science, technology and industry. The NIS is often defined in several ways, but in general, its approach stresses innovation and technological development as the results of a complex set of relationships among actors in a larger system, which includes enterprises, universities and government research institutes (OECD 1997: 11). In order to describe capitalism as a whole, the NIS framework establishes the need to investigate certain features of a developing country. Among them, a national education system is undoubtedly a key aspect.

The fathers of the NIS, Freeman and Bengt-Åke Lundvall, evoke List's *National System* as a precursor. Their concept of 'national systems of production' includes education and training in a wide set of national institutions (Freeman 1995: 6) and focuses on the development of productive forces rather than on allocation issues (Lundvall 1992: 897). In an unpublished 1982 OECD report on Japan's successful technological catching-up and the role the state played in this, Freeman refers for the first time to List's contribution (Freeman 1982). According to Freeman, List's book on *The National System of Political Economy* might as well have been entitled 'The National System of Innovation' since it anticipates many of the concerns of this contemporary literature (Freeman 2002: 193).[3]

Throughout, Christopher Winch does not quote Freeman's 1995 article; rather, he goes beyond hypothesising the existence of an articulate educational system in List's thought and comparing it with Smith's vocational one. He puts the development of productive powers at the centre of economic concern because of their future competitive advantages in the long term. The general goal is to establish an industrial nation with high-skills equilibria where the workers are remunerated enough for full access to market consumption. Winch points out that the prevailing character of work production in the capitalist system, Taylorism, remains a practice with a low-skill workforce, leading to a significant running down of List's productive powers (Winch 1998: 376).

If a high-skill economic system does not arise through the operation of market forces, the public aspects of this system compel an outside intervention through the state. Winch concludes that this does not imply that vocational education should be provided by the state, but that the state provides the conditions necessary for it in order to promote a high-skill equilibrium. He imagines how List's model of vocational education might look, with designated schools for pre-vocational education, technical institutes, and universities for nurturing commercial institutions and promoting skills development linked to education and occupational context. Accordingly, government has a positive role to play in List's schema; it is the chief instrument through which non-economic institutions and the economic infrastructure can take full advantage of a nation's development potential (Fusfeld 1977: 745).

The positive role played by the state in order to realise the conditions necessary to promote a high-skill equilibrium is complex and articulated. With the theory of productive powers, List's analysis points out that not only is economic success in industry dependent upon education (skills, knowledge, and so on), but that a 'good' education is the result of the growth of industry. Classical economic theory – cosmopolitan theory – assumes that this can be achieved by leaving individuals free to pursue their own private interests. They can do this by using personal attitudes and evaluating them with market prices. From this perspective, 'government action to stimulate the establishment of industries does more harm than good' (List [1837] 1983: 70). On the contrary, in List's opinion it is the logical and chronological progress of industrialisation that requires higher and higher levels of skill and education. This happens because: 1. he pinpoints the mental component of the productive powers as decisive; 2. he finds in the productive powers the engine of the progress of a nation;[4] and 3. he continuously advances in drawing the best progression from an ignorant agricultural society to an educated and industrial nation.

While points 1 and 2 are discussed above, point 3 means that List is aware of the complexity of the institutions required to coordinate education and training and to match them with the development of productive powers. Agrarian and manufacturing workers have an important part to play in the development of the economy, but the state can create the conditions to favour this process. Winch is right to assert that all this requires state planning or, at least, institutional preservation in economics. List's planning corresponds with the theory of the economic stages in development. In Chapters 9 to 12 of the *Natural System,* we find the best planned progression from an ignorant agricultural society to an educated industrial nation. We can see the sequence.

In the first fully agricultural stage of economic development, human beings

> depend entirely upon farming and live in isolation. [...] Lacking contact with each other, they are ignorant folk who have no appreciation of the arts [...] Their physical and mental powers are never adequately used or properly developed [...] The intellectual powers of such a people are hardly awakened and are put to little use. There are no opportunities for latent talents to be developed.
>
> (List [1837] 1983: 52–3)

In a nation devoted entirely to agriculture, the whole range of intellectual forces is virtually absent. In the second stage, apparently, there are no direct references to education, but some external manufactured goods are exchanged with internal agricultural products. Therefore, farmers can produce with more efficient machines and tools, reaching a better standard of living and beginning to demand, for the first time, manufactured products. At first, manufacturers join with farmers in supporting free trade, which is advantageous to both. Then the industrialists need protection, and in the third stage of economic development 'the industries of the nation dominate the whole – or nearly the whole – of the home market' (List [1837] 1983: 60). Here the planned road map towards economic development becomes very interesting. At this stage, there is an opportunity to reach high-skill equilibrium levels because industry calls forth and promotes the growth of intellectual and moral forces of every kind. In this stage, education is really the result of the growth of industry because 'the development of manufactures demands a great many skills and those who possess such skills have the opportunity of using their abilities in various branches of manufacture' (List [1837] 1983: 63). Moreover,

> as a nation becomes more industrialised it becomes more necessary to secure the services of suitable trained people in the factories and workshops [. . .] It is clear that all branches of knowledge – particularly those which can be applied to industrial pursuits – are making rapid progress.
> (List [1837] 1983: 67)

Finally, the high skill equilibrium becomes dynamic because when workers engaged in industry 'become more familiar with the advances made in scientific knowledge' more discoveries and inventions are applied to industry.

## Coordination and planning

According to List, the productive powers of industry awaken in both industry and agriculture the spirit of innovation. They motivate the expansion of all kinds of skills and abilities. With the macro and complex function of the stages analysis, the German theorist discovers a peculiar coordinating agent that attempts to reach an optimum equilibrium. This coordinating agent moves far from a purely agricultural society and counts on the relationship between importing foreign technology and domestic technical development. Surely, these two aspects are the basis of German economic success in contemporary history. In a wider sense, List devises a system of theoretical and real innovation in interaction between the various components of research, technical change, innovation and learning. As in the NIS, List's national system brings to the forefront the central role of the coordinating agent in the process of the economic stages. The agent, in this case, is the role of education by economic planning. Precisely, it is similar to the indicative planning because it lacks the command element. Even in a market capitalist economy – as in List's system – one can refer to a planning programme operated not directly by the government but through the state. This is indirectly involved in favouring the realisation of the stages of progress through indicative planning, carried out scientifically and accompanied by the use of market mechanisms in order to achieve benefits in a knowledge-based economy.

List is rarely regarded as an economist advocating economic planning.[5] Nevertheless, he is a supporter of state interventions to promote development, and his ideas are systematic in their perspective on education and knowledge. In List's determination to 'show the way', Sai-wing Ho looks for a parallel with the economic indicative planner approach, for example that of Gunnar Myrdal. In his opinion, when List comes to the areas that are more traditionally regarded as economic, especially the promotion of industries, education becomes a main policy indication (Sai-wing Ho 2006: 362–4). Some features in educational planning, however, cannot definitively exclude the German economist from the group of the educational thinkers who are able to operate in the framework of provisional economic growth.

In particular, the manpower forecasting approach (MFA) (Spalletti 2015) has some features in common with List's educational thought. First of all, both List and manpower forecasting analysis start from the standpoint that an economic system in expansion, especially in the manufacturing sector, needs to involve more of its labour force. Secondly, when List states that industrial skills partially fall back in agriculture, he draws a framework in which the labour requirements can be translated into educational requirements, indirectly assuming that each job corresponds to a determined occupational level and type of education. Specifically, for industrial skills List raises the localisation question, its theory and its planning:

> [...] the population of an industrialised society is brought together in a few conurbations in which are concentrated a great variety of technical skills, productive powers, applied science, art and literature. Here are to be found great public and private institutions and associations in which theoretical knowledge is applied to the practical affairs of industry and commerce.
>
> (List [1837] 1983: 69)

Thirdly, List's predictions about stages attempt to provide a comparative projection of future outcomes and events. This is the case of the MFA and a part of its 'modus operandi'. Indeed, in the international comparison method, manpower forecasting for a particular country is done by borrowing historical manpower examples from countries in higher stages of development. This is the case of Germany in relation to the English model.

According to Blaug, the economic policy of MFA involves demand and supply in the education market and demand and supply in the labour market (Blaug 1966: 166). Only the supply in the education market is a pure policy-variable, and it is influenced indirectly by List's theory of economic and education stages in relation to the development of the temperate nations. List's plan is indicative of two things: on one side of the coin there is the perceptible need to elevate the overall level of education of the population, stimulated by efficiency concerns; on the other side, there is the need to have technically skilled people available to induce investment in physical capital. Therefore, List's plan is 'all-inclusive' in nature and looks for a social objectives approach. List is also aware that education plays a decisive role in achieving non-economic goals and his approach assumes that a better educated labour force can promote certain goals taken for granted, such as the eradication of illiteracy.

## Conclusion

The above reading of List's economic thought shows a certain benevolence, with the assumption of a common manpower growth path for all the developmental nations. In List's vision this path matches up with the economic stages theory; therefore, one may assume the existence of an educational stage theory roughly compatible with some universal 'Rostow's stages of economic growth'.[6] Different stages are linked to technology and labour force also in List's socio-economic analysis of progress. Although he is silent about the methods that would be useful in forecasting the manpower impact of technology in the progression of the economic stages, he is aware that technology affects manpower needs in terms of occupational shifts and skill requirements.

From this perspective, he is comparable to a socio-economic planner, even if he does not focus on achieving narrowly defined objectives with predetermined devices. His planning is rather a systematic process of envisioning a desired future, and he attempts to translate this vision into broadly defined goals (for example in international trade) and, moreover, into a sequence of economic stages. List appears to bring forward the Harbison and Myers target-setting approach in manpower forecasting, a procedure centred on a large-scale analysis of education. This target setting is not explicitly oriented to make projections based on limited assumptions regarding achieving one or two specific objectives. Its purpose is rather to influence the future course of development, indicating a target only as a direction (Harbison, Myers 1964: 204), and hopefully accelerating its fulfilment. The quantitative predictions, in this sense, are less important of the indicative direction. Therefore, List attempts to guide future development that spreads out from industrial production, and he is aware that factories give workers 'the opportunity to use their skill so that their productive powers are multiplied by 10 or even by 100' (List [1837] 1983: 68). This result appears to be List's major contribution to the economics of education, together with the target-setting concept as an approach for making long-term manpower estimates.

## Notes

1 In defining capital, Adam Müller's *Elemente der Staatskunst* (*Elements of State Art*, 1809) underlines the importance of several economic, cultural and social elements (Müller 1922: 2, lectures 25, 26, 27). Thus, Müller's theory of productivity contains a 'fourth' factor of production, called 'thought capital' (Hutter 1994: 297).

 In Thünen's *Der isolierte Staat in Beziehung auf Landwirtschaft und Nationalökonomie* (*The Isolated State in Relation to Agriculture and Political Economy*, 1875), the author expresses the idea of education as capital (*Erziehungskapital*) (Thünen 1875: 3, ii, 145–9). According to Kiker (1969), Thünen treats human beings as capital and emphasises the relationship between educational costs and labour productivity.

2 Some nationalist implications of List's thought are sometimes in contrast with a certain internationalist (cosmopolitan) approach he uses in his work. A year after the publication of the *National System*, Carlo Cattaneo, a leading exponent of the Italian federalist culture, expresses his opinion about List in the *Politecnico*, a review of original studies and critiques founded by Cattaneo himself. Cattaneo's closest affinity with List is his theory of 'associated minds' that, although deriving from philosophy, refers to the organic concept of the economic strength of a nation. Mind association means mind knowledge, and List's policies are concerned with learning the new technology and applying it. In this sense, List draws from another Italian economist, Antonio Serra (1570–?) and his *Breve trattato delle cause che possono far abbondare li regni d'oro e d'argento dove non sono miniere* (*Discourse on the Sources of the Wealth of Nations without Gold and Silver Mines*, 1613). When Serra distinguishes the category of 'accidenti communi' in the wealth creation process, he judges the 'quality' of the population in mentality, education and culture as decisive. The increase of the crafts is influenced by the educational level of the population, and the state policy would provide for economic knowledge because this is linked to production of goods.

3 Soete (2009) pinpoints another seminal List quotation taken from the 1995 Freeman paper, arguing that industry should be linked to the formal institutions of science and education. The quotation is:

> There scarcely exists a manufacturing business which has no relation to physics, mechanics, chemistry, mathematics or to the art of design, etc. No progress, no new discoveries and inventions can be made in these sciences by which a hundred industries and processes could not be improved or altered. In the manufacturing State, therefore, sciences and arts must necessarily become popular.
>
> (List [1841] 1904: 142, quoted in Freeman 1995; quoted in Soete 2009)

4 Even wars and conflicts are useful events in developing productive powers (Spalletti 2017).

5 Among the exceptions: Carr (1947: 23–4), who pinpoints List as the 'father' of national planning; Ellman (2014: 341) for the supranational investment planning based on comparative costs.

6 Expression is in Blaug (1966: 11).

# References

Becker, G.S. (1964) *Investment in Human Capital: A Theoretical and Empirical Analysis with Special Reference to Education*, Columbia University Press, New York.

Blaug, M. (1966) 'An Economic Interpretation of the Private Demand for Education', *Economica*, 33(130), 166–182.

Blaug, M. (1984) 'Friedrich List, Economist and Visionary 1789–1846', by W. O. Henderson and Friedrich List, The Natural System of Political Economy 1837, Translated and edited by W.O. Henderson, *Economica*, 51(203), 368–369.

Bronk, R. (2009) *The Romantic Economist. Imagination in Economics*, Cambridge University Press, Cambridge.

Carr, E.H. (1947) *The Soviet Impact on the Western World*, The Macmillan Company, New York.

Ellman, M. (2014) *Socialist Planning*, Cambridge University Press, Cambridge.

Freeman, C. (1982) 'Technological Infrastructure and International Competitiveness, OECD Ad Hoc Group on Science, Technology and Competitiveness', Reprint for 'Innovation Systems and Development Strategies for the Third Millennium' Conference, November 2–6, 2003, Rio de Janeiro.

Freeman, C. (1995) 'The National System of Innovation in Historical Perspective', *Cambridge Journal of Economics*, 19, 5–24.

Freeman, C. (2002) 'Continental, National and Sub-National Innovation Systems-Complementarity and Economic Growth', *Research Policy*, 31, 191–211.

Fusfeld, D.R. (1977) 'The Development of Economic Institutions', *Journal of Economic Issues*, 10(4), 743–784.

Ganilh, C. (1812) *An Inquiry into the Various Systems of Political Economy*, H. Colburn, London.

Greenfeld, L. (2001) *The Spirit of Capitalism. Nationalism and Economic Growth*, Harvard University Press, Cambridge, MA.

Harbison, F. and Myers, C.A. (1964) *Education, Manpower and Economic Growth. Strategies of Human Resource Development*, McGraw-Hill, New York.

Hartog, J. (2000) 'Human Capital as an Instrument of Analysis for the Economics of Education', *European Journal of Education*, 35(1), 7–20.

Helleiner, E. (2002) 'Economic Nationalism as a Challenge to Economic Liberalism? Lessons from the 19th Century', *International Studies Quarterly*, 46(3), 307–329.

Henderson, W.O. (1983) *Friedrich List. Economist and Visionary 1789–1846*, Frank Cass, London.

Hutter, M. (1994) 'Organism as a Metaphor in German Economic Thought', in Mirowski, P. (ed.) *Natural Images in Economic Thought*, Cambridge University Press, Cambridge, 289–321.

Ince, O.U. (2013) *Imperial Origins of the National Economy*, Annual Convention of the American Political Science Association, Chicago, September.

Kiker, B.F. (1968) *Human Capital in Retrospect*, University of South Carolina, Columbia, SC.

Kiker, B.F. (1969) 'Von Thünen on Human Capital', *Oxford Economic Papers*, 21(3), 339–343.

Levi-Faur, D. (1997) 'Friedrich List and the Political Economy of the Nation-State', *Review of International Political Economy*, 4(1), 154–178.

List, F. (1831) 'Idées sur les Réformes Économiques, Commerciale et Financières Applicables à la France', *Revue Encyclopédique*, 49, 473–490; 50, 37–52.

List, F. ([1827] 1909) 'Outlines of American Political Economy', in Hirst, M. (ed.) *Life of Friedrich List and Selections from His Writings*, Smith, Elder & Co., London, 147–286.

List, F. ([1816] 1971) 'Gedanken über die württembergische Staatsregierung', in *Friedrich List Werke*, Scientia Verlag, Aalen, 1, 87–148.

List, F. ([1837] 1983) *The Natural System of Political Economy*, Henderson, W.O. (ed.), Frank Cass, London.

List, F. ([1841] 1904) *The National System of Political Economy by Friedrich List*, Nicholson, J.S. (ed.), Longmans, Green and Co., New York and Bombay.

Lundvall, B.-Å. (1992) 'National Innovation Systems: From List to Freeman', in Hanusch, H. and Pyka, A. (eds.) *Elgar Companion to Neo-Schumpeterian Economics*, Edward Elgar, Cheltenham (UK) and Northampton (US), 872–881.

Müller, A.H. (1922) *Die Elemente der Staatskunst*, Fisher Verlag, Jena.

OECD Committee for Scientific and Technological Policy. (1997) *National Innovation Systems*, OECD, Paris.

Sai-Wing Ho, P. (2006) 'Analysing and Arresting Uneven Development: Friedrich List and Gunnar Myrdal Compared', *Journal of Economic Issues*, 40(2), 359–367.

Schumpeter, J.A. (2006) *History of Economic Analysis*, Perlman, M. (ed.), Routledge, London.

Selwyn, B. (2009) 'An Historical Materialist Appraisal of Friedrich List and His Modern-Day Followers', *New Political Economy*, 14(2), 157–180.

Soete, L. (2009) 'The National Innovation Systems and the Role of the OECD: Two Decades Later', in OECD TIP Workshop, *Future Orientations for Science, Technology and Innovation Policy*, OECD, Paris.

Spalletti, S. (2015) 'The Manpower Forecasting Approach. Notes in Retrospect', *History of Economic Thought and Policy*, 1, 39–57.

Spalletti, S. (2017) 'Productive Powers and War in Friedrich List's Theory of Economic Development', in Bientinesi, F. and Patalano, R. (eds.) *Economists and War: A Heterodox Perspective*, Routledge, New York, 173–188.

Thünen, J.H. (1875) *Der isolierte Staat in Beziehung auf Landwirtschaft und Nationalökonomie*, Wiegandt, Hempel and Parey, Berlin.

Tribe, K. (1988) 'Friedrich List and the Critique of Cosmopolitical Economy', *The Manchester School of Economic and Social Studies*, 61(1), 17–36.

Turunen, O. (2016) *The Emergence of Intangible Capital Human, Social, and Intellectual Capital in Nineteenth Century British, French, and German Economic Thought*, Jyväskylä University, Jyväskylä.

Wendler, E. (2014) *Friedrich List (1789–1846). A Visionary Economist with Social Responsibility*, Springer, Berlin.

Winch, C. (1998) 'Two Rival Conceptions of Vocational Education: Adam Smith and Friedrich List', *Oxford Review of Education*, 24, 365–378.

Yeh-Yun Lin, C. and Edvinsson, L. (2010) *National Intellectual Capital: A Comparison of 40 Countries*, Springer, Berlin.

# 8 Manufacturing matters

## From Giovanni Botero (c.1544–1617) to Friedrich List (1789–1846), or: The history of an old idea

*Philipp Robinson Rössner*

Friedrich List's system of political economy rested, amongst others, upon three premises: (a) he defined, mainly in his *Das Nationale System der politischen Ökonomie* (1841),[1] and *Das Wesen und der Werth einer nationalen Produktivkraft* (1839)[2] the nation state as an active protagonist, located between the human individual and mankind (whereas the 'classical' economists in the wake of Adam Smith and David Hume had leaned somewhat towards the former); (b) he saw manufacturing and industry as *conditiones sine qua non* which every country or national economy needed in order to grow rich (again something which Adam Smith's thinking did not develop in similar clarity, suggesting instead, if implicitly, that all economic activities were the same); and that (c) the wealth of a nation was not primarily dependent upon accumulated riches and treasure but rather founded on the development of her productive powers. The source or origin of this development lay in institutions, law and good governance – in other words *cultural* factors such as training and education.[3] Whereas List called agriculture 'lifeless' or sterile, it was manufacturing – with its higher level of market integration; higher requirements for skill and knowledge; a more differentiated and higher level of division of labour; its higher demand for useful knowledge and potential capacity for productivity-enhancing innovation strategies and thus, ultimately, its higher capacity to generate added value – that would, in the end, be the most important activity to enhance per capita output and total factor productivity. 'Manufactures', he wrote in a letter that represented part of his *Outlines of American Political Economy* (1827), 'moreover, are the nurses of arts, sciences and skill, the sources of power and wealth'. (Notz 1931, p. 105). Amongst the major tasks to achieve this goal there were the creation of an integrated national market (*Volkswirtschaft*), as well as setting up protective import duties until a comparable productivity level with the rest of the world had been achieved. By no means was List an outright protectionist or opposed to free trade in principle. But it was the *timing* of adopting free trade that was crucial for economic development (List 2009, p. 43).

However, List's ideas – which recent research has identified as important for modern economic growth and current issues in development (Reinert

2007) and (Chang 2003) – were neither new nor particularly original at the time he wrote them down. They had been developed in European political economy discourse since the Middle Ages. List in a sense stood on the shoulders of giants that got lost in subsequent development of modern economics but who had laid out the basic principles of his theory long before. He merely supplied the capstone towards a building of theory whose construction had started long ago but which was now to be made fit for late-comers in an age of industrialization. The purpose of this chapter is to sketch the broad outlines of this age-old discourse (I), to test it against the empirical economic record (II), so as to demonstrate, by ways of a brief conclusion, the common ground List shared with his ancestors that had come before him (III).

# I

Two basic ideas were once held important in Europe's transition to capitalism, but got forgotten over time as economic discourse and economic theory evolved, attaining their characteristically modern shape during the last two centuries or so. These ancient insights were, first, that manufacturing mattered, and second that a strong and pro-active state was important to safeguard and nurture the precarious plant which became later on known, in modern linguistic use, as *economic growth and development*. Names have been given to these ideas, as well as the theories embodying them, such as 'mercantilism', 'Colbertism' (in France) or 'cameralism', denoting differences only in terms of nuance and context-specific economic practice rather than principal content. We may subsume them under the more neutral term 'economic reason of state',[4] reflecting mutual interest and feedback processes between state, finance and economy that influenced the writing of these theories. These ideas were widely shared across Europe. Their pedigree is ancient. And they continue to matter today – particularly, as we may add, in the light of the current crises in the world economy.

If we look at pre-industrial Europe we see that many of the key ingredients and ideas usually identified as crucial to 'modern' economic growth, even the often invoked 'European Miracle' and 'Great Divergence' – were already to be found. They had been for a long time.[5] A strong manufacturing base? Known to sixteenth-century Italian economic writers. The role of knowledge management, technology and science? Known to early seventeenth-century Swedish thinkers. The notion that infinite growth is principally possible? Again, Sweden, around 1600 A.D. A strong state that safeguards its subjects' economic interests and property rights, up to the point of actively promoting growth and development? We find this idea in seventeenth-century and eighteenth century German economic discourse, but, of course, much earlier in Renaissance Italy. We also find states that repeatedly tried to apply these ideas in practice. The best example perhaps is post-1688 England. Here we find, as new research has pointed out, an increasingly developmental-protectionist state that laid the foundations for the subsequent transition into the 'first industrial nation'.[6] Less-well understood, however, is how deeply influenced continental Europe's intellectual landscape was by these ideas. We also lack a deeper understanding of the interaction between these ideas and economic practice and policy. The present section will make a very modest contribution, by sketching out the idea of the prominence of manufacturing in European economic discourse from Italian writer Giovanni Botero (c.1544–1617) to Friedrich List (1789–1846).

Botero – whom List apparently never quoted[7]– said, in Book Eight of his *Ragione di Stato*, originally part of his other opus magnum *Delle cause della grandezza delle città* (Rome, Martinelli, 1588) but since 1589 included in the *Reason of State*:

> Over and above all this a ruler must ensure that money does not leave his country unless this is quite essential. If considerable expense is entailed in obtaining something in his own dominion the money will at least remain within his country or will ultimately return to the exchequer by way of taxes and dues; whereas once money is sent out of the country it is lost and its potentialities are lost too.
>
> (Giovanni Botero, 1956 [1588])

This was standard fare in contemporary bullionist and early mercantilist economic thought. But in the section 'On Industry', Botero wrote

> Nothing is of greater importance for increasing the power of a state and gaining for it more inhabitants and wealth of every kind than the industry of its people and the number of crafts they exercise. Some of these are essential or useful for civilised living, others are required for pomp and ornament and others for luxuries and for the enjoyment of leisure. These crafts cause a conflux of money and of people, some of whom work, some trade in the finished products, some provide raw materials and others buy, sell and transport from one place to another the fruits of man's ingenuity and skill. (...) Since art is the rival of nature I must consider which is of more importance to make a state great and populous, the fertility of the soil or the industry of man. Without hesitation I shall say industry. Firstly, the products of the manual skill of man are more in number and of greater worth than the produce of nature, for nature provides the material and the object but the infinite variations of form are the result of the ingenuity and skill of man. (...) Moreover a far greater number of people live by industry than by rents, as the many cities of Italy bear witness – in particular Venice, Florence, Genoa and Milan, whose greatness and magnificence are manifest, and almost two-thirds of whose inhabitants live by the silk and woollen industries. (...) But this becomes obvious with each raw

material we consider. The revenues derived from iron mines are not very large, but the processing of iron and trade in that metal support an infinite number of persons, some engaged in excavating, refining or casting it, some selling it wholesale or retail, making of it engines of war, defensive and offensive weapons, innumerable instruments for agriculture, architecture and every other art, and for the everyday necessities of life, for which iron is as essential as bread. So that comparing the gain which the owners derive from the iron-mines with the profit which craftsmen and merchants make from the iron industry and the wealth which accrues also to the ruler by way of taxes, it is clear that industry is far in advance of nature. (...) And how many people depend for their livelihood upon their skills rather than directly upon nature. Such is the power of industry that no mine of silver or gold in New Spain or in Peru can compare with it, and the duties from the merchandise of Milan are worth more to the Catholic King than the mines of Zacatecas or Jalisco. Italy is a country in which, as I have mentioned above, there is no important gold or silver mine, and so is France: yet both countries are rich in money and treasure thanks to industry. Flanders too has no metals, but so long as the country was at peace such were the many various and wonderful works of art and ingenuity which were produced there that she had no cause to regard with envy the mineral wealth of Hungary and Transylvania. (...) A prince, therefore, who wishes to make his cities populous must introduce every kind of industry and craft by attracting good workmen from other countries and providing them with accommodation and everything convenient for their craft, by encouraging new techniques and singular and rare works, and rewarding perfection and excellence. But above all he must not permit raw materials, wool, silk, timber, metals and so on, to leave his state, for with the materials will go the craftsmen. Trade in goods made from these materials will provide a livelihood for a far larger number of people than will the raw materials; and the export of the finished manufactured article will provide the ruler with greater revenues than will the material alone.

(Giovanni Botero 1956 [1588])

It is important to quote Botero at length here, not only because with this quote he formulated some key theoretical stances held by later mercantilism, cameralism, up to the German historical school and others, but also because most of the subsequent authors in European economics seem to have built upon Botero – not always without reference or explicit acknowledgement.[8] This also includes Friedrich List. Botero – a Jesuit monk who has become known for his theory and treatises on demography – has never been held, let alone claimed, by modern historians and economists to have been an 'economist' in the proper sense, in terms of his contribution to modern economic knowledge and theory. But arguably he provided a cornerstone of modern economic thinking with his ideas on the role of manufacturing in the economic process, coupled with – as in the passage above – a strong pro-active government and state that would support the process of import substitution and economic development.[9]

The importance of adding value and creating employment was also noted by Veit Ludwig von Seckendorff (1626–1692), sometimes hailed as the 'Adam Smith of cameralism' (A. Small), a jurist and state official in the services of, amongst others, Ernest I 'the Pious' of Saxony-Gotha since 1645. Seckendorff wrote, in the *Additiones* to his magnum opus on the *Theutsche Fürstenstaat* (originally published in 1655) in 1665 after a telling visit to the Netherlands, the economic leader of the day[10] that employment and income were only likely to rise where wages, and thus rewards to factor inputs of labour, were high, be that in agriculture or elsewhere (Seckendorff 1703, p. 166). One implication was that by no means would it be a goal worthwhile to pursue – as has been said in the literature on mercantilism – to keep wages and thus general incomes low. That would have been a totally wrong economic strategy.

> Diesem nach folget/daß es in FriedensZeiten an Leuten nicht ermangeln werde/wenn man dem gemeinen Mann ein erkleckliches und bestaen-diges Verdienst schaffen kann. Es stehet aber eben die Kunst und difficultaet darinnen/was man vornehme und erfinde/uem solchen Ver-dienst/Tag oder Jahr Lohn zu schaffen.(It follows from this that at times of peace there will be no shortage of men, if they can be provided with a reasonable, proper and steady income. But the very challenge and art is to create the necessary preconditions for such a sufficient and ample daily or yearly income for everyone.[11]
>
> (Seckendorff 1703, pp. 166–167)

Seckendorff stressed the importance of *adding value* (Reinert 2007) using the negative example of pastoral agriculture. Manufactures were only worthwhile to pursue if the value added came close to the value added in the production of the primary good or raw material itself. Where the focus was on the production (and export) of raw wool, only the owner of the sheep, the carrier, hauler and the merchant trading the raw wool would earn something on top of the value generated in pastoral agriculture; the general income multiplier effects, so to speak, of this activity were low. But where the wool was processed *within* the country using domestic manufactures and factor employment, 'ten or twelve men might be nourished for one year', as Seckendorff maintained (ibid.). One sector where this virtuous cycle was most easily and likely to be achieved was, in Seckendorff's opinion, woollen stuff manufactures (ibid.), something that was also highlighted in Philipp Wilhelm von Hörnigk or Hornick's *Oesterreich über alles wann es nur will* (1684) (see below). Economic activity (*Nahrung*) should be 'free' (*frey*), Seckendorff went on, i.e. free from guild incorporation and other restrictive regulations characteristic of *Ancien Régime* Europe[12] restricting output and number of producers and businesses with access to the market (ibid.). The beneficial aspects of guild incorporation – caring for the poor and widows; keeping up good order in the respective trade and trader's community, ceremonial and burial arrangements – were far outweighed by the negative effects or tendency of guild incorporation to create monopoly and rent seeking (*Zwang/monopolium*; ibid., p. 169). These harmed the common good and created Pareto-suboptimal scenarios of resource allocation. In the *Additiones* to his *Theutscher Fürstenstaat* Seckendorff also highlighted very clearly the same ideas regarding import substitution and infant industry protection that are to be found in Hörnigk's work and literally all cameralist economics textbooks of the later seventeenth and the eighteenth century. Foreign skilled workers and craftsmen should be lured into the country. The importation of 'useful knowledge' should be encouraged. Promising new branches of industry should be protected by temporary monopoly privileges. The editor of the 1720 edition, Andres Simson Biechlingen, stressed, in his annotations to Seckendorff's *Additiones* (it was fairly common for later editors to add and modify the original texts considerably), that 'to concede a permanent monopoly would be as wrong as, even worse than, the artisans' and craft guilds';[13] highlighting the cameralists' principal creed and *plaidoyer* for the free market. Valuable raw material imports should be taxed only lightly, and no commodity that could be procured or produced at reasonably comparable quality at home should be imported from foreigners (Seckendorff 1720, pp. 172–3). Manufacturing should be located in cities but not through orders, limitations and punishment but rather by spontaneous development. Where cities are populous and flourish manufacturing would automatically be attracted and withdrawn from the countryside, and industrial by-employment on the countryside would wither away, as would rivalry and competition with urban manufacturing industry (ibid., pp. 176–8). For this one would only need skilled 'population management' as well as the forces of the free, meaning reasonably unregulated, market.[14]

The anonymous *Bedencken von Manufacturen* (1683), a pamphlet which Philipp Wilhelm von Hörnigk knew well and which must have enjoyed some popularity in the German lands during the 1680s, usually ascribed to Johann Daniel Crafft or Krafft – a seventeenth-century Saxon 'project-maker' (Forberger 2015), whom Hörnigk met several times and on whose work *Oesterreich über alles* (1683) drew considerably – reiterated this topos. Crafft maintained that

> where cities decline and become desolate, the surrounding countryside will decline as well; but where cities are populous peasants will be rich.
> (Crafft/Krafft 1683, pp. 3–4)

This axiom had been in European economic discourse since the days of Giovanni Botero – Philipp Wilhelm von Hörnigk, in his *Oesterreich über alles Wann es nur will,* published one year after Crafft's 'anonymous' pamphlet, his famous 'Nine Rules of Economics':

- All corners of the land, both above the earth, as well as subterranean, should be surveyed carefully and put to productive use;
- all raw materials that cannot be used or consumed domestically should be processed into manufactures domestically because the value added by manufacturing surpasses their initial value 'by two, three, ten or twenty, nay, even hundred times' (*zwey/drey/zehen/zwantzig/auch wol hundert-fach*). Hörnigk speaks of a transformation or transmutation (... *Inländischer rohen Güter oder deren Verwandelung in Manufacturen*); he explicitly mentioned quicksilver, which in Venice and Amsterdam was worked into 'vermillion or sublimate' (*sublimat, praecipitat und Zinober*), as well as some other chemicals; or Pilsen wool that was processed in Saxony (Vogtland) and the Palatinate into proper woollen stuffs; or Annaberg and Dutch Spitzen, made from Silesian yarn with a final value increased by more than 100 times;
- there should be as large a population as large as possible given constraints of incomes and living standards; idleness should be taken care of and abolished; technology transfer should be promoted by hiring foreign experts;
- all native precious metal reserves should be mined and brought into circulation; no money was to be spent on unnecessary imports;
- foreign imports should be minimized and limited to the absolute minimum necessary;
- if imports from abroad were to take place, they should be made in return for exports of goods; exports of specie in payment for imports should be avoided at all cost;
- imports of foreign semi-processed goods should be finished at home;
- exports should be encouraged and maximized, especially of manufactures;
- no goods must be imported that can be produced domestically. It would be better to spend two *thalers* on a domestically made good, Hörnigk says, that is lesser in terms of quality than to spend one *thaler* for importing a better substitute.

These rules were 'no invention of a speculative mind'; the nature of things gives them away to everyone who is in their right mind, Hörnigk said. He then formulated a principle of protectionism and import substitution that sounded similar to List's *Erziehungszoll* (Hörnigk, *Oesterreich über alles*, Chapter XV). Chapter XXI of *Oesterreich über alles* was even more Listian in nature. Hörnigk said that if he were in the position to put the process of development into motion, he would start with the fifth rule, stipulating that 'the inhabitants should make every effort to get along with their domestic products',[15] regardless how bad or deficient domestic products were, so long as would be necessary to improve and build up what modern usage has called 'comparative advantage'. This was, of course, mercantilism at its crudest and most primitive – which Hörnigk was fully aware of. But once implemented as a general strategy, other branches of the economy would follow, setting in motion a synergetic process and virtuous circle with spill-overs from one sector into other branches of the economy. These spill-over effects were so exceedingly obvious to Hörnigk that he did not spill much ink to explain why. Upon hindsight we can say that the idea goes back to Giovanni Botero. Hörnigk also maintained that if only Austria's manufactures were well developed and competitive, a lessening of the strict prohibitions may be feasible and prohibitive measures replaced by moderately protective duties and a gradual introduction of the free market. This, of course, is again similar to what List would argue about 150 years later.

Wilhelm von Schröder, another eminent Austro-German or early camera-list, wrote in his *Fürstliche Schatz und Rentkammer* (Leipzig 1686), that it was eminently clear (*sonnenklar*) that countries without much useful soil but flourishing commerce and manufacturing would do much better than countries with good soil and flourishing agriculture but without much manufacturing:

> Die sache ist an sich selbst sonnenklar; dann man aestimire ein pfund eisen in seiner m i n e r a wo es waechset/so wird solches gar einen schlechten werth gelten. Wann aber ein uhrmacher oder dergleichen kuenstler dieses pfund eisen in seine hand nimmt/und arbeitet es nach seiner kunst/so ist das pfund eisen wohl hundert mahl so viel werth/als es vorhero gewesen; dann die manufactur/so daran ist/und nicht das eisen/wird so hoch aestimiret. (It is a crystal-clear matter: estimate a pound of iron in its mineral stage, i.e. ore, and you will see that its initial value will be low. But as soon as the watch-maker or comparable artisan takes it into his hands, working it up into a manufactured good according to his respective trade, and it will be worth a hundred times more. This value added comes from manufacturing the iron, not from its raw state.)
>
> (Schröder 1705, p. 344)

Johann Heinrich Gottlob von Justi (1717–1771), then, a towering figure of eighteenth-century Austro-German 'high' cameralism – in Justi's works cameralism finally came closest to what we could nowadays describe as a full or closed economic theory – stressed the significance of manufacturing. This should include manufactories or *Manufakturen*, i.e. large centralized workshops that featured all major characteristics of the modern factory apart from the fact that the energy source was still organic (animal, horse or wind power; no steam engines). Such ventures were depicted in Diderot's rich *Encyclopedie* from which Adam Smith took the inspiration for his Book One (of the *Wealth of Nations*). But in Justi's theory '*Manufacturen*' also referred to industrial production in more general terms, including handicraft industries and decentralized manufacturing processes within the individual homes of the producers, frequently situated within an agrarian context and usually captured under the term *Verlag* or putting-out system. In his *Staatswirthschaft*, Vol. I (Justi 1755), Justi made the point that manufactures were fundamentally important for raising domestic economic activity (GDP) and particularly exports, which were seen as a stimulus to economic growth and development; manufacturing industry usually originated spontaneously within bigger countries or economies. A flourishing economy needed all types of manufacturing, but – in order to capture new and foreign markets – it was crucial that innovative products and processes were implemented. Here the element of what scholars have called, in a slightly different context, 'useful knowledge' comes into play, i.e. the generation of innovative ideas and production processes *within* the system (today known colloquially as R&D). The introduction of new manufacturing industry would increase the level (transaction volume) and speed of monetary circulation (velocity). But in order for these processes to work optimally, all areas of economic activity should be left as free of regulation as possible, especially by an absence of guilds as holders of monopolistic powers and other restrictions to economic activity. Again the free market as we know it stood at the centre of this reasoning. The state had to play a crucial role in this process, by monitoring and steering the development in manufacturing; for instance by the creation of statistical bodies recording output and productivity within the industry (so-called *Manufactur-Collegia*). We find such institutions in many a continental state since the later seventeenth century, from France under Colbert, to Austria under Emperor Leopold, to Scotland in 1727, when the Board of Trustees for the Fisheries and Manufactures was erected, whose main task was to produce yearly production statistics for the linen industry as well as to spend money and efforts within the industry to raise productivity and average quality of the product. These measures matched what modern development economics has labelled 'infant industry protection'.

By abolishing the strong focus on agriculture still inherent and manifest for instance in the late bloom of the German *Hausväterliteratur* or agrarian economics around 1700, Justi developed cameralism into a full-blown theory of economic growth and development. In the sections on 'urban economics' (Justi 1755; § 485) he formulated (in 1755) the very same principles Adam Smith would later use to open his (1776) *magnum opus* on the division of labour:

> Da auch viele Waaren, die in den Stadtnahrungs-Geschäfften zu ihrer Vollkommenheit gebracht werden, aus einer Menge von Theilen bestehen, deren jeder seine besondere Bearbeitung erfordert: so hat man angemerket, daß die Arbeit des Ganzen viel geschwinder und besser von statten geht, wenn ein jeder Arbeiter seinen besondern Theil zu

bearbeiten hat, bey welchem er beständig gelassen wird, so daß einer dem andern immer in die Hände arbeitet, wobey gar viel Zeit, Neben-geschäffte und Anstalten ersparet werden. (Since many goods manufac-tured and finished in cities consist of a multitude of inputs and other materials which all need to go through separate stages of preparation and processing, it has been noted that each step in the process of production will go ahead much faster if assigned to a separate worker each, rather than one worker doing all necessary steps; from which it follows that each worker will work for someone else, meaning that savings of time, effort and other labour will be considerable.)

Instead of a pin factory (Adam Smith) Justi referred to a mint. He even suggested that vertical integration might be an important way to increase profitability and productivity in large enterprises (§ 487), prefiguring in a sense R. D. Coase's theorem of the firm. By all standards Justi's *Staats-wirthschaft* was a work as modern as Smith's *Wealth of Nations* (1776) or Steuart's *Political Oeconomy* (1767).

Justi's *Staatswirthschaft* may therefore easily translate as 'Principles of Economics'. Good economics required the existence of a strong and fiscally wealthy state. Invariably the state had to be impersonated by an absolute ruler, who, invariably male (§ $11^{16}$), was bound to the commitment to do everything in his power to promote his subjects' *Glückseligkeit* ('public happiness') – a term and concept that is absent from modern mainstream economics, and which had been replaced, until recently, by the rational utility maximizer (*homo oeconomicus*).[17] Increasing the wealth of the economy or nation was contingent upon increasing the wealth of the state. The two were intrinsically linked. But by no means were – as a common misrepresentation goes – the power and wealth of the state or prince put, in the cameralist conception, on top of or before the goal of raising national welfare and per capita GDP. In the same way as a strong and flourishing free market economy today needs a strong state safeguarding the 'rules of the game' in all ways and areas necessary, pre-industrial economic theory had little room for spontaneously unfolding Pareto-optimality on atomistic free unregulated markets.

On commerce and manufactures Justi said that he knew of no country, however primitive, that would have *no* external trade whatsoever (Justi 1755, I, § 180). The composition and size of the trade volume was dependent upon factor endowment, somewhat resonating the modern Heckscher-Ohlin factor proportion theorem, or relative productivity levels (resembling Ricardian comparative advantage):

Nein, es ist wohl kein Land in unserem Welttheile, das nicht seine Kaufleute hat, die zur Nothdurft und Bequemlichkeit des menschlichen Lebens eine Menge solcher Waaren in das Land einführen, und wieder einzeln verhandeln, die entweder die Natur ihrer Himmelsgegend versagt hat, oder, die die Einwohner aus Unwissenheit und Mangel der Anstalten nicht zu verfertigen wissen. (I know of no nation in our part of the world where there are no merchants, who will be needed for human convenience as well as necessities. They will import and sell and thus supply us with those goods that nature has failed to supply us with in situ, or which this nation lacks due to a lack of useful knowledge or suitable production facilities for making said goods.)

(Justi 1755, § 180)

Here Justi was in line with the later mercantilists who accepted that a nation's trade balance may be partially passive; only overall there must be a surplus for the economy to be healthy. It was unreasonable (and unenforceable) to entirely prohibit the exportation of money as payment for imports, at least for those imports that could by no means produced at home (ibid., § 182). Overall, however, the national economy must strive to obtain a positive balance on current account (ibid., § 183). He made, earlier (ibid., §159–161) some important qualifications with regard to the structure of the trade balance. Even if it was positive but dominated by raw material and unprocessed exports this would be detrimental for the national economy:

> Wenn der Kaufhandel mit innländischen Waaren geführet wird; so gewinnt zwar der Reichthum des Landes allemal etwas dabey: allein diese Art der Commercien kann dem ohngeachtet dem Staate nachtheilig seyn. Denn wenn die Waaren roh und unverarbeitet aus dem Lande geführet, oder von fremden Nationen selbst abgeholet warden: so verliert das Land ein Beträchtliches an dem Gewinnste und an der Nahrung der Unterthanen, die man davon hätte genießen können. (If there is an export of domestic goods, the nation's wealth will increase in consequence, but may still bring the balance into the negative and be to the nation's detriment. That is because we export the goods in their raw state, or let foreigners take them from us by purchase in their raw state, the nation forfeits the value added and profit gained from exporting such materials in their finished, i.e. manufactured, state.)

(ibid., § 161)

Justi identified two options to turn a passive trade balance into a positive one, either to reduce imports or increase exports; in practice the chosen strategy would depend upon a combination of the two (ibid., §185). The basic starting point would be to have someone (a government board) compile a reliable set of statistics derived from toll, customs and excise accounts (ibid., §186). These would indicate which goods would have to be imported, and which could, by a strategy of import substitution, be relocated into the domestic production landscape (ibid., §186; see also § 281 on manufactures). For this he identified the manufactories as a panacea, drawing on native raw materials, such as raw wool (for cloth manufactures), as well as foreign raw materials where applicable (English cloth producers would regularly import fine Spanish wool). Justi acknowledged that it would be difficult to surpass the neighbouring countries, such as the Netherlands, England, France and Italy (the *Welschen*) in this game, i.e. to catch up with their higher productivity levels and to completely substitute native commodities for imports. But it would be nice to at least reduce these expenses to the absolute necessary (ibid., §188). At least those items weighing heavily on the import balance, and where the largest sums of money left the country, should be taken care of so as to relocate as many of them as possible into the domestic economy (ibid., §189). The key to creating a competitive advantage was, in Justi's opinion, to create new manufactures, new types or ranges of goods (or colours in textiles); to develop new techniques and processes of production (ibid., §188). Here he mentioned the example of a new colouring and printing process for medium-type Saxon textiles which 'seven or eight years ago' (i.e. around 1747) would have secured a considerable level of sales in Italy and elsewhere (ibid., §188). In order to promote the reduction of imports, a strategy of technology transfer and promotion of inventions would be essential: *Erfindungen* (inventions) should be turned into useful applications in the productive landscape (*das, was sie täglich erfinden, zu nutzen, und ihnen Gelegenheit zu verschaffen, daß sie ihre gute Nahrung dadurch finden können*). Again, this sounds very modern.[18] The state should expend money, even risk small losses in certain cases to promote general climate of invention, because '*Wer gar nichts wagen will, der wird auch sein Vermögen niemals vergößern*' ('who does not dare will not win anything') (ibid., §185, note). It was the state's role to safeguard export markets by enforcing certain standards of quality and price (ibid., §187). Export commodities should be inspected by government officials (*Auffseher*) before sale; good quality work fit for export would be marked or stamped accordingly (ibid., §198). This was very common during these days, not only within the German lands but Scotland (and Ireland) as well.[19] Only the good quality pieces should be exempted from all excise and customs duties upon export (ibid., §198). Incentives such as premiums and bounties on well-made piecework should be granted (ibid., § 198). Foreign experts should either be hired and re-located into the country; or their useful knowledge should be imported by questioning them in a detailed way about best practice methods abroad, inquired of if necessary in an illicit manner (industrial espionage) (ibid., § 198). Conversations between craftsmen and intellectuals or scholars (*Gelehrte*) should be encouraged, so as to facilitate technology transfer, innovation and emulation:

> Es würde von großem Nutzen vor den Staat seyn, wenn man die unter den Handwerkern so sehr eingerissene Meynung, daß sie bloß bey ihrem alten Schlendrian, den sie von ihren Meistern gelernet haben, ohne Abänderung verbleiben müßten, ausrotten könnte, und wenn sie

dahin zu bringen wären, daß sie sich bemüheten, ihre Arbeiten immer schooner, geschickter, dauerhaftiger und vollkommener zu machen. Der Umgang derselben mit den Gelehrten und ein engerer Zusammenhang mit denselben würde hierzu nicht wenig beytragen.(It would be of great benefit to the nation if the rut, traditionalism and sluggishness characteristic amongst so many a tradesman and artisan were uprooted and each and every manufactured were forced to work and produce only to the highest standard, more skilful, more durable, more perfectible. Some intercourse of artisans with learned men and men of letters would certainly help.)

(ibid., § 302.)

This was different from the English model on the generation and promulgation of 'useful knowledge' in the age of Enlightenment sketched, for instance, by J. Mokyr (2009). Experts and master craftsmen should be appointed as chief inspectors (*Aufseher*) for the respective trades. The erection of schools should be encouraged (ibid., § 303). The state should also promote the people's spirits of industry and commerce.

Other cameralist authors – and many an English mercantilist – followed suit. There is little need to quote let alone study them in entirety. Suffice it to say that in Justi's age high cameralism had– as a subject taught in universities – reached its highpoint as a full-blown economic theory which failed to make it, for reasons that cannot be discussed at present, into the modern canon of economic sciences.

## II

To what extent had such ideas any meaningful practical effect? Some evidence of their translation in practice has already been given in the previous section, but generally speaking it is difficult to reconstruct transmission mechanisms between theory (say: cameralism, mercantilism, or Boterian economic reason of state) and practice; that is, economic policy, meaning theory applied in practical economic policy and development.[20] First of all, modern research has agreed that prior to 1800 there was no such thing as the modern state. So there cannot have been a modern economic policy. This, however, is a truism and therefore quite trivial. What we could call economic policy of the emerging 'proto-states' in the early modern period (c. A.D. 1500–1800) chiefly extended to *market regulation* and *stabilization* of the common good (*bonum commune*), or what the German language has as '*Ordnungs- und Stabilitätspolitik*'. This ranged from coin valuations (directed at the stabilization of spot exchange rates of the hundreds and thousands of different coins circulating in medieval and early modern Germany (Rössner 2014)); the regulation of weights and measures; the building of roads and other transport infrastructure; the unification of the territorial economies by an (attempted) standardization of customs and toll duties; the building up and redistribution of grain reserves to the public in times of dearth;[21] up to prohibitions of rent-seeking and usurious behaviour in the market place (such as forestalling, charging unduly high prices, the granting of monopolies on certain economic activities which may obviously clash with the previously-mentioned activities; as well as price level stabilization for essentials, such as foodstuffs, in times of dearth). Such measures were intended to 'get the property rights right', in order to attract foreign capital and make the inhabitants richer and safer – mainly, perhaps, for fiscal needs.[22]

But is it always either possible, or even meaningful, to disentangle the 'fiscal' from the 'economic' in the policies of the early modern state? Is this even permissible to do in the modern context? If we define 'economic policy' as in the previous paragraph, we find good examples of it since the Middle Ages. The only thing we do not find, however, in reality are states that actively interfered with the economic process in the modern sense. In theory we do: economic discourse had held since the Renaissance and the days of Giovanni Botero, that the state should interfere with the economy where necessary; the only problem being that pre-industrial states were weak, soft and lacking the tools of government steering and intervention that have made contemporary states and government so powerful at times (Magnusson 2009, ch. 1 and 2).

Secondly, good ideas do not necessarily *have to* turn into good practice spontaneously or automatically. That is, a theory may be 'good' whilst being totally inapplicable in practice. Or else a theory or strategy may not be so axiomatically refined or complex as many modern models in the economic sciences and still yield exceedingly good practical results. Schumpeter was well aware of this, remarking pointedly that economic theories were mostly elegant or useful, but never both at the same time. Some scholars would, just to take one example, conclude that literally all 'mercantilist' measures aimed at creating a unified and uniform Prussian market under Frederick the Great (1712–1786) ultimately failed, as did attempts at effectively promoting domestic industry in the dispersed lands that made up the composite Prussian state. Both were cornerstones of the cameralist-mercantilist faith. But does this mean that mercantilist ideas were 'bad'? Or did they simply not unfold as intended, in the repeated attempts to implement them, because the contexts were bad – the set of prevailing social customs and legal institutions usually denoted as 'feudalism'? Prussia managed, after the 1830s, one of the fastest transitions towards industrialization, as Magnusson's 2009 volume on the *Invisible Hand* argues (Magnusson 2009) – but only after basic restrictions on individual economic activity, which had little to do with the mercantilist-cameralist creed but more with somewhat unfavourable property rights, were lifted by the abolition of 'feudalism' and serfdom (*villainage*, manorial system) in Prussia in 1806/1811. In fact the cameralists were viciously opposed to feudalism and any restrictions to economic activity in what we would call the 'free market'. So perhaps we need to turn the problem back on its feet, then. It was not mercantilism and cameralist economic theory that didn't work – it was the *context,* the prevailing legal, institutional and sometimes socio-economic circumstances, that often didn't do the trick.[23]

There is the obvious problem of 'translating' ideas into different contexts. Grafe has argued that in seventeenth- and eighteenth-century Habsburg Spain, mercantilist ideas of domestic industry promotion and protection circulated widely. But it was the institutional structure of multi-ethnic and regionalized Spanish society, which prevented the effective application of a national economic policy promoting Spain's common wealth (Grafe 2013). A strong tradition of institutional fragmentation in Spain created a bias towards promoting municipal policies at the expenses of the royal or national interest, thus failing to either create an integrated national economy, or to promote industrial policy on the national level. Similar restrictions prevailed in early modern Prussia as well as elsewhere. Once the basic restrictions had been lifted, however, many European states after 1800, during the process of industrialization, applied the old, pre-modern cameralist and mercantilist ideas and strategies of import substitution and national market integration increasingly effectively (Magnusson 2009). In fact, most economic historians nowadays agree that European industrialization during the nineteenth and twentieth century, with Britain being the first-comer, followed by Belgium, France, Germany; later on Austria, Sweden, Denmark etc., then, towards the turn of the twentieth century Russia etc., would not have taken place without the intervening of an emerging strong and pro-active modern state.[24]

So Boterian ideas of economic reason of state must have resonated reasonably well amongst the brains of politicians, rulers and kings – as well as entrepreneurs – in early industrial Europe, c. 1600–1900. But their full effective translation into practice had to await the arrival of the modern nation state and national economies (*Volkswirtschaften*) à la List – i.e. market economies that were integrated economically *as well as* politically.

## III

Therefore, what we have come to know as Listian economics – an economic model and strategy that influenced modern heterodox, as well as modern growth and development studies – was neither new nor terribly original. The core structure of the Listian development strategy had been formulated in the works of Giovanni Botero, by Antonio Serra (in his *Breve Trattato...*, 1613)[25] and many others, to be taken up and developed into a full-blown economic theory by the emerging discourse and academic science known as 'German' (which it never was) cameralism, c. 1660s–1800. We may label this tradition of economic reasoning 'economic reason of state'. These ideas focused around the stance that sustained modern economic growth was impossible to achieve without strong manufactures, and that it was quite unlikely for such processes to unfold spontaneously according the working mechanisms of the physiocratic or *Invisible Hand* model (or the modern neoclassical market mechanism) but were most likely to be achieved by a strong interventionist if not dirigiste state that would protect, as long as necessary, those industries and manufacturing branches that were deemed the most promising or 'leading sectors' of the domestic economy.

## Notes

1 List (1851).
2 List (1926, pp. 367–436).
3 It is interesting in its own right that List called agriculture 'lifeless' or sterile (*leblos*) and thus quite unsuited to generate lasting economic spill-over effects that would lead to sustained economic growth and development. This was mainly due to the limited productivity-enhancing capacities, which were much lower than in other sectors. This line of reasoning was obviously quite different from what the physiocrats said regarding agriculture. Accordingly List was critical of physiocracy, see Friedrich List (1851, pp. 201–236 and 330–333). On the other hand List maintained, in his *Wir wollen keine Fabriken!* (1843) that for Germany he wished a balanced economy, with equal contributions of the three sectors – agriculture, manufacturing/industry and services – to national wealth (see List 1926, pp. 594–626, at 596). And in his *Über die Beziehungen der Landwirtschaft zur Industrie und zum Handel* (1844) (List 1926, pp. 627–683, at 629) he called agriculture the most important and foundational sector of the economy without which none of the other two would be able to flourish. On List, see, e.g. Brauer (1985), Brinkmann (1959), Daastøl (2011), Stieda (1928), Gehrig (1956), Henderson (1989) and Reinert (2007).
4 A term coined by Weststeijn and Hartman (2013).
5 See Rössner (2016a) for detailed case studies and an update on current research in the history of modern political economy.
6 See, e.g., Parthasarathi (2011), Ashworth (2003), Ormrod (2003). For the pre-industrial period, especially the middle ages, see also Epstein (2000).
7 See List (1851, Vol. 10).
8 See Reinert and Carpenter (2016).
9 On Botero, from the viewpoint of his 'demographics', see the recent study by Nipperdey (2012) with references to literature on Botero on pp. 65–66.
10 Reinert (2005).
11 All translations are the author's.
12 Epstein (2000) and Epstein and Prak (2008).
13 Seckendorff (1720, p. 238).
14 For a pointed view, see Harcourt (2011). For a historical discussion see Rössner (2016).
15 This and the following quotes are based on the translation by Arthur E. Monroe.
16 Where he said that it was 'scientifically proven' that the female gender would be unfit for ruling; ironically the *Staatswirthschaft* (1755) was dedicated to Maria Theresia of Austria (frontispiece)!
17 Priddat (2008), Burkhardt and Priddat (2005) See also Tribe (1995, ch. 1), Schefold (1993) and Bog (1981).
18 E.g. Reinert (2007) and Chang (2003).
19 E.g. Durie (1979) and Whatley (2000).

20  This section draws on my introduction to the forthcoming translation of Philip Wilhelm von Hörnigk's *Oesterreich über alles wann es nur will* (Rössner 2018).
21  Something we find as far away as China, see Wong (1997).
22  On Germany in the early modern period, see, e.g., Blaich (1970, 1973). An interesting case study for Württemberg around 1500 is Weidner (1931). For early modern Britain, see Parthasarathi (2011), Ashworth (2003), Hoppit (2011a, 2011b), Sickinger (2000), Gambles (2000), and Dudley (2013). In a wider context, see Reinert (2007) or Vries (2002). On states and property rights in terms of general models, see, e.g., North and Thomas (1973).
23  This paragraph draws on Rössner (2015).
24  For eighteenth-century Britain, see Parthasarathi (2011) and for late-comers or catch-up development, the classic by Alexander Gerschenkron (1962).
25  Antonio Serra (2011).

# References

Ashworth, W.J. (2003), *Customs and Excise: Trade, Production, and Consumption in England, 1640–1845*, Oxford and New York, NY: Oxford University Press.

Blaich, F. (1970), *Die Epoche des Merkantilismus*, Wiesbaden: Steiner.

Blaich, F. (1973), *Die Wirtschaftspolitik des Reichstags im Heiligen Römischen Reich: Ein Beitrag zur Problemgeschichte wirtschaftlichen Gestaltens*, Stuttgart: G. Fischer.

Bog, I. (1981), 'Ist die Kameralistik eine untergegangene Wissenschaft?', in: *Berichte zur Wissenschaftsgeschichte*, 4, 61–72.

Botero, G. (1956 [1588]), *The Reason of State/Della ragione di stato*, transl. P. J. and D. P. Waley, New Haven: Yale University Press, 150–153.

Brauer, W. (1985), 'List, Friedrich', in: *Neue Deutsche Biographie (NDB)*, Vol. 14, Berlin: Duncker & Humblot, 694–697.

Burkhardt, J. and Priddat, B.P. (eds.) (2005), *Geschichte der Ökonomie*, Frankfurt am Main: Deutscher Klassiker Verlag.

Chang, H. J. (2003), *Kicking Away the Ladder: Development Strategy in Historical Perspective*, London: Anthem.

Crafft/Krafft, J.D. (1683), *Bedencken von Manufacturen in Deutschland*, Jena: Bauhofer.

Daastøl, A.M. (2011), *Friedrich List's Heart, Wit and Will: Mental Capital as the Productive Force of Progress*, Ph.D. Diss, Universität Erfurt, Erfurt.

Dudley, C. (2013), 'Party Politics, Political Economy, and Economic Development in Early Eighteenth-Century Britain', in: *Economic History Review*, Second Series, 66 (4), 1084–1100.

Durie, A.J. (1979), *The Scottish Linen Industry in the Eighteenth Century*, Edinburgh: John Donald.

Epstein, S.R. (2000), *Freedom and Growth: The Rise of States and Markets in Europe, 1300–1750*, London: Routledge.

Epstein, S.R. and Prak, M.R. (eds.) (2008), *Guilds, Innovation, and the European Economy, 1400–1800*, Cambridge and New York: Cambridge University Press.

Forberger, U. (2015), 'Crafft (Kraft), Johann Daniel', in: Institut für Sächsische Geschichte und Volkskunde e. V./Martina Schattkowsky (ed.), *Sächsische Biografie*, Online issue: www.isgv.de/saebi/ (last accessed 20 January 2015, 14:13 p.m.)

Gambles, A. (2000), 'Free Trade and State Formation: The Political Economy of Fisheries Policy in Britain and the United Kingdom, circa 1780–1850', in: *Journal of British Studies*, 39 (3), 288–316.

Gehrig, H. (1956), *Friedrich List und Deutschlands politisch-ökonomische Einheit*, Leipzig: Koehler & Amelang.

Gerschenkron, A. (1962), *Economic Backwardness in Historical Perspective: A Book of Essays*, Cambridge: Belknap Press of Harvard University Press.

Grafe, R. (2013), 'Mercantilism and Representation in a Polycentric State: Early Modern Spain', in: P.J.Stern and C.Wennerlind (eds.), *Mercantilism Reimagined: Political Economy in Early Modern Britain and Its Empire*, Oxford: Oxford University Press, 241–262.

Harcourt, B. (2011), *The Illusion of Free Markets: Punishment and the Myth of Natural Order*, Cambridge, MA: Harvard University Press.

Henderson, W.O. (1989), *Friedrich List: Der erste Visionär eines vereinten Europas. Eine historische Biographie*, Reutlingen: Verlagshaus Reutlingen, Oertel u. Spörer.

Hoppit, J. (2011a), 'Bounties, the Economy and the State in Britain, 1689–1800', in: P. Gauci (ed.), *Regulating the British Economy, 1660–1850*, Farnham, Surrey and Burlington, VT: Ashgate.

Hoppit, J. (2011b), 'The Nation, the State, and the First Industrial Revolution', in: *The Journal of British Studies*, 50 (2), 307–331.

Justi, von J.H.G. (1755), *Staatswirthschaft oder Systematische Abhandlung aller Oekonomischen und Cameral-Wissenschaften, die zur Regierung eines Landes erfodert [sic!] werden: In zween Theilen ausgefertiget*, Leipzig: Breitkopf, Vol. I, 144–268.

List, F. (1851), 'Das nationale System der politischen Ökonomie', in: L. Häusser (ed.), *Friedrich List's gesammelte Schriften, III*, Stuttgart and Tübingen: Cotta.

List, F. (1926), *Friedrich Lists kleinere Schriften, I: Zur Staatswissenschaft und politischen Ökonomie*, Friedrich Lenz ed., Jena: Gustav Fischer.

List, F. (2009), *Das nationale System der politischen Ökonomie in Rüdiger Gerlach, Imperialistisches und kolonialistisches Denken in der politischen Ökonomie Friedrich Lists*, Hamburg: Kovač.

Magnusson, L. (2009), *Nation, State and the Industrial Revolution: The Visible Hand*, London and New York: Routledge.

Mokyr, J. (2009), *The Enlightened Economy: An Economic History of Britain, 1700–1850*, New Haven: Yale University Press.

Nipperdey, J. (2012), *Die Erfindung der Bevölkerungspolitik: Staat, politische Theorie und Population in der Frühen Neuzeit*, Göttingen: Vandenhoeck & Ruprecht, 65–98.

North, D.C. and Thomas, R.P. (1973), *The Rise of the Western World. A New Economic History*, Cambridge: Cambridge University Press.

Notz, W. (ed.) (1931), *Friedrich List. Grundlinien einer politischen Ökonomie und andere Beiträge der Amerikanischen Zeit 1825–1832*, Berlin: Reimar Hobbing.

Ormrod, D. (2003), *The Rise of Commercial Empires: England and the Netherlands in the Age of Mercantilism, 1650–1770*, Cambridge and New York: Cambridge University Press.

Parthasarathi, P. (2011), *Why Europe Grew Rich and Asia Did Not: Global Economic Divergence, 1600–1850*, Cambridge and New York: Cambridge University Press.

Priddat, B.P. (2008), 'Kameralismus als paradoxe Konzeption der gleichzeitigen Stärkung von Markt und Staat. Komplexe Theorielagen im deutschen 18. Jahrhundert', in: *Berichte zur Wissenschaftsgeschichte*, 31, 249–263.

Reinert, E.S. (2007), *How Rich Countries Got Rich – And Why Poor Countries Stay Poor*, London: Constable.

Reinert, E.S. and Carpenter, K. (2016), 'German Language Economic Bestsellers before 1850, with Two Chapters on a Common Reference Point of Cameralism and Mercantilism', in: P.R. Rössner (ed.), *Economic Growth and the Origins of Modern Political Economy: Economic Reasons of State, 1500–2000*, Milton Park and New York: Routledge.

Reinert, S.A. (2005), 'Cameralism and Commercial Rivalry: Nationbuilding through Economic Autarky in Seckendorff's 1665 Additiones', in: *European Journal of Law and Economics*, 19 (3), 271–286.

Rössner, P.R. (2014), 'Monetary Instability, Lack of Integration and the Curse of a Commodity Money Standard. The German Lands, c.1400–1900 A.D.', in: *Credit and Capital Markets*, 47 (2), 297–340.

Rössner, P.R. (2015), 'Heckscher Reloaded? Mercantilism, the State and Europe's Transition to Industrialization (1600–1900)', in: *The Historical Journal*, 58 (2), 1–21.

Rössner, P.R. (ed.) (2016a), *Economic Growth and the Origins of Modern Political Economy: Economic Reasons of State, 1500–2000*, Milton Park and New York: Routledge.

Rössner, P.R. (2016b), 'Freie Märkte? Zur Konzeption von Konnektivität, Wettbewerb und Markt im vorklassischen Wirtschaftsdenken und die Lektionen aus der Geschichte', in: *Historische Zeitschrift*, 303 (2), 349–392.

Rössner, P.R. (2018), 'Introduction', in: P.R. Rössner (ed.), *Austria Supreme, If It So Wishes 1684: A Strategy That Made Europe Rich*, London and New York: Anthem.

Schefold, B. (1993), 'Glückseligkeit und Wirtschaftspolitik: Zu Justis "Grundsätze der Policey-Wissenschaft"', in: B. Schefold (ed.), *Vademecum zu einem Klassiker des Kameralismus: Johann Heinrich Gottlob von Justi, Grundsätze der Policey-Wissenschaft*, Düsseldorf: Verlag Wirtschaft und Finanzen.

Schröder, Wilhelm Freiherr von (1744), *Fürstliche Schatz- und Rent-Cammer* (Leipzig: Christoph Gottfried Eckart) (first ed. 1684).

Seckendorff, Veit Ludwig von (1703), *Teutsche(r) Fürsten- Stat* (Frankfurt/Main: Meyer).

Seckendorff, Veit Ludwig von (1720), *Teutsche(r) Fürsten- Stat*. Jena no publisher (first ed. 1655), Jena: Johann Meyers Wittwe.

Serra, A. (2011), *A Short Treatise on the Wealth and Poverty of Nations*, S.A. Reinert ed., London and New York: Anthem.

Sickinger, R.L. (2000), 'Regulation or Ruination: Parliament's Consistent Pattern of Mercantilist Regulation of the English Textile Trade, 1660–1800', in: *Parliamentary History*, 19 (2), 211–232.

Small, Albion (1909). *The Cameralists. The Pioneers of German Social Polity* (Chicago: University of Chicago Press).

Stieda, W. (1928), 'Friedrich List', in: *Berichte über die Verhandlungen der Sächsischen Akademie der Wissenschaften zu Leipzig, Philologisch-historische Klasse*, 80 (1), 1–44.

Tribe, K. (1995), *Strategies of Economic Order: German Economic Discourse, 1750–1950*, Cambridge: Cambridge University Press.

Vries, P. (2002), 'Governing Growth: A Comparative Analysis of the Role of the State in the Rise of the West', in: *Journal of World History*, 13, 67–193.

Weidner, K. (1931), *Die Anfänge einer staatlichen Wirtschaftspolitik in Württemberg*, Stuttgart: Kohlhammer.

Weststeijn, A. and Hartman, J. (2013), 'An Empire of Trade: Commercial Reason of State in Seventeenth-Century Holland', in: R.Sophus and R.Pernille (eds.), *The Political Economy of Empire in the Early Modern World*, Houndmills, Basingstoke, Hampshire: Palgrave Macmillan, 11–31.

Whatley, C.A. (2000), *Scottish Society. Beyond Jacobitism, Towards Industrialization*, Manchester and New York: Manchester University Press.

Wong, R.B. (1997), *China Transformed: Historical Change and the Limits of European Experience*, Ithaca: Cornell University Press.

# 9 Two early views on railway regulation in Germany
## Friedrich List and David Hansemann

*Bernhard Wieland*

## 9.1. Introduction

The literature on German railway economics in the 19th century is dominated by the name of Friedrich List. And indeed, there can be no doubt that List through his tireless agitation for a German railway system, both in writing and practice, deserves an outstanding position in German railway history. If there ever was a technological visionary List certainly qualifies. Almost every German railway historian knows the famous drawing in his classic pamphlet *On a Railway System in Saxony as Basis of a General German Railway System* (List, 1833). The pamphlet was written in the early 1830s when the first small railway lines in Germany had just started to operate. But the drawing shows already all major railway connections which are still relevant and in operation today. Other perhaps more important prophecies of List turned out to be true as well. In his essays *The World is Moving* (List, 1837) and *The German National Transport System* (List, 1838), and also in his major theoretical work *The National System of Political Economy* (List, 1841a) he made predictions on the societal and economic effects of railways which almost all proved to be right. What distinguishes List in this regard from most of his contemporaries is the fact that his predictions and prophecies were firmly rooted in the dominant economic theories of his time, be they his own or those of others (including those of his supposed intellectual adversary Adam Smith, on which List nevertheless frequently relies).

In this chapter List's intellectual monopoly on German railway economics in the 19th century will be challenged a bit. The chapter will draw attention to another outstanding German railway pioneer, David Hansemann (1790–1864) who, apart from his interest in railways, was also an important industrialist, banker and politician. In many biographical accounts of Hansemann his railway activities are counted just as a minor part of the various business activities of this many-sided man. But Hansemann wrote several treatises on railway policy which intellectually live up to List's standards and which, in the parts dealing with regulatory matters, are surprisingly modern. Thus, Hansemann, as early as 1837, advocated the separation of network and operations and developed ideas which are very close to the concept of Demsetz auction, a concept which was introduced by Harold Demsetz in the modern economics literature in 1968 (Demsetz, 1968). It is known that Demsetz's ideas were anticipated in some sense by Edwin Chadwick (1859), but as will be seen below, Hansemann's contribution was not only earlier but far more specific. But these priority considerations may not be so important in the end. The main purpose of this contribution is to show that the thinking about railway regulation, not only by List but by others too, had developed already to a surprising degree of sophistication at a time when the building of railroads in Germany had barely begun.[1]

The rest of this chapter is organized as follows. The next section discusses List's ideas on railway regulation, mostly as laid down in his work *The German National Transport System* of 1838 and his *The German Railway System as an Instrument for the Perfection of German Industry, the German Customs Union and German Unity in General* of 1841. Section 9.3 will give a short sketch of Hansemann's life, which in many ways was the precise opposite of List's tragic career. Section 9.4 contains an exposition of Hansemann's regulatory proposals, drawn from his *The Railways and their Shareholders in Relation to the State* (Hansemann, 1837) and reflects shortly in how far Hansemann can be thought of as a precursor of Demsetz and Chadwick. Section 9.5 concludes.

## 9.2. List on railway regulation

When List writes on railways he usually spends most of his time on the economic and societal benefits of railways in general or of a specific railway connection in particular. He calculates costs and benefits of special railway links in great detail and gives much thought to the influence of the competing modes, notably canals. However, there are also several places in his writings where he deals with economic regulation in the modern sense of the word, notably in his *The German National Transport System* of 1838 (henceforth quoted as *Transport System*). But there also hints in his *The German Railway System as an Instrument for the Perfection of German Industry, the German Customs Union and German Unity in General* of 1841 (henceforth quoted as *Railway System*), particularly with respect to externalities.

The modern literature gives the following possible reasons for regulation:

(1) Existence of a natural monopoly
(2) Ruinous Competition
(3) Substantial external effects (positive or negative)
(4) Universal Service
(5) Information asymmetries
(6) High transaction costs.

As far as I can see List devotes his thoughts mainly to the first four of these issues. Issue (5), information asymmetries, comes into play mostly in the form of (a) asymmetries between the railroad firms' management and the shareholders and (b) asymmetries between the firms and the regulators. As far as I can see, List never mentions asymmetries between customers and firms of railway companies. In fact, List doesn't even seem to care much about the hazards to health that were so widely discussed at his time with respect to railway transport, especially in Germany. One may conjecture, that this neglect was perhaps due to his experience in America, were he had already seen railroads in operation.

Concerning transaction costs, issue (6), one might say metaphorically that List's railway writings, in principle, deal with little else. The whole of his writings is full of descriptions of how railways will reduce transport costs, communications costs, or search costs, which are all elements of transaction costs. Accordingly, Wendler in his biography of List quotes the contemporary German economist Müller as contending that List may be regarded as a precursor of transaction cost economics (Wendler, 2013: 209). There is certainly a grain of truth in this view, but the claim seems to be a little far-fetched. The same claim could be made, and perhaps with more justification, for Adam Smith, notably for his analysis of the relation between the division of labour and the extent of the market (Smith, 1776, Book I, Chapter 3). But transaction cost theory in the technical sense of the term has to do with the influence of transaction costs on the choice of institutions (see for example Williamson, 1985), and it is in my view doubtful that List makes any contribution to this type of analysis. It has to be admitted, however, that his arguments for the public financing of railroads given below may be interpreted as a transaction cost type of analysis, but this is probably not what Wendler and Müller have in mind. I therefore shall neglect the transaction costs rationale for regulation in what follows.

What does List have to say on the remaining above reasons (1) to (4) for regulation?

In discussing this question it has to be kept in mind that List, despite his general farsightedness, did not know these concepts although he certainly had a feeling for the type of market failures they are designed to describe. All one can do is therefore to screen his writings for places which might be interpreted in the light of these concepts. It goes without saying that there is always an element of arbitrariness in such a procedure. We just saw an example in the concept of transaction costs.

Concerning natural monopoly it is important to note that List, notwithstanding his emphasis on creating a national German railway system, mainly thinks of the establishment of railways on the territories of the 19th century's German federal states. It has to be borne in mind that Germany as a nation-state did not yet exist. (Remember that List died in 1846.) The *national* railway system, which List was aiming at, was to come about through cooperation among the regional railway systems, preferably within or parallel to the activities of the Zollverein. To remember one of List's most famous quotes: "The railways and the Zollverein are Siamese twins." (*Railway System* 4)

In discussing the natural monopoly problem with respect to these regional railways List was not so much worried about the aspect of wasteful duplication but rather about excessive transport tariffs and profits. He seemed to believe that transport markets in the 19th century would develop so rapidly and to such an extent that they would simply outgrow the area of subadditivity of the cost function (the cause for wasteful duplication). List even argues that in many cases it would be profitable to build a new railroad parallel to an already existing canal (*Transport System* 20). In part this was due to complementarity between road and waterborne transport and in part due to the differing characteristics (heterogeneity) of the goods being transported. Thus, the railroad would be able to take over transport during winter times or times of low water. In addition, goods whose delivery was not time sensitive would permanently be shipped via steamboats. It can be concluded from this analysis that, apart from natural monopoly, ruinous competition, issue (2) above, was not a problem to List either.

List was far more worried about another problem of monopoly: excessive tariffs. In *Transport System* he devotes several paragraphs to this question.

He first points out that the beneficial effects of railway building will not materialize if transport tariffs are too high. (*Transport System* 45). He explains how this problem was dealt with in England and North America at his time.

In England the maximum level of tariffs was set in the charters granted to the railway operators at their establishment by the local parliament. He cites the example of the Liverpool–Manchester railway, whose parliamentary charter stipulated that dividends should never exceed 10%. In modern terms one would describe this arrangement as rate-of-return regulation. List already notes the major defect of this type of regulation. In setting the charters it was tacitly supposed by the local parliaments that in the case where the rate of return on capital invested would exceed 10% the companies would use the surplus profits to lower tariffs or to improve quality of service. What in effect happened, was that instead the Liverpool–Manchester railway took to "a splendid administration" (*Transport System* 45). In modern terminology this is known as "gold plating", a special feature of the so called Averch-Johnson effect. (List did not mention overuse of capital.)

List then turns to the example of France where the problem of tariff regulation was solved by auctioning off railway projects to the bidder promising the lowest tariffs. In modern terminology this tendering procedure would be designated as a Demsetz auction. List points out that in order to function properly both procedures, the North American as well as the French, require detailed knowledge of cost and demand.

In order to calculate transport prices in the way most advantageous to the entrepreneur and the state, or rather the general public, one would have to know the level of the cost of capital, maintenance and transport on the one hand and the volume of transport of passengers and goods on the other – all unknown magnitudes!

*(Transport System* 45)

In other words, there exists substantial uncertainty and there are informational asymmetries between firms and regulators. Mistakes are unavoidable. If these mistakes occur to the disadvantage of the entrepreneurs the share-holders will suffer. If, on the other hand, share-holders gain excessively, "the public will have to pay the large dividends" and in addition will be deprived of cheap transport and "the thousand benefits it entails" *(Transport System* 45). Considering that the railroad will be the source of many spill-over effects and innovations in the economy at large, the dynamic losses will even be greater than the static ones. List therefore advocates regulatory procedures which allow adjustments of tariffs, both downwards and upwards. But he believes that such procedures will solve the above problems only in a very unsatisfactory manner. He therefore opts strongly in favour of public ownership: "All the evils named above will thereby be prevented forever". *(Transport System* 47) Given List's frequent complaints about bureaucracy this conclusion comes somewhat as a surprise. Moreover, it is not quite clear what List really means by public ownership. The original wording is "auf Rechnung des Staates" which can be translated literally as "financing by the state". This would be compatible with several arrangements, for instance (a) a vertically integrated public enterprise (integrating both the network and the operation of trains) or (b) a vertically integrated private enterprise funded entirely by the state, much in the sense of a modern PPP (Public Private Partnership). Hansemann, as will be seen in the next section, opted for a third solution, namely public financing and ownership of the infrastructure combined with the private operation of trains. From what transpires between the lines it seems that, in contrast to Hansemann, List thought of a vertically integrated private concessionaire whose network was financed entirely by public loans. Be that as it may, he believed that public ownership would speed up the building of new lines and, in contrast to a private firm, would use the ensuing revenues either to lower transport tariffs or to extend the railway network.

But the government could, of course, use the revenues for budgetary purposes as well. List is aware of this possibility but argues that it would be unwise for the state to act like this. In the long run low transport tariffs will stimulate the economy so much that tax revenues will far outweigh railway profits. For the same reason List opposes cross-subsidies to the postal services which had been demanded in particular by the Thurn und Taxis in compensation for the diminished travel demand for postal coaches.

List has nothing to object, however, to internal subsidies from "dense" to "thin" railway links. (*Transport System* 50) This type of cross-subsidy, of course, is closely related to the regulatory issue of "universal service" in modern terminology, issue (4) above. List is not quite clear whether he advocates internal subsidies for distributional reasons or in order to exploit network externalities. In *Transport System* there are formulations which support both views. In his later *Railway System* the focus is clearly on the network externalities effect (see below). He frequently repeats that the individual railways only make sense as parts of a total nationwide network.

List has a further argument for state-ownership in railways: speculation in railway shares. He complains that bankers and major stock brokers had amassed large fortunes in the emission business. In several cases the same bankers held top positions in the very railway companies whose shares they were trading. Hansemann, by the way, was a case in point. As a consequence substantial insider trading had occurred. To prevent such speculation List proposed that railway shares should be issued only by the government and that revenues should be distributed according to the following fixed rules: (1) the government guarantees a minimum return of 3% of capital invested to the concessionaire for building and operating the railway; (2) returns over 3% but less than 6% should entirely go to the share-holders; (3) returns over 6% but below 10% should be divided equally between government and share-holders; and (4) from all revenues beyond 10% one third should go to share-holders and two thirds to the government. In the latter case the government should use these proceeds for internal subsidies from thin to dense routes and to extend the railway network (*Transport System* 48).

List thought that these rules would reduce speculation to a minimum. Basically he believed that they would make railway shares unattractive to professional speculators and that therefore they would mainly be bought by "the custodians of widows and orphans" and other risk-averse investors (*Transport System* 49–50).

Let us now take up the last reason for regulation that was mentioned in the introduction to this section, namely external effects. List hardly ever mentions *negative* external effects but *positive* externalities are his big topic, of course. In fact, List almost gets poetical when he describes the big advantages of railroads. The corresponding passages (for example in *The World is Moving* or in *Transport System*) are too well known to need repetition here. It is worth mentioning, perhaps, that in the present author's view Bröcker (2013) has succeeded to reduce the poetry to more prosaic terms by building an important part of List's intuition into a Romer-like endogenous growth-model. Broadly speaking, in this model, investment in transportation infrastructure, notably high-speed trains, helps to reduce communications costs and thereby amplifies the spill-over effects of agglomeration of industry. In the context of the theory of regulation, positive externalities like these would provide a reason for government subsidies. In a similar vein, List in *Railway System* argues that the state should build the railways because the macroeconomic spill-over effects are so widely spread that they never can be appropriated by any private entrepreneur. But, as he asserts, this does not mean that railway building is not profitable *for the state*. In his view, most railway lines will be cost-covering in a very short time after they have been built (already after one year, *Railway System* 23) and, in addition, after a few years more will generate the substantial positive externalities which are his permanent topic.

Apart from financing by the state List also advocates low tariffs, as we have seen, but to my knowledge he never advocates that in the operational phase railways should price below costs and that the loss should be made up by the state. The only exception are cross-subsidies to the "thin" lines mentioned above in connection with the argument of universal service.

So much for externalities on the economy at large. Concerning network externalities in the narrow sense List formulates his position most clearly in *Railway System*. At several places in this work (*Railway System* 12, 17, 22, 23) he points out that the profitability of single lines will strongly depend on the degree to which a nationwide network has been achieved. He therefore urges that this nationwide network should as far as possible be built all at once. This furnishes one more argument that the railroads should be built by the state (*Railway System* 24).

## 9.3. Biographical notes on David Hansemann[2]

Readers of this volume are likely to be well acquainted with List's life.[3] Hansemann's life is probably less known. I therefore omit biographical material on List in this chapter and concentrate on Hansemann. Readers not interested in biographical detail may immediately jump to Section 9.4. To avoid confusion it should also be noted that David Hansemann must be distinguished from his son Adolph von Hansemann who (like his father) was an important banker but whose main activities spanned the Bismarck area, and who (unlike his father) was not a liberal.

Hansemann's life was in many respects the very opposite of List's. Whereas List's life was a continuous personal tragedy leading from failure to failure (with the exception of List's American period) Hansemann's can be called a glorious triumph leading from success to success, both in business and politics. In many ways it may be said that Hansemann's life was the life that List was longing to lead. Hansemann succeeded in holding top positions during the establishment of several profitable railway firms in the short time between 1836 and 1845 when he occupied himself primarily with railway questions. It is tempting to speculate what it was that made the psychological difference between these two men, a temptation that shall be resisted in this chapter.

Hansemann was born 1790 in a small village, named Finkenwerder near Hamburg. (Today it is a suburb of Hamburg.) His father, a Protestant priest, could not afford a university education for all four of his sons. So it was decided that David, being the youngest, was to become a businessman. His first job was as a travelling salesman in the wool trade. In 1817 he established his own firm in this trade in Aachen, close to the Belgian border, which was a major centre of the textile industry at that time. Hansemann, however, soon diversified into other fields of business, in particular insurance. Thus in 1824/25 he established the Aachener Feuer-Versicherungs-Gesellschaft, which today after several transformations and renamings is a part of AMB Generali. In this period of his life Hansemann had already become a wealthy man.

In 1837 Hansemann turned his attention to railways. One of the main political and economic questions about railways at that time concerned the appropriate role of the state in the construction and operation of railways. Not only List, as described above, but also other observers feared excessive profit-making and speculative bubbles in railway shares if railways were left to private industry; others were concerned about the financial burdens governments would have to shoulder when railways were to become public enterprises. Hansemann, who had studied the private railway system of the USA as well as the state-operated railways in the neighbouring Belgium, advocated a differentiated middle-of the road position as will be shown below.

But Hansemann was not only a profound thinker on railway matters, he was also involved in the practical realization of several railway projects, as mentioned already above. Unlike List, who was mobbed out of several projects after his ideas had been gladly exploited, Hansemann succeeded in staying at the top management level and in reaping the gains of his activities. Two of these projects deserve special mention here.

Around 1830 Belgium sought railway access to the Rhineland which (as a result of the Napoleonic wars) was under Prussian government at that time. A plan existed to link Antwerp and Cologne by a railway connection which, however, would bypass Aachen, the city where Hansemann had meanwhile become an influential figure. Hansemann managed through skilful negotiations to ensure that this plan was changed into a new plan which included Aachen as a major stop. The corresponding new railway firm obtained its concession in 1837 under the name of Rheinische Eisenbahngesellschaft (Rhenish Railway Company) and grew into one of the most important German railways in the 19th century. Hansemann held the post of vice-president from 1837 until 1844.

The Rhenish Railway Company operated to the west of the River Rhine. Hansemann, however, was also involved in two major projects which were designed to operate on the east of the River Rhine. In 1843 the Cologne–Minden Railway (Köln-Mindener Eisenbahngesellschaft) started operations and in 1844 (the year of Hansemann's and List's encounter in Aachen – see endnote 1) the Bergisch-Märkische Eisenbahn-Gesellschaft obtained its concession. All of these three big railways in the western part of Germany started as private companies. In 1850, however, the Bergisch–Märkische Bahn came under state control. Notwithstanding that it was run by civil servants it showed a highly competitive spirit in the following years and is frequently cited as an example that public enterprises can be very dynamic too. In 1879 The Cologne–Minden-Railway and in 1880 the Rhenish Railway were nationalized. At nationalization these railways operated a track-length of around 1100–1300 kilometres each.

Meanwhile Hansemann had become a well-known public figure in the Rhineland and been elected to several political bodies. In 1843 he became a member of the Rhenish Regional Diet (Rheinischer Provinziallandtag) and in 1847 member of the Prussian Diet (Preussischer Vereinigter Landtag). He was regarded as one of the leading spokesmen of liberalism in Germany. For a brief time, from March 1848 (after the "March Revolution" of 1848) to September 1848 he held the position of minister of finance in the Prussian cabinet, first under Ludolf von Camphausen and then under Rudolf von Auerswald. After dissolution of the "Cabinet Auerswald-Hansemann" he was appointed president of the Prussian Central Bank, a post which he held until 1851. Interestingly enough, he had advocated the privatization of the bank and the private emission of bank notes, proposals which certainly were not suited to win him many sympathies, be it on the right or the left of the political spectrum. Karl Marx, incidentally, called Hansemann a "liberal bootlicker" (Marx, 1858).

After his presidency of the central bank Hansemann increasingly moved back into the private sector and resumed his business activities. In 1851 he founded the "Direction of the Disconto-Gesellschaft", (later only Disconto-Gesellschaft) which subsequently turned into one of the first German "mega-banks" and which merged with Deutsche Bank in 1929.

In 1847, during his political period, Hansemann had moved to Berlin. Since the middle of the 1850s he had started to live in a stately villa in Berlin-Tiergarten which was a major meeting point of the Prussian society, not only of businessmen and politicians but also of artists and men of science. He died in 1864 during a holiday trip in a small town close to Wiesbaden. He is buried in the graveyard of Matthäus Church in Berlin in the grandiose tomb of the Hansemann family, which still exists.

## 9.4. Hansemann on railway regulation[4]

In a treatise written in 1837 entitled "The Railways and their Shareholders in their Relation to the State" (henceforth cited as "Railways") Hansemann investigated whether it was preferable for a country to have a public or a private railway system (Hansemann, 1837).[5] As mentioned already, this question was one of the most hotly debated issues of railway policy at that time in Germany.

Hansemann gives a surprisingly modern and differentiated answer to this question. Already at a time when the first railroads in Germany had scarcely begun to exist he draws the sharp distinction between the network level of railroading and the operational level which is at the centre of modern regulatory discussions today. The network level comprises the planning, building and maintaining the network. The operational level comprises the movement of trains over a given network. When Hansemann speaks of "the railways" he usually refers to "ways" in the literal sense, i.e. the network level. In Section 3 of "Railways" where he advances arguments for state-ownership of railways he always refers to the network level. § 54 of Chapter 10, for instance, states:

> But don't let me be misunderstood. It is not my intention at all that the state should engage in the *operation* on the railroads. This type of business is not unlike running a big factory where managerial and technical knowledge and special monitoring are necessary requirements. In order to be economically viable a business of this type must be supported by private interests in a major way and its management must have a degree of freedom and latitude which never can be given to a public administration.
>
> ("Railways" Chapter 10, § 54 italics added)

This quotation shows that Hansemann argues that the operational level should be left to private firms. The network, in contrast, could either be built by the state or by private *concessionaires*. Hansemann considers both options. Section 3 of his treatise is devoted to a system where railways are financed and built by the state. Section 4 deals with privately financed and operated railways. His sympathies are with the first option but he takes into account that this option might not be politically feasible due to budgetary constraints.

In line with many modern authors Hansemann argues that the gains of the new technology would be greatest if usage of the tracks were free of charge or rather if charges were set at marginal cost such as to cover repair and maintenance ("Railways", Chapter 9, § 45). His reasons for marginal cost pricing are very similar to List's views on the positive externalities of railroads mentioned above but also reminiscent of his well-known analysis of "productive forces". Hansemann contends that investments in railway infrastructure generate two types of capital. The "first capital" is the railway infrastructure itself. The "second capital" consists of the economic gains which are generated by the first type of capital.

> The increase in the national capital which is the indirect and inevitable consequence of the use of the railways … is a second capital which is generated in addition to the newly created railway capital. Experience shows that this capital is larger than the railway capital. The states have built roads and canals to generate this second capital.
>
> (Hansemann, 1837: 46)[6]

This argument in itself, of course, is not sufficient to make state ownership inevitable. The deficit incurred by marginal cost pricing could be made up by the state via transfers to private railway companies. Hansemann, however, does not discuss this possibility, perhaps because of reasons of political acceptability at his time. From the viewpoint of the history of economic thought it is worth noting that marginal cost pricing for public utilities in general became the focus of the so-called marginal cost controversy, which started in the '30s of the last century with a contribution by Hotelling and which continues to our day.[7] Hansemann was not a theoretical economist, however, and his argument for marginal cost pricing is mainly the classical gains of trade which accrue due to a cheaper transportation technology (see "Railways", Chapter 5, §§ 27–33). Another argument for state ownership advanced by Hansemann is the possibility of cross-subsidization. Even though track access charges should cover only marginal costs, the state can still use tax revenues from the operations of the profitable railroads to finance railway networks in the less developed parts of the nation ("Railways" Chapter 9, § 47). Hansemann, like List, fears that private firms would not be prepared to build "thin" lines at all. This concern was well founded, as later experience showed that private firms were not prepared to connect the thinly populated areas in East Prussia to the main network. (The question of the *"Ostbahn"*.)

Hansemann's distinction between train operations and network ownership appears certainly very modern today. To be fair, it has to be noted, however, that in making this distinction Hansemann was not alone. The Prussian Railway Act of 1838, drew this distinction as well. § 27 of the Act stated that once a track had been built by a certain concessionaire other companies should have access to the network too, provided they had applied for a corresponding licence from the Ministry of Commerce and after a waiting period of three years (Fremdling and Knieps, 1993: 133). In return, they were required to pay a track access charge (*"Bahngeld"*) to the track owner (Fremdling and Knieps, 1993: 144). The law also specified the precise methodology for calculating the track access charges.

Hansemann, however, rejects "competition on the track" (or "open access" in modern terms) in favour of a monopoly on the operational level. He cites evidence from other countries (notably Pennsylvania) that accidents would occur more often under open access ("Railways", § 87, Chapter 18). But he also anticipates the modern argument of "synergies between wheel and rail" and argues that the costs of maintenance depend critically on the technical characteristics and the quality of the rolling stock. In order to optimize cost therefore, only one transport company should be allowed.[8]

But how should the monopoly firm on the operational level be selected? Here Hansemann proposes a bidding process which is remarkably similar to a Demsetz auction.

He suggests that a corresponding concession should be put out to tender in such a way that "the state obtains the most favourable conditions" ("Railways", Chapter 10 § 56). To make this condition more precise he distinguishes three cases:

(1) The state's sole aim is to achieve the lowest transport tariffs possible. In this case the concession should go to the operator who offers the lowest transport tariffs. This is probably the case that comes closest to the textbook notion of a Demsetz auction. It should be noted, however, that in his whole treatise Hansemann proposes that railway tariffs should be differentiated according to types of goods. More specifically, he advocates the principle of "value of service" pricing (i.e. valuable goods should be priced higher than low value goods). He does not say according to which criterion in such a situation of differentiated tariffs the "best" bidder should be selected. Still it can be said that apparently his idea of "most favourable conditions" is more subtle than just a uniform tariff.
(2) The state only wants to obtain a certain minimum rate of return on the invested capital. In that case the concession should go to the bidder who guarantees this rate of return but who at the same time proposes the lowest transport prices.
(3) The state's aim is to maximize revenues. In this case he should select the candidate who offers the highest price for the concession subject to the condition that he can guarantee continuity of operations at that price.

In § 56 of Chapter 10 of "Railways" Hansemann (1837) is even more specific about the bidding process by adding further details to his tendering proposal. The duration of the concession, for example, should be long enough that "in the public interest operations can be perfected as much as possible". He suggests that 20 years might be enough to achieve this goal which, again, corresponds remarkably well to the time frames applied today. In order to solve the problem of barriers to entry due to sunk cost the next concessionaire should be forced to acquire all facilities from his predecessor at a price for which special calculation rules have to be developed.

Obviously an auction along these lines resembles very much the auction proposed by Demsetz, notably in the first case. The present author, therefore, has argued elsewhere (Wieland, 2007) that Hansemann should be considered as a forerunner of Demsetz, even more so than Edwin Chadwick who published an article in 1859 with similar ideas and who is therefore given priority over Demsetz (see Kitch, 1983). Still, as was mentioned above in Section 9.2, List points out that auctions like these were already routinely used, for instance in France, not only for the tendering of railway projects but in other industries as well. Chadwick mentions this fact too when he compares the British regime of "competition in the field" to the French regime of "competition for the field". Thus, it seems pointless to argue about priority with respect to Demsetz auctions. As far as Demsetz himself is concerned, his focus lay much more on auctioning as an alternative to the regulation of natural monopolies than on the tendering process per se. Hansemann, vice versa, nowhere mentions the problem of natural monopoly, even though this holds for Chadwick too.[9] He is far more interested in making sure that railway operations on an already given track are carried out in an innovative and efficient way, as the first quote above makes abundantly clear. I therefore propose to put the priority question to rest. List's and Hansemann's views on regulation are of sufficient interest in themselves to merit description, even without the priority question.

## 9.5. Conclusion

In the literature on railway policy in 19th Century Germany, the topic of regulation is rarely addressed. Exceptions are, for example, Blankart (1987) or Fremdling and Knieps (1993). Most contributions focus on the railway technology in use at that time, the major connections, the major railway companies, the political debates surrounding the various projects or the macroeconomic consequences of railroad building. Moreover, intellectually the picture is always dominated by the outstanding figure of Friedrich List. In this chapter it has been shown that discussion of regulatory issues had already developed to a high degree of sophistication in the first part of the 19th century, at a time when railways had barely started to exist in Germany. Some of the proposals that were debated are surprisingly modern. Using the example of David Hansemann it has also been shown that List was not alone in his efforts, but that besides him there existed other outstanding writers whose thoughts on regulation were in part even more detailed than List's.

## Notes

1  Did Hansemann and List know each other? Wendler, in his comprehensive biography of List, mentions that both men met on August 13, 1844, in Aachen, to discuss a customs treaty between Belgium and Prussia (Wendler, 2013: 277). We do not know whether railway matters were discussed at this meeting too. Considering, however, that Hansemann at that time was actively engaged in the construction of the railway connection between Cologne, Aachen and the Belgian frontier this seems quite likely. There are apparently no other reports of any further meeting between Hansemann and List.
2  This section draws heavily on Section 9.5 of Wieland (2007). With permission of Springer Science+Business Media. Well known biographies of Hansemann are Däbritz (1960), Malangré (1991), Ottman and Poll (1964) and Müller-Jabusch (1960). Malangré (1991) cites extensively from the first Hansemann biography of Bergengrüen (1901).
3  For a recent biography see Wendler (2013) with many more references.

4 This section again draws heavily on and partly quotes Wieland (2007), this time Section 9.4. With permission of Springer Science+Business Media.
5 Hansemann's second important contribution to railway policy in Germany was a critique of the Prussian Railway Act of 1838 ("Kritik des Preußischen Eisenbahn-gesetzes vom 3. November 1838") which was published in 1841.
6 "Die Zunahme des Nationalvermögens, welche indirekt unausbleiblich die Folge der Benutzung von Eisenbahnen, nämlich der verbesserten Kommunikations-mittel, sein muss, ist ein zum neu geschaffenen Eisenbahnkapital erworbenes zweites Kapital, das erfahrungsgemäß mehr als jenes selbst beträgt. Die Staaten haben Kunststraßen und Kanäle gebaut, um das vorbezeichnete zweite Kapital zu erwerben" (Hansemann, 1837, § 52, p.46) English transla-tion by the author.
7 For the marginal cost controversy see for instance Laffont and Tirole (1993), Section 3.3.
8 Both arguments are open to discussion of course. But this is not the topic of the present note.
9 Chadwick's focus was less on public tendering as a substitute for regulation of natural monopolies than on excessive entry, ruinous competition and wasteful duplication of facilities. This opinion seems to be shared by Crain and Ekelund: "In the cases so far considered, *waste* due to natural monopoly was the rationale ... for the proposed new institutional arrangements in water and gas distribution systems, postal service and railroads" (Crain and Ekelund, 1976: 156, italics in the original).

# References

Bergengruen, A. (1901) *David Hansemann*. Berlin: Guttentag.
Blankart, C. (1987) Stabilität und Wechselhaftigkeit politischer Entscheidungen: Eine Fallstudie zur preußisch-deutschen Eisenbahnpolitik von ihren Anfängen bis zum Zweiten Weltkrieg. *Jahrbuch für neue politische Ökonomie* 6, 74–92.
Bröcker, J. (2013) Wider Economic Benefits from Communication-Cost Reductions: An Endogenous Growth Approach. *Environment and Planning B: Planning and Design* 40(6), 971–986.
Chadwick, E. (1859) Results of Different Principles of Legislation and Administration in Europe; of Competition for the Field, as Compared with the Competition within the Field of Service. *Journal of the Royal Statistical Society* 22, 381–420.
Crain, W. and Ekelund, R. (1976) Chadwick and Demsetz on Competition and Regulation. *Journal of Law and Economics* 19, 149–161.
Däbritz, W. (1960) David Hansemann 1790–1864. *Rheinisch-Westfälische Wirtschafts-biographien, Band 7*. Münster: Aschendorffsche Verlagsbuchhandlung.
Demsetz, H. (1968) Why Regulate Utilities? *Journal of Law and Economics* 11, 55–65.
Fremdling, R. and Knieps, G. (1993) Competition, Regulation and Nationalization: The Prussian Railway System in the Nineteenth Century. *Scandinavian Economic History Review* 16, 129–154.
Hansemann, D. (1837) *Die Eisenbahnen und deren Aktionäre in ihrem Verhältnis zum Staat*. Leipzig and Halle: Renger'sche Buchhandlung.
Kitch, E. (1983) The Fire of Truth: A Remembrance of Law and Economics at Chicago, 1932–1970. *Journal of Law and Economics* 26, 163–234.
Laffont, J.J. and Tirole, J. (1993) *A Theory of Incentives in Procurement and Regulation*. Cambridge, MA: MIT Press.

List, F. (1833) *Ueber ein sächsisches Eisenbahn-System als Grundlage eines allgemeinen deutschen Eisenbahn-Systems und insbesondere über die Anlegung einer Eisenbahn von Leipzig nach Dresden.* Leipzig: Liebeskind.

List, F. (1837) *Die Welt bewegt sich (Le Monde Marche).* Göttingen: Vandenhoeck und Ruprecht.

List, F. (1838) *Das deutsche National-Transport-System in volks- und staatswirtschaftlicher Beziehung.* Altona und Leipzig: Verlag von Friedrich Hammerich.

List, F. (1841a) *Das Nationale System der politischen Ökonomie.* Baden-Baden: Nomos. 2008 edn.

List, F. (1841b) *Das deutsche Eisenbahnsystem als Mittel zur Vervollkommnung der deutschen Industrie, des deutschen Zollvereins und des deutschen Nationalverbandes überhaupt.* Stuttgart und Tübingen: J.B. Cotta'scher Verlag.

Malangré, H. (1991) *David Hansemann 1790–1864.* Aachen: Einhard Verlag.

Marx, K. (1858) Das neue Ministerium. In *New-York Daily Tribune.* No. 5492, 27 November 1858, reprinted in Karl Marx, Friedrich Engels, Werke, (Karl) Dietz Verlag, Berlin, Band 12, Berlin/DDR 1961, 636–639.

Müller-Jabusch, M. (1960) David Hansemann – Finanzmann eigener Prägung. *Zeitschrift für das gesamte Kreditwesen* 13, 815–854.

Ottmann, K. (1964) Hansemann als Eisenbahnpolitiker. In Poll B (ed.) *David Hansemann, Zur Erinnerung an einen Politiker und Unternehmer,* Aachen: Wilhelm Metz. (Im Auftrag der Industrie- und Handelskammer für den Regierungsbezirk Aachen).

Smith, A. (1776) *An Inquiry into the Nature and Causes of the Wealth of Nations.* Volume I. Indianapolis: Liberty Funds. 1981 edn.

Wendler, E. (2013) *Friedrich List (1789–1846): Ein Ökonom mit Weitblick und sozialer Verantwortung.* Wiesbaden: Springer/Gabler.

Wieland, B. (2007) A Note on David Hansemann as a Precursor of Chadwick and Demsetz. In Baake P and Borck R (eds.) *Public Economics and Public Choice, Contributions in Honor of Charles B. Blankart,* Berlin and Heidelberg: Springer, 243–255.

Williamson, O. (1985) *The Institutions of Capitalism.* New York: Free Press.

# 10 Friedrich List and the non-financial origins of the European crisis

*Erik S. Reinert and Rainer Kattel*

## 10.1. A taxonomy of economic integrations

In Friedrich List's writings we can find three basic principles that largely summarize the development consensus up to 1980s, including the founding documents of the EU[1]:

*First Listian principle*: The preconditions for wealth, democracy and political freedom are the same: a diversified manufacturing sector subject to increasing returns (which would historically mean manufacturing, but also includes a knowledge-intensive service sector). This was the principle upon which the United States economy was built, promoted by the first US Secretary of the Treasury, Alexander Hamilton, and this same principle was rediscovered by George Marshall in 1947 as the foundation for the Marshall Plan. Also the 1988 Cecchini Report, which laid the foundations of the EU, assumed that most of the benefits from the single market would come from increasing returns. It is not unreasonable to argue that Cecchini would have understood that nations which lost their manufacturing industries would not benefit from the union.

*Second Listian principle*: A nation first industrializes and is then gradually integrated economically into nations at the same level of development.

*Third Listian principle*: Economic welfare is a result of synergy. Already in the 13th century Florentine Chancellor Brunetto Latini (1210–1294) explains the wealth of cities as a *common weal* ('un ben comune'). Investments in infrastructure, education and science are an integral part of this type of policy.

The European Union, as it came to exist over the 1990s and 2000s, perhaps unwittingly but certainly willingly came to negate all Listian principles as neo-classical economics came to totally dominate the economic discourse. In order of the listing above: within the European policy framework the following assumptions took over from the previous understanding:

- All economic activities are qualitatively alike, so it does not matter what you produce;

- Free trade is a goal per se, even before the required stage of industrialization is achieved;
- And 'There is no such thing as society' (Margaret Thatcher 1987).

It can be argued that much of the pre-Smithian history of economic thought is filled with treatises trying to understand why certain types of trade with certain regions bring beneficial results and other types do not, i.e. in effect being extremely concerned with the dangers of asymmetrical integration. The role of manufacturing as being the key to wealth is found all over Europe, starting with Giovanni Botero (1589) and Antonio Serra (1613) (see E. Reinert 2007 and S. Reinert 2011 for in-depth discussions).

An early statement of this theory in English is found in the first pages of Charles King's three-volume work (1721), a compilation of works published in the previous decade, which was to enjoy unique authority for decades. It is important to note that his theory is based on a possible discrepancy between the interest of the merchant and the interest of the nation itself: 'There are general Maxims in Trade which are assented to by every body (*sic*). That a Trade may be of Benefit to the Merchant and Injurious to the Body of the Nation, is one of these Maxims' (1721:1). This is, of course, very different from the later teachings of Adam Smith and his followers, who assume an automatic harmony of interests between merchant and nation. In King's scheme, the normal pre-Smithian scheme, the vested interests of some economic actors will coincide with those of the nation-state – mainly those of the manufacturers – while the vested interests of other economic actors will be at odds with the interests of the nation-state. Yet, it is precisely this crucial link between the interest of the state (higher wealth) and that of industry which is essential to the success of modern nation-states in Europe and North America (a point already made by Schmoller in ([1884] 1944). Development – in short – required that the vested interests of the capitalists were forced in line with the vested interest of the nation-state itself. Import tariffs on 'good' economic activities – encouraging higher value added activities – and export tariffs on 'bad' economic activities[2]– making raw materials more expensive to foreigners than to domestic industry – were the main tools used in achieving this.

This pre-Smithian taxonomy of 'good' and 'bad' trade was based on the observation of the obvious urban bias of economic development that was found everywhere in Europe. The taxonomy is based on the fundamental understanding that economic development is activity-specific, at any point in time available in some economic activities rather than in others. Development was seen as a goal created by increasing returns and innovations and an ever-increasing division of labor in manufacturing which could not be achieved in agriculture, where stagnant productivity, diminishing returns, monoculture and the absence of division of labor and of synergies prevented growth.

This accumulated wisdom was taken over in the economics of Friedrich List (1841), who was the theoretical economist behind the industrialization of continental Europe. List is conventionally regarded as a protectionist, but this is a mistake on two accounts. First, inside Germany he is seen as the great free trader; he broke down the tariff barriers among the more than thirty German states which existed at the time, and secondly he was the first visionary of European economic integration once all nations had achieved a comparative advantage in manufacturing (increasing returns industries) (see Reinert 1998).

As a continuation of King's principles, and with the experience of 300 more years of economic history, we can establish the taxonomy – based on 'ideal types' – of economic integrations. There are two main types: symmetrical free trade areas (i.e., integration among nations at a similar level of economic development and economic sophistication), and asymmetrical free trade areas (i.e., integration of nations with widely different economic structure at different levels of development).

There are two further, essentially mixed types of integration: First, the welfare colonialism type of integration. Secondly, there can also be an integrative and asymmetrical type of economic integration. This is a type of economic integration that differs from the classical colonial version above in that it attempts to integrate the asymmetrical partners – countries at different levels of economic development – into a welfare state. We discuss the taxonomy briefly below.

### 10.1.1 Symmetrical free trade areas

#### 10.1.1.1 Listian integration (From Friedrich List)

Examples of Listian economic integration are 19th century Germany and the 'old' European Union (up to 1992, the year of the Maastricht Treaty that laid the groundwork for the euro zone and enlargement conditionalities). Listian economic integration is between nations on roughly similar levels of GDP per capita, that all have a comparative advantage in increasing returns activities. This insures that economic integration will not de-industrialize, de-skill or create large-scale unemployment in any of the partner countries. Large Listian areas can, however, absorb small units of relatively more backward countries to the benefit of all parties. An example of this is the integration of Portugal in the old EU, where mature and labor-intensive industries could be farmed out to Portugal, increasing real wages both in Portugal and in the rest of the EU (see also Priewe 2006, 160–162 on waves of European enlargement). In this case integration can be seen as a variant of the flying geese type (see below).

Two main variables determine the ability of a Listian integration to absorb poorer partner countries to mutual benefit. Firstly: the Schumpeterian dynamism of the core (wealthy) countries; i.e., the more dynamic the core countries, the more mature industries they can farm out to the poorer partners without hurting their own employment and wage level. This is also related to the stage in which the region finds itself in the dynamics of techno-economic paradigms (Perez 2004). The second variable is the size of the poorer country/countries to be integrated; i.e., the smaller the pool of people to be integrated, the easier the integration becomes.

A symmetrical Listian free trade area can be converted into an integrated welfare state at a relatively low cost. Listian integration is a typical win–win strategy if it does not deteriorate into welfare colonialism (see 1.3 below).

### 10.1.1.2 Peripheral symmetrical integration

Examples of 'peripheral symmetrical integration' are Pacto Andino and Mercosur. These are cases of economic integration of peripheral nations whose international comparative advantage does not lie in increasing returns industries, but that wish to grow such activities and need a bigger market. Included in successful schemes of this type are preferences for relatively lagging countries, as was planned for Ecuador and Bolivia in the Pacto Andino. The Latin American Free Trade Association (LAFTA/ ALALC) is an example of such an integration that failed. Indeed the present problems of Spanish-speaking Latin America may be seen as resulting from going from a highly protected national manufacturing sector directly to global competition. In the logic of Friedrich List an intermediary step of continental integration (i.e. LAFTA) would have been needed in order to strengthen the manufacturing base before exposing it to global competition.

One problem with this type of integration is often that such nations have similar economic structures and relatively little to sell to each other, and the countries remain dependent on foreign earnings to import newer technologies and capital goods. However, this type of regional integration is probably a necessary stepping-stone before reaching global free trade. Peripheral symmetrical integration is also a win-win strategy if the right dynamics are achieved.[3]

### 10.1.2 Asymmetrical free trade areas

### 10.1.2.1 'Colonial' and non-integrative

In the classical colonial relationship, a dynamic industrial nation integrates with a periphery which – whether explicitly stated or not – is not to specialize in innovation and increasing returns activities. Traditionally, 'colonies' specialized in supplying raw materials, with the 'bad' characteristics listed above.

With the current techno-economic paradigm that enables increasing specialization as well as outsourcing, a more sophisticated neo-colonial division of labor appears as both manufacturing and agriculture sectors split up in high-tech/capital intensive/innovative/high wage segments on the one hand, and low-tech/low capital intensity/non-innovative/low wage segments on the other (Kattel 2012). Mexico is the country where this development is most visible. The old manufacturing sector, containing 'complete' industries is shrinking and being replaced by the *maquila* sector consisting of unmechanizable fragments of a global value chain seeking low-wage and low-skilled labor. This development finds its parallel in the Mexican agricultural sector, where highly subsidized US imports of mechanizable grain – produced with exceptionally advanced technology including unmanned tractors using global positioning equipment – are replacing Mexican agriculture not only in wheat but even in a traditional product like corn (maize) while Mexico specializes in exporting unmechanizable agricultural produce, such as strawberries and cucumbers. Such changes bring about lower prices and higher gains to consumers, but in this case the consumer is in the US and the producer in Mexico. The benefits accrue to US customers, while the Mexican farmer – working under perfect competition, diminishing returns and unlimited supply of labor – will not see his income raised. The Mexican national innovation system is deteriorating accordingly, and returning to a center-periphery relationship with the United States (Cimoli 2000; Gallagher and Zarsky 2007).

In asymmetrical trading areas the Vanek-Reinert Effect[4] starts operating, and the least advanced nation concentrates in the low-skilled and low capital-intensity areas both in manufacturing and in agriculture. In the worst case this can lead to rampant de-industrialization and plummeting real wages (Reinert 2004). In Mexico a deteriorating sequence can be observed: first de-industrialization, subsequently de-agriculturalization (even of the country's most traditional crop, maize) and finally de-population. In many areas of Southern Mexico only the population above 60 years of age and below 12 is left. The others are working in the United States or further north in Mexico. We find a similar pattern in the European periphery; in Moldova we find a demographic pattern similar to that of Southern Mexico.

The success of this strategy from the colonizing nation's point of view depends on the same variables as mentioned above. If the Schumpeterian dynamics in the rich country are high enough, and the supply of labor to be absorbed is not too big, or protection can be kept at a point securing employment, the rich country may have all the advantages of producing technologically mature and labor-intensive crops with cheap foreign labor, but not the disadvantages. In other words: the periphery specializes in staying poor.

Classical colonialism is a win-lose strategy: the colonial power wins while the colony loses. However, this is potentially a lose-lose strategy if the colonial power loses control or loses dynamism. Potentially, Mexican real wages may fall while, at the same time, wages fall in the US, when the 'giant sucking sound' hits US employment and real wages – as US 1992 presidential candidate Ross Perot used to talk about. If the world moves towards factor-prize equalization, this now appears to be downwards. One factor keeping wages up was national labor unions, which now have lost most of their power. In this sense, David Ricardo may be proven correct that the 'natural' price of labor is close to human subsistence. The integration of the Baltic countries seems to fall in this category, with only Estonia – due to its pockets of high-tech activities like Skype – showing elements of the next category, Flying Geese.

### 10.1.2.2 *Flying geese, or sequential technological upgrading*

The flying geese metaphor for economic integrations first appears in a 1935 article by Kaname Akamatsu, published in Japanese. His views became known to the West in his 1961 article in *Weltwirtschaftliches Archiv*, and during the 1980s Japanese economist and foreign minister Saburo Okita propagated the concept. The essence of the flying geese pattern of economic integration is that nations upgrade and catch up technologically by sequentially riding the same technological wave. It essentially describes the way East Asian nations grew. The model builds on Friedrich List's stages of integration. Its dynamics are similar to Michael Porter's stages of national development (Porter 1990), to Ray Vernon's life-cycle theory of international trade (Vernon 1966) and to Jane Jacobs' import-replacing development of cities (Jacobs 1984).

To illustrate the process, follow a product: a hairdryer is produced in Japan and exported to the rest of the world. When Japan upgrades its technology and wage level, the production of hairdryers passes on to Korea and is exported from that country. As Korean production after a while also gets more sophisticated, the production of simple hairdryers passes on to Taiwan, where the phenomenon is again repeated. Hairdryer production moves on to Malaysia and Thailand, and finally to Vietnam. On the way all nations have sequentially increased their wealth and upgraded technologically, all based on the same product.

The flying geese strategy has proved spectacularly successful in East Asia – a true win-win form of economic integration – where Korea moved up from being poorer than Tanzania and even Somalia in the 1950s. However, the strategy was only possible because it was in the interest of the United States to build a *cordon sanitaire* of well-to-do countries around the communist world. The strategy of protectionism and heavy-handed government intervention allowed at the time is impossible to initiate today under the rule of the Washington Institutions and the World Trade Organization (WTO). Latin American import-substitution initially contained strong elements of flying geese, creating a win-win situation where US companies prolonged the life cycle of their products by producing in Latin America. However, Latin America failed to move to the next Listian stage – into regional integration – through the failure of LAFTA/ALALC, and lost its dynamics. It should be noted, however that even the inefficient manufacturing sectors built up in countries like Peru and Mongolia provided much higher real wages than does global capitalism in the same countries today. This is the lesson which will now hit the European Union: the periphery which is now being de-industrialized provided much higher living standards with their 'inefficient' industries than without them.

## 10.2. EU enlargements

In our previous articles we have argued that the integration of the European South (Portugal, Spain and Greece) in the 1980s was fundamentally based on *symmetrical integration*: countries with similar levels of development joining into a common economic area (although the Greek industrial sector was relatively weak) (Reinert and Kattel 2004, 2007, 2014). Integration was slow; in some cases tariffs were gradually lowered over a period of 10 years, while massive funds were made available for industries in the joining countries to gear up to the technological level of the core countries before free trade was introduced.

The Eastern European enlargement followed a completely different pattern: an instant free trade shock after the fall of the Berlin Wall had virtually de-industrialized the ex-Soviet periphery. Integration was consequently very asymmetrical: poorer nations were integrated into a common economic space with much wealthier economies. In what follows we aim to show that the asymmetrical Eastern enlargement turned the previously symmetrical integration of the South also into a much more asymmetrical integration, as competition and labour migration from low-wage Eastern European economies undermined the upgrading of many South European companies. Increasing competition from China and East Asia strengthened the cumulative negative effects inside the European Union.

Over the past few decades, the European periphery has gone through remarkable changes in economic fortunes. Figure 10.1 shows dynamics of labor productivity compared to Germany in three European peripheral areas that also coincide with regions the European Union integrated with over the last three decades: Southern Europe (Portugal, Spain and Greece), Scandinavia (here Finland and Sweden) and Central Europe.

Far from seeing European-wide convergence in productivity – a key assumption behind the European integration processes in the 1990s (see Boyer 1993) – we see different regions faring rather differently. First, after three decades of trailing Germany relatively closely in the post-war era, Finland and Sweden take advantage of joining the EU (1995) and of the German reunification shock, and rapidly forge ahead of Germany; second, Central Europe experiences its first lost decade between 1988 and 1998. Then – with the start of the 1998 accession talks – follows a sharp increase towards catching up; and third, Southern Europe was steadily catching up with Germany up to the mid-1980s,[5] fell behind anew during most of the 1990s and started to catch up again albeit very slowly in the 2000s. In

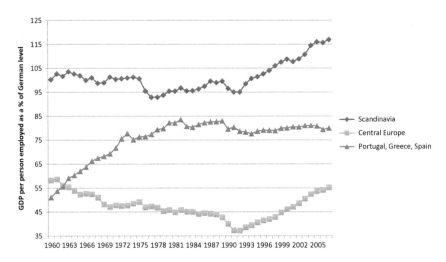

*Figure 10.1* GDP per person employed as a % of German level, in 1990 GK $ (regional averages), 1960–2010

Source: The Conference Board Total Economy Database, www.conference-board.org/data/economydatabase/; calculations by the authors.

terms of our taxonomy, it can be argued that the integration of Scandinavia was a very successful Listian integration. Our thesis is that the integration of Southern Europe is an interrupted Listian integration and that the interruption results from a combination of the Eastern enlargement and from massive technological catching-up in China, without the corresponding growth in wages that used to accompany such technological change in the West. The deadly combination of austerity and the frozen exchange rate – the euro – contributes, quite unnecessarily, to the deepening of the European crisis.

The Southern European catching-up process stalled with the creation of a common market that, it can be argued, laid the basic groundwork for later enlargements based on the ideology of liberalizing markets and limiting public sector debt and borrowing. Yet, the European Commission's white paper from 1985, titled *Completing the Internal Market*, sees the main reason for large internal markets in significant enhancement of the EU's 'economic and industrial dimension by enabling industries to make economies of scale and therefore to become more competitive' (The European Commission 1985, 6). The underlying assumption behind single market creation was indeed one of symmetrical integration, extending increasing returns activities to the whole territory.

Indeed, it seems relatively likely that without the Eastern enlargement, European integration of the Southern economies would have followed a relatively common Vernonian life-cycle path of maturing industries moving to cheaper locations, and in the late 1980s this would have been the South (Vernon 1966). For instance, think of Fiat and Volkswagen cooperating with Seat in Spain during the 1970s and 1980s respectively. However, with the sudden fall of the Berlin Wall and rapid opening of the Central European and Baltic economies, maturing industries in the West all of a sudden had vastly better opportunities in the East. In addition, as argued above, change in the techno-economic paradigm allowed for a rapid breaking-up of the value chain and a consequent dispersion of manufacturing functions (*outsourcing*) (See Perez 2002, 2006).

While unlocking the potential of Eastern Europe as destination for Western maturing and outsourcing industries took roughly a decade – that very lost decade we can observe in Figure 10.1 – it was the European integration processes, starting officially in 1998 with the opening of accession talks, that virtually ensured that the Soviet industrial structure was not slowly upgraded but relatively rapidly replaced – the Vanek-Reinert effect – with Western factories operating within the Western value-chain. The similarities with Mexico are clear here.

Figure 10.2 shows how the EU has become a veritable valley of tears for Eastern and Southern economies.

The gulf between low- and high-productivity countries is filled with countries where innovations are not that important for companies and where more hierarchical organization types prevail. In other words, as Eastern European and Baltic economies are highly integrated with German and Northern European economies respectively, this is also reflected in their innovation profiles as these are converging, but without being accompanied by productivity growth. The channel for such convergence is, on the one hand, high share of foreign ownership, and, on the other, tightly interwoven trade networks. Southern European countries seem to have distinctly different innovation profiles and hence integration patterns.

At the same time, however, because many production companies in the East do not in fact exhibit domestic linkages of any importance, industrialization processes in the region remain relatively slow and exhibit clear characteristics of a Latin-Americanization and primitivization. Indeed, Eastern European and in particular Baltic export companies exhibit the same pattern of being isolated economic enclaves, which was considered a sign of underdevelopment already in the 1930s. In addition, since the financial systems in the Eastern economies are dominated by subsidiaries of foreign universal banks, these financial sectors remain locked into financing predominantly consumption, potentially fuelling more current account deficits and new boom-bust cycles (Kattel 2010).

The result of both processes is that during downturns (due to automatic stabilizers of the welfare state, potential banking sector problems, capital flight, and so on) public finances deteriorate – also because under the Maastricht criteria, public finances behave pro-cyclically – and without a

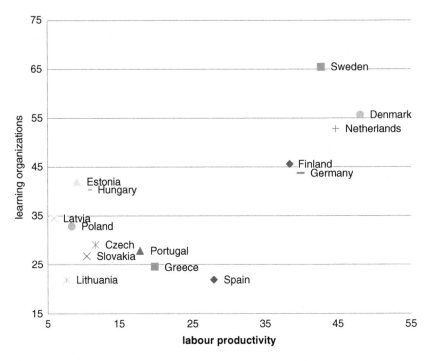

*Figure 10.2* Share of learning organizations (innovations) and labor productivity, 2005[6].

Source: Eurostat; Holm et al. 2010.

clear lender of last resort, economies in the South and in the East are prone to recurring systemic crisis and without actual significant convergence in livings standards with the core economies. This is what we call integrative and asymmetrical integration.

As we see it such asymmetrical processes of integration created huge structural imbalances within the EU, which for almost a decade were offset by the convergence of interest rates resulting from a common currency. This convergence produced declining interest rates in Southern and Eastern Europe, as well as in Ireland, fuelling public and private asset bubbles, and funding growing demand and increasing imports of goods and services of the core European economies, chiefly Germany. (Kregel 2011) However, with the highly peculiar financial structure of the euro zone – a single currency, but segmented sovereign and private capital markets, no uniform deposit guarantee scheme and the absence of a real lender of last resort – as well as with a highly uneven national economic restructuring in terms of presence or lack of Schumpeterian dynamics, such imbalances were bound to lead to huge problems as the Union essentially became a mix of a Ponzi scheme (sustaining private sector income growth by increased borrowing) and a beggar-thy-neighbor policy, in the form of German wage constraints throughout the 2000s.

The present blame-game of 'irresponsibility' from the core of the EU towards the Southern periphery fails to capture and understand the origins of the underlying mechanisms. After decades of terrorism from the right and from the left – the period Italians call *gli anni di piombo* or the 'leaden years'[7] – social peace was achieved through compromises that would only be fulfilled through increased inflation: the government made more commitments that could be met with domestic resources, given the constraints of the then ruling exchange rate mechanism. Inflation was, in a real sense, the price of democracy and peace. Those with experience in Latin America will recognize this as a typically democratic phenomenon: the countries which early experienced high inflation were Chile and Costa Rica, the most democratic countries of all. Dictatorships – like Alfredo Stroessner's in Paraguay – never saw problems of inflation.

Before the EMU (Economic and Monetary Union) was converted into the straightjacket enforced by the euro – the 'irresponsible' inflationary systems in Southern Europe had their own dynamic logic: inflationary budget spending led to falling exchange rates and to depreciation within the European Exchange Rate Mechanism ERM. In this way the intra-European competitiveness of the real economy was saved. Government debt also tended to be issued in local currency, so government debt was devalued with the currency. In Latin America these mechanisms would lead to a default on debt in foreign currency, so frequent devaluations and defaults on debt were necessary correction mechanisms in the 'cycles of irresponsibility'. Flexible exchange rates were an integral part of keeping the system going. Introducing the euro – i.e. a fixed exchange rate – had the effect of completely sealing the safety valve in the system. In the EU periphery the choice is now either to force down real wages further, which will cause more migration, or devaluation and sovereign default. Sooner or later 'something's gotta give', either the population or the exchange rate. As in any Ponzi scheme, the default will eventually have to come anyway; the question is how much damage and human suffering will be caused before default is admitted.

The internal dynamic of Europe is in some ways a microcosm of the same type of problems confronting the entire global economy governed by the WTO rulebook and, perhaps even more importantly, bilateral free trade agreements: the key problem of uneven development in the productive structure, especially of the de-industrialized or non-industrialized peripheries, is marginally – if at all – addressed. Similarly to the European situation, flaws in the productive structure are temporarily 'offset' by financial inflows and/or asset bubbles, engendering Ponzi-scheme-like dynamics where further growth relies on continuing inflow of foreign savings (Kregel 2004). The poorly developed industrial structure in respective peripheries fails to create the necessary demand that would create a high value-added service sector. Economic problems in the peripheries are solved by the migration of labor, rather than by addressing their structural and financial requirements for development. Contrary to the mainstream discourse in economic integration that predicts a convergence towards 'factor-price equalization', asymmetrical integration may lead to 'factor-price polarization' – that is, increasing gaps in real wages and growing inequality.

## 10.3. Conclusion

If our argument is correct – that asymmetrical economic integration is undermining the evolution of Schumpeterian dynamics in the European periphery – then it also follows that the European Union cannot recover from its current crisis without significantly rethinking some of its basic ideas in terms of what policies regions and countries with lower income levels and less dynamic economic structures should pursue and how these policies should be financed. We think it is safe to argue that the European integration through the 1980s was still constructed in the post WW II logic of 'transnational mercantilism' (Graz 2004): every country needed a sector of Schumpeterian dynamics ('industrialization' for short) in a system of symmetrical integration.

Integration after the fall of the Berlin Wall, on the other hand, was marked by neoliberal triumphalism – seeing markets as the great equalizer – and wishful political thinking. But this approach was applied in name only as the German government intervened to influence labor market conditions and reduce wage growth so as to enhance German competitiveness within the EU through a beggar-my-neighbor wage policy. The mind shift from the initial plan that saw the euro as a currency for the strong economic core only, to also including the Southern periphery as 'an act of solidarity' towards the South, shows the utter ignorance of basic economic phenomena among the European political elites and, also, among their economic advisors.

Today the combined effect of austerity and the euro act like a plot to kill off effective demand in Europe. It appears as if capitalism has declared war on its own customers: indeed an attempted economic suicide as we suggested in the title of our 2007 paper. Indeed, returning to the pre-neoliberal mindset and a renewal of industrial policy, rather than interference in the labor market, in some form or other – with domestic development finance – seems to be a *conditio sine qua non* for European recovery.

## Notes

1 This article builds on our previously published work, Reinert and Kattel 2004, Reinert and Kattel 2007, and most recently, Reinert and Kattel 2014.
2 It can be argued that the 'Tudor Plan' of Henry VII and Elizabeth I, gradually increasing the export tariffs on raw wool while encouraging domestic

manufacturers of cloth, laid the foundation for the later English success and ruined the Italian woolen industry (Reinert 2007).

3 We would suggest that the former Soviet economies (Council for Mutual Economic Assistance; COMECON) fell into this symmetrical category because of the emphasis on geographical and national distribution of increasing returns activities. Of course, all trade was controlled and thus also, arguably, integration and its results. It can be argued that this understanding survived in the Soviet Union through the insights of Count Sergei Witte (1849–1915) who translated Friedrich List into Russian and served as Minister of Economy under the last two Tsars.

4 In rapid liberalization of trade and markets between countries/regions with strongly unequal levels of development, the first industries to suffer from competition and to close down are *the most advanced industries of the less developed country/region.* This is a key mechanism in understanding economic primitivization, see Reinert 1980 and 2007 for detail.

5 Greece joined the EU in 1981, Spain and Portugal in 1986; single market legislation was introduced in 1986 and in 1992.

6 Holm and Lorenz have utilized the European Working Conditions Survey – which is based on individual interviews with employees about working conditions – to come up with a taxonomy of organizations (Holm and Lorenz 2014). Their taxonomy is based on the way work is organized at the shop level: how hierarchical are decision making processes (for instance, when something goes wrong, who decides how and what should be done?); how complex are tasks?; how much team work is there?, etc. And they show that there are four key types of organization, from discretionary learning-based organizations, through lean and Tayloristic organizations to simple organizations. Particularly the former are interesting for the purposes of the current paper as these organizations – here called learning organizations – are geared toward continuous and incremental learning and innovations (See also Holm et al. 2010). To put it very simply: the more such learning organizations there are in an economy, the more innovative the economy is.

7 http://en.wikipedia.org/wiki/Years_of_Lead_(Italy), accessed April 16, 2015.

## References

Akamatsu, Kaname. (1961), A Theory of Unbalanced Growth in the World Economy, *Weltwirtschaftliches Archiv*, 86, pp. 196–217.

Botero, Giovanni (1589), *Della Ragion di Stato: Libri dieci, con Tre Libri delle Cause della Grandezza, e Magnificenza delle Città*, Venice: Appresso i Gioliti.

Boyer, Robert. (1993), 'The Convergence Hypothesis Revisited: Globalization but Still the Century of Nations?', available at www.cepremap.ens.fr/depot/couv_orange/co9403.pdf.

Cimoli, Mario. (ed.) (2000), *Developing Innovation Systems: Mexico in a Global Context*, New York: Continuum International Publishing Group.

European Commission. (1985), *Completing the Internal Market*, Brussels: European Commission.

Gallagher, Kevin P. and Luyba Zarsky. (2007), *The Enclave Economy. Foreign Investment and Sustainable Development in Mexico's Silicon Valley*, Cambridge, MA: MIT Press.

Graz, Jean-Christophe. (2004), 'Transnational Mercantilism and the Emergent Global Trading Order', *Review of International Political Economy*, 11, 3, August 2004, pp. 597–617.

Holm, Jacob R. and Edward Lorenz. (2014), 'Has "Discretionary Learning" Declined During the Lisbon Agenda? A Cross-Sectional and Longitudinal Study of Work Organisation in European Nations', electronic copy available at: http://ssrn.com/abstract=2487849.

Holm, Jacob R., Edward Lorenz, Bengt-Åke Lundvall and Antoin Valeyre. (2010), 'Organizational Learning and System of Labor Market Regulation in Europe', *Industrial and Corporate Change*, pp. 1–33. doi: 10.1093/icc/dtq004.

Jacobs, Jane. (1984), *Cities and the Wealth of Nations: Principles of Economic Life*, New York: Random House.

Kattel, Rainer. (2010), 'Financial and Economic Crisis in Eastern Europe', *Journal of Post Keynesian Economics*, 31, 1, pp. 41–60.

Kattel, Rainer. (2012), 'Catching Up and Knowledge Governance', in R. Kattel, L. Burlamaqui, and A.C. Castro (eds.), *Knowledge Governance: Reasserting the Public Interest*, London: Anthem Press, pp. 49–78.

King, Charles. (1721), *The British Merchant or Commerce Preserv'd*, 3 vols, London: John Darby.

Kregel, Jan. (2004), 'External Financing for Development and International Financial Instability'. G-24 Discussion Paper No. 32. October 2004.

Kregel, Jan. (2011), 'Debtors' Crisis or Creditors' Crisis?', Levy Institute Public Policy Brief 121, available at www.levyinstitute.org/publications/?docid=1431.

List, Friedrich. (1841), *Das Nationale System der Politischen Ökonomie*, Stuttgart & Tübingen: Cotta.

Perez, Carlota. (2002), *Technological Revolutions and Financial Capital: The Dynamics of Bubbles and Golden Ages*, Cheltenham, UK: Edward Elgar.

Perez, Carlota. (2004), 'Technological Revolutions, Paradigm Shifts and Socio-Institutional Change', in E.S. Reinert (ed.), *Globalization, Economic Development and Inequality: An Alternative Perspective*, Cheltenham, UK: Edward Elgar, pp. 217–242.

Perez, Carlota. (2006), 'Respecialisation and the Deployment of the ICT Paradigm: An Essay on the Present Challenges of Globalisation', in R. Compañó et al. (eds.), *The Future of the Information Society in Europe: Contributions to the Debate*, Seville, Spain: European Commission, Directorate General Joint Research Centre, Institute for Prospective Technological Studies (IPTS), pp. 27–56.

Porter, Michael. (1990), *The Competitive Advantage of Nations*, London: Macmillan.

Priewe, Jan. (2006), 'Exploring the Future Borders of the European Union', in E. Hein et al. (eds.), *European Economic Policies Alternatives to Orthodox Analysis and Policy Concepts*, Marburg: Metropolis, pp. 151–180.

Reinert, Erik S. (1998), 'Raw Materials in the History of Economic Policy; or, Why List (the Protectionist) and Cobden (the Free Trader) Both Agreed on Free Trade in Corn', in G. Cook (ed.), *The Economics and Politics of International Trade: Freedom and Trade*, Volume 2, London: Routledge, pp. 275–300.

Reinert, Erik S. (2004), 'Globalization in the Periphery as a Morgenthau Plan: The Underdevelopment of Mongolia in the 1990s', in E. Reinert (ed.), *Globalization, Economic Development and Inequality: An Alternative Perspective*, Cheltenham, UK: Edward Elgar, pp. 157–214.

Reinert, Erik S. (2007), *How Rich Countries Got Rich… and Why Poor Countries Stay Poor*, London: Constable.

Reinert, Erik S. and Rainer Kattel. (2004), 'The Qualitative Shift in European Integration: Towards Permanent Wage Pressures and a "Latin-Americanization" of

Europe?', PRAXIS Working Paper No. 17, available at www.praxis.ee/data/WP_17_20042.pdf.

Reinert, Erik S. and Rainer Kattel. (2007), 'European Eastern Enlargement as Europe's Attempted Economic Suicide?', The Other Canon and Tallinn University of Technology Working Papers in Technology Governance and Economic Dynamics, no. 14, available at www.technologygovernance.eu.

Reinert, Erik S. and Rainer Kattel. (2014), 'Failed and Asymmetrical Integration: The Baltics and the Non-Financial Origins of the European Crisis', in J. Sommers and C. Woolfson (eds.), *The Contradictions of Austerity. The Socio-Economic Costs of the Neoliberal Baltic Model*, London: Routledge, pp. 64–86.

Reinert, Sophus A. (2011), *Translating Empire. Emulation and the Origins of Political Economy*, Cambridge, MA: Harvard University Press.

Schmoller, Gustav von. ([1884] 1944), *Das Merkantilsystem in seiner Historischen Bedeutung. Städtische, Territoriale und Staatliche Wirtschaftspolitik*, Frankfurt: Klostermann.

Serra, Antonio. (1613), *Breve trattato delle cause che possono far abbondare li regni d'oro & argento dove non sono miniere*, Naples: Lazzaro Scorriggio.

Thatcher, Margaret. (1987) 'Interview', in *Woman's Own,* 31 October, available at: www.margaretthatcher.org/document/106689.

Vernon, Raymond. (1966), 'International Investment and International Trade in the Product Cycle', *Quarterly Journal of Economics*, 80, pp. 190–207.

# 11 Noboru Kobayashi's research on Friedrich List

## A contribution on List's reception and interpretation in Japan*

*Tetsushi Harada*

## I

This contribution does not deal with the reception of Friedrich List, in its various forms, in Japan in general, but focuses on the reception of List by the historian of economic thought Noboru Kobayashi (1916–2010). However, the following three periods provide a general overview of research on Friedrich List in Japan:

### The first period: from the Meiji Restoration to the beginning of the 1930s

After the Meiji Restoration (1868) – the establishment of the modern empire in place of the Tokugawa Shogunate – the Japanese attempted to adopt numerous European and American economic doctrines, especially via textbooks such as those of Francis Wayland and Millicent Garnett Fawcett. Most of these were based on British classical political economy, but the Japanese found the content too abstract and inaccessible. They therefore also turned their attention to German economic thought, such as the Historical School and Friedrich List. In this context, List's main work *The National System of Political Economy* (*Das nationale System der politischen Ökonomie*) (1841) – or strictly speaking its English translation (1885) by Sampson S. Lloyd – was translated into Japanese by the economic protectionist Sadamu Ōshima (1845–1914).[1]

List's ideas were not understood to their full extent before the beginning of the Second World War. The reasons for this were: firstly, even his idea of domestic free competition as a pre-condition for protectionism[2] was difficult to accept in Japan under the dirigistic control of the government at that time; secondly, there was no particular necessity for protectionist measures for the export of Japanese industrial products to China (mainly because of the cheap Japanese textile commodities produced by women working for low wages); and finally, List's thought as a whole was very difficult to understand before the publication of the large edition *Friedrich List: Works/Speeches/Correspondence* (*Friedrich List: Schriften/Reden/Briefe*) of 1927–1935, edited by Erwin von Beckerat, Edgar Salin and Arthur Sommer, among others.[3]

## The second period: during the Chinese-Japanese war (1937–1945)

The discipline of "the history of economic thought" brought together Japanese scholars of economics who were critical of militarism and expansionism. This was because they were, to a certain extent, allowed to discuss liberal and occasionally even Marxist economic thought under the pretext of historical research. They expressed their own opinions through their research, even though they did this covertly. They debated not only Adam Smith but also Friedrich List. This group of scholars also included some people who became very influential after the war, for example, Kazuo Ōkōchi (president of the University of Tokyo after the war), Zenya Takashima (founder of the Faculty of Sociology of the Hitotsubashi University after the war) and, last but not least, Noboru Kobayashi.

Takashima, for example, emphasized in his book *Fundamental Problems of Economic Sociology: Smith and List as Economic Sociologists* (in Japanese, 1941) that despite Friedrich List's support for a temporary protective tariff policy, he had ultimately sought a free-market economy such as that pioneered by Adam Smith. In 1935 Takashima had translated E. Salin's *History of Political Economy* (*Geschichte der Volkswirtschaftslehre*) (2nd ed., 1929) into Japanese. So he already knew the aforementioned large List edition, but he almost exclusively used its 6th volume, namely *The National System*, in his *Fundamental Problems*.[4]

In addition to this, there were Japanese economists in the period who addressed other themes from other volumes of the large List edition:

- The constitutional dispute in Württemberg, from part 1 of volume 1, by Yoichi Itagaki;
- The traffic system, from volumes 3 and 4, by Yūji Tominaga;
- World powers in competition, from volume 7, and the colonial movement, from volume 5, particularly List's treatise on "The Agricultural Constitution, Dwarf Agriculture and Emigration" (Die Ackerverfassung, die Zwergwirtschaft und die Auswanderung), first published in its entirety in volume 5 by Kobayashi; and
- The German Trade and Commerce Union (deutscher Handels- und Geberbeverein), from part 2 of volume 1, by Tomoo Matsuda.

However, these various research studies could not provide enough of an overall view of List's politico-economic thought because they were rather disconnected and lacked a systematic, comprehensive approach.[5]

## The third period: after the end of the Chinese-Japanese, or the Second World War

After the Second World War, Kobayashi regarded it as his task to grasp and convey List's thought in its totality. He attempted to achieve this not merely by synthesizing German and Japanese politico-economic research, but also through his own thorough and precise reading of the large List edition. This attempt by Kobayashi was quite successful in various respects.

I will now present Kobayashi's research on Friedrich List. I will not be able to explain his extensive, comprehensive and profound research on List in its entirety here, but I can at least demonstrate its important points.

## II

Noboru Kobayashi was the leading historian of economic thought in Japan. Because most of his works are published in Japanese, he often remained unknown to foreign scholars, with such exceptions as the historian of economic thought Bertram Schefold and the List researcher Eugen Wendler. Kobayashi dominated as the "secret king of the history of economic thought in Japan"[6] (Schefold), not only because of his outstanding works, but also due to his membership of the Japan Academy (the highest organization of Japanese scholars under the government) as the only member from the field of the history of economic thought. List researcher Eugen Wendler was "deeply impressed" with the venerable character of Kobayashi, whom he calls "the ideal scholar in the Humboldt sense".[7] Wendler attempted to learn the Japanese language in order to access Kobayashi's List research.[8]

Kobayashi had three main research fields: first, James Steuart (1713–1780) and other British mercantilists; second, Adam Smith (1723–1790); and third, Friedrich List. He described and analyzed each of these precisely. However, because he was always sympathetic toward thinkers of tragic destiny due to his own bitter experiences of the war,[9] he seemed to have more of a psychological interest in Steuart (forced to emigrate) and List (ended with suicide) than in Smith, who had been financially successful in his lifetime. We may also assume that Kobayashi favored List over Steuart from the fact that in 1964 he did not choose a Scottish University for Steuart and Smith research, but the University of Tübingen and the Friedrich List Archive in Reutlingen City Archive for List Research as his place of research and residence abroad (this period abroad is permitted for each Japanese scholar, normally for only one sabbatical year).[10] Already in this sense, then, Friedrich List was the most important figure for Kobayashi.

The eleven-volume *Works of Noboru Kobayashi on the History of Political Economy* (in Japanese, 1976–1989) contains three volumes (vols. 6, 7 and 8) which deal exclusively with Friedrich List. Furthermore, he published the book *East-West Debates on List* (in Japanese, 1990) and many other papers on List, as well as Japanese translations of two of List's most important works: one is the book *The National System of Political Economy* and the other is the treatise "The Agricultural Constitution, Dwarf Agriculture and Emigration", which is – according to Kobayashi – crucial to understanding List's thought, as I will explain later. Despite (or "because of" – he would perhaps say!) his deep sympathy toward List and his fate, Kobayashi took a solid, scholarly approach, attempting to analyze and explain List's thought always without prejudice and down to the last detail, so he often warned other researchers to avoid rash, thoughtless fondness for List and the crude argumentation that might ensue from this. Numerous theories within Kobayashi's interpretation of List are based on his "complete reading of the large List edition",[11] i.e. all its volumes, so the Japanese economic historian Minoru Morota considers Kobayashi's research on List a "reliable lexicon of List".[12]

## III

### Kobayashi's publications in English or German

Kobayashi wrote most of his works in Japanese, but he published some works on Friedrich List in English and German:

- *Die List-Forschung in Ostdeutschland* (*Economic Series*, vol. 29, ed. by Science Council of Japan, Division of Economics, Commerce & Business Administration), 51 pages, Tokyo 1962.
- *James Steuart, Adam Smith and Friedrich List* (the same *Series*, vol. 29), 37 pages, Tokyo 1967.
- "Forschungen über Friedrich List in Japan", In: *Economic Journal*, Daito Bunka University, Tokyo, No. 46, 1988, 1–21.
- Friedrich Lists System der Sozialwissenschaft – von einem japanischen Forscher betrachtet", In: Bertram Schefold (Ed.): *Studien zur Entwicklung der ökonomischen Theorie*, vol. 10, Berlin 1990, pp. 63–77.

Above all, the two latter articles and Schefold's reminiscence "Über Herrn Noboru Kobayashi (1916–2010) und seine Friedrich-List-Forschung"[13] provide a rough outline of Kobayashi's interpretation of List in the German language. Although these three do, to a certain extent, convey its key points, reading these alone does not provide enough of an understanding from the Japanese point of view. In my opinion, Kobayashi's German articles are not very polemical, particularly when it comes to his discussion in a foreign language. This is due to his courteous Old Japanese character. Schefold, despite his sharp insight and pointed discussion, was not able to convey Kobayashi's Japanese works any more directly because of the language barrier. Furthermore, each of the three is merely one article in comparison with Kobayashi's research on List, which spans several volumes.

The principal characteristics of List's thought, which were grasped and demonstrated by Kobayashi, are based mainly on his chief work on List *Friedrich List's Theory of the Powers of Production* (1948). I will explain these presently, but I will also mention other works by Kobayashi and other authors.

## The protective tariff policy of the large nations in the temperate zone and their rise to world powers

Friedrich List's model of stages of development – whereby industrialization would be promoted by a temporary protective tariff – could indeed, in theory, be applied to all developing countries equally. And it is often believed that List wanted to balance and harmonize all nations after their industrialization. According to Kobayashi, however, upon a closer reading of List's discussion in his main work *The National System* and in his later writings, a rather more problematic – at least in today's eyes – world view emerges of a dominance of the great powers. List was indeed entirely progressive in the sense of increasing national welfare.[14] However, from today's perspective of the equal rights of all nations, there are some negative aspects to his thinking: List's development model is not applicable to all nations according to List's original concept.

Kobayashi regards the ideal – often attributed to List – of "free trade as the final goal" among all nations as his "window-dressing of the ideas, List's so-called 'philosophy'" or "a mere passing disguise".[15] For, according to Kobayashi,

> The world politics postulated in his book *The National System* [1841] was the establishment of a union of the European continent in opposition to England. By contrast, he called for opposition to France and Russia through a union between Germany and England in the newspaper *The Tariff Union Newspaper* [*Das Zollvereinsblatt* from 1843]. This newer political line of thought is also based on his understanding of the powers of production within high capitalism, but it denies his [previous] ideal of the world united through free trade, which was his final goal in *The National System*.
>
> (Kobayashi, 1948, pp. 100–101)

It is particularly in List's newer standpoint – after this "change"[16] – that Kobayashi recognizes his obvious "global-political concept of establishing a German empire in the future world of coexisting great powers".[17] And this later standpoint of List's can, according to Kobayashi, be clearly seen in List's article of 1842 on agriculture, "The Agricultural Constitution, Dwarf Agriculture and Emigration" (List, 1927–1935, vol. 5. p. 418–547).

I will discuss this work on agriculture by List in more detail in section IV, but beforehand I would like to look at his book of 1841, *The National System of Political Economy*, to some extent by way of background knowledge. List's tendency toward a large hegemonic state is, according to Kobayashi, apparent not only in works of his later period, but also already in *The National System*.

In this book, at first glance, List seems to explain the five stages of economic development of nations merely in general: "[1] stage of original barbarism, [2] pastoral stage, [3] agricultural stage, [4] agricultural manufacturing stage, and

[5] agricultural manufacturing commercial stage", and the necessity of the protective tariff during the shifting periods from the third (especially from the fourth) to the fifth stage. But upon closer reading, List stresses that the protective tariff measures are suitable only for "large nations of the temperate zone",[18] and he rejects the possibility of industrialization in two categories of countries: firstly, countries in the polar regions and the tropics, and secondly, small countries in the temperate zone.

According to List, the countries in the first category cannot industrialize because of their difficult geographical location. These countries should function almost exclusively as suppliers of raw materials and agricultural products to the large countries of the temperate zone. List says:

> Even if a country in the tropical zone were to want to increase its own manufacturing power, it would be highly detrimental to it to set about doing so. Having not been called to this vocation by nature, it will make much greater progress in its material wealth and in its culture by exchanging manufactured products of the temperate zone for its agricultural products of the tropical zone.
>
> (List, 1927–1935, vol. 6, pp. 52–53)

> The countries *of the world* that are *most favored by nature* in terms of their national and international division of labor, are evidently [...] *the countries of the temperate zone.* For in these countries it is primarily manufacturing power that thrives, by means of which the nation is not only able to achieve the highest degree of intellectual and social growth and political power, but is also, to a certain extent, able to make the countries of the tropical zone and the nations of inferior civilization tributary to itself.[19]
>
> (List, 1927–1935, vol. 6, p. 198)

The countries in the second category too, in List's view, cannot industrialize independently because of their lack of potential powers of production. They should be subsumed into a large country (in other words, a large state or a large nation). Only after that will they be able to industrialize as part of the large country. According to List, this applies even to the Netherlands and Denmark:

> Protectionist measures are justifiable only for the purpose of promoting and protecting domestic manufacturing power, and only in the case of nations which, due to their extensive and consolidated territory, large population, possession of natural resources, well advanced agriculture, and high degree of civilization and political development, are qualified to rank equally with the principal agricultural manufacturing commercial nations [...].
>
> (List, 1927–1935, vol. 6, pp. 322–323)

It is only through its Tariff Union [Zollverein since 1834] that the German nation has arrived at one of the most important attributes of its nationality. But this measure cannot be considered complete so long as it does not extend over the whole coast, from the mouth of the Rhine to the Polish frontier, including *Holland* and *Denmark*.

(List, 1927–1935, vol. 6, p. 211)

What Friedrich List calls the "normal nation" at the highest "agricultural manufacturing commercial stage", where "agriculture, manufacture and commerce are [...] developed equitably",[20] is therefore the large industrialized nation in the temperate zone, which includes neighboring smaller countries and has its own colonies in the tropical zone. So we may regard List's image of the nation as an early manifestation of the imperial great power. It is lacking only a concept of balance between several great powers, a concept List will address in his later period. On this, Kobayashi says:

As far as his apparently static image of the normal nation is concerned, its framework will be burst open by its inherent dynamic power. It is precisely this stage that is described as the fifth and highest stage in *The National System of Political Economy*. From an economic point of view, this is the stage of the export-industrial state; more generally, it is the stage of the imperial nation.

(Kobayashi, 1948, p. 130)

List's famous world view of the association of industrialized "normal" nations leads therefore to a balance between the great powers in the temperate zone, of which each has its own colonies, especially in the tropical zone. From his progressive and national standpoint, Friedrich List is concerned above all with the development of the German nation. So we have to interpret this, even if unwillingly, as a sort of first step toward later German imperialism, at least from the perspective of the countries of the polar regions and the tropics, as well as of the smaller countries neighboring the large nations.[21]

## IV

*List's quasi expansionist proposals, originally aimed at domestically balanced economic development and at ensuring the survival and political participation of the peasants*

Kobayashi points out, further, a paradoxical conjunction between the democratic intentions and the quasi expansionist proposals in List's works on agriculture and emigration. From the early period when he was a government official in the territorial state of Württemberg to the late period of the 1840s, List was always determined to ensure the survival of the impoverished peasants who were inevitably engaged in "dwarf agriculture" (Zwergwirtschaft), in other words agriculture on land that was too small, due to inheritance distribution. They could barely secure the minimum level of subsistence, so a lot of them reluctantly emigrated – mainly to North America. We find this issue addressed by List in his earlier period,. for example in "Against the Unlimited Division of Agricultural Estates" ("Wider die unbegrenzte Teilung der Bauerngüter")[22] of 1816, when he attended, as "a Swabian 'democrat'",[23] the so-called "Constitution Dispute" (Verfassungsstreit) in Württemberg (Swabia), as well as in his later period, especially in his article "The Agricultural Constitution, Dwarf Agriculture and Emigration" of 1842. In the latter, List also strongly attacked the "unrestricted dismemberment of estates" promoted by "Jacobinism" in France, calling it an unpleasant case.[24]

But before a close analysis of "The Agricultural Constitution, Dwarf Agriculture and Emigration", we should consider that in *Das nationale System* (1841) List already emphasizes the balance of agriculture and industry in a national economy, or the significance of agriculture itself. He therefore believes that active domestic agricultural production is necessary, not only in order to ensure the survival of the impoverished peasants but also for the ideal balance between the two sectors, considering the industrial sector is becoming stronger. He says in *The National System*:

> [...] Every improvement in domestic agriculture, every new cultivation acts as a stimulant on domestic manufacturing, because every increase in domestic agricultural production must result in a proportionate increase in domestic manufacturing production. This reciprocal action therefore guarantees progress to both these main sources of subsistence for the nation for all time.
>
> (List, 1927–1935, vol. 6, p. 218)

Even though List considered national industrialization up to the level of exportation as the mainspring of economic development, he did not forget to emphasize that "the domestic market [mainly between the two sectors] of a nation is ten times more important than its foreign market, even where the latter is flourishing".[25]

Now we turn to "The Agricultural Constitution, Dwarf Agriculture and Emigration" (which from now on I will refer to as "The Agricultural Constitution").

The productivity of dwarf agriculture, above all in south-west Germany, was very low. The peasants were scarcely in a position to actively participate in the domestic market, and therefore had neither motivation nor opportunity for participation in national progress and politics.

> We are of the conviction that the agricultural constitution within which smaller- and medium-sized agriculture is the rule but large- and dwarf-sized agriculture is the exception, – such an agricultural constitution

best corresponds to both the [democratic] representative system and the agricultural and economic principle.[26]

(List, 1927–1935, vol. 5, pp. 435–436)

To solve the problem, in "The Agricultural Constitution" List proposed first the dissolution of the inherited field constitution, and then the "realignment of estate boundaries" (Gutsarrondierung), in other words, field redistribution.

> We know that the remedy against the spread of dwarf agriculture is the partial and gradual dissolution of the village constitution, specifically of its mixed field constitution, and the introduction of a realignment of estate boundaries or a farm constitution.
>
> (List, 1927–1935, vol. 5, p. 451)

But because List was aware of the inadequacy of this measure, he proposed another: "emigration" (Auswanderung), namely resettlement in the "hinterland",[27] so that the impoverished peasants could acquire their own land again by reclaiming wasteland and become independent smaller- and middle-sized farmers on this land.

It is worth noting that List understood "hinterland" in contrast to North America, where people often settled from Germany at that time, and which he considered "a quite unnatural"[28] place, especially for southern Germans. He explained the "hinterland" as follows:

> What mighty stream of power south-east Germany allows to flow into the ocean [to North America]! What might be achieved if it were to be channeled into the Danube Canal? In truth, nothing less than the establishment of a powerful German-Magyar eastern empire [Austro-Hungarian Empire], lapped by the waves of the Black Sea on one side and by the waves of the Adriatic Sea on the other, and animated by the German and Hungarian spirit.
>
> (List, 1927–1935, vol. 5, pp. 499–500)

> Do not the countries on the right and the left banks of the Danube – from Bratislava unto its estuary, the northernmost provinces of Turkey and the western shore of the Black Sea – offer the German emigrants an expanse of unused but naturally fertile land that is not difficult to access [...]?
>
> (List, 1927–1935, vol. 5, p. 499)

> We have hinterland (blackwoods) as good as that of the Americans – the countries on the lower Danube and the Black Sea – the whole of Turkey – the whole of the south east beyond Hungary is our hinterland.[29]
>
> (List, 1927–1935, vol. 5, p. 502)

And furthermore:

> For if the High Gate [the government of the Ottoman Empire] should fall – and it is as certain to fall as the withered leaves in the Fall –, then to whom will nature grant this part of its inheritance? – To the Italians, who still have not established any colonies anywhere? – To the French, who only started colonizing everywhere so they could demonstrate how incompetent they are at it? – To the Russians, who have more to colonize and civilize within themselves and their own country than they will ever be able to bring about for centuries? – To whom, other than the Hungarians united with the Germans?[30]
>
> (List, 1927–1935, vol. 5, p. 500)

Here we find an early concept of the balance between the great powers, in the form of the German confrontation with Italy, France and Russia for the supremacy of the Balkans and Turkey. In actual fact, in the period when he was writing his article "The Agricultural Constitution" List's own standpoint on international politics was changing. Whereas previously he had argued for the need to construct and enlarge the German tariff union against the most industrialized state, England, as well as to establish a continental union as its enlarged form, now he was arguing for the need to unite with England against France and Russia. In 1846 he even went to London and made a vain attempt to talk to Peel about an alliance between Germany and England.[31]

### The characteristics of the "national citizen" that were also expected of emigrants in the "hinterland"

List believed the cultivated areas in the "hinterland" should belong to the mother country. This would enable the mother country to strengthen its domestic agriculture against the industrial sector, balancing out both sectors. Because the new smaller- and middle-sized farmers in the areas would be highly qualified – not only economically but also intellectually – as independent landowners and producers, they would be suitable for participation in national politics. List regarded this as worth striving for, especially because the number of impoverished workers had increased during industrialization, similar to the "proletarians" (Proletarier) in England. Among these people, "a sort of spirit [has] stirred, beginning to question whether freedom and national greatness have any value for someone who, every two or three years, is in danger of starving to death along with his family".[32]

The new farmers would form an effective counterweight to these workers in the political sphere and would build up a sound, unified German state. List thought it necessary for proper "national citizens" (Staatsbürger) to have the following three characteristics, which the new farmers would also have:

We expect *three* main characteristics of the national citizen [...]: *Firstly*, that he is so sufficiently independent in his economic competence as to need neither favor nor aid, nor to fear disfavor, and that he is so sufficiently prosperous as to make his own contribution [...] toward the promotion of public welfare and the maintenance of order in times of stability, and also to provide extraordinary assistance in maintaining law and order [...] and retaining national integrity in times of turbulence. *Secondly*, that he is intellectually qualified to take part effectively in the administration of the municipality [Gemeinde] and the higher self-governing bodies [höhere Korporationen], to understand his rights as a national citizen, to assert these firmly in a legal manner, and to wholly fulfill his obligations as a national citizen (e.g. in the function of the representative, the voter, the juror or the military defender of the estate [Landwehrmann]). *Thirdly*, that he is capable of equipping his children economically and intellectually so that as many of them as possible are capable of fulfilling the obligations of the fully fledged national citizen.[33]

(List, 1927–1935, vol. 5, p. 449)

Where the newly cultivated areas had previously not belonged to German territory, the new smaller- and middle-sized farmers, the ex-peasants who had settled there, should – according to List – defend their estate against their enemies with weapons, thereby fulfilling their national citizen's obligation of military defense of the land. As land owners they would have a fairly strong awareness of and a strong desire for national defense because this defense would, at the same time, apply to their own lands. It would be directed, of course, against the previous inhabitants – if there were any there – and above all against those under the influence of the French and the Russians. The emigration List recommends, therefore, is connected with such secondary matters as this, yet it is also remarkable that this emigration takes place not merely at a private level but through its "expedient organization" (zweckmäßige Organisation) with the understanding of German "governments".[34]

The quotation above makes clear List's intention to not only maintain the Austro-Hungarian Empire – which did indeed stand outside the German Tariff Union dominated by Prussia but still represented the German countries in some respects through its chairmanship in the Federal Assembly of the German Confederation (Deutscher Bund) – but moreover to expand it to "the whole of the south east beyond Hungary" including "the whole of Turkey".

Can we perhaps, to some degree, interpret List's proposed emigration as a harmless settlement intended as mere reclamation? An appropriate answer to this question – whether yes or no, and if yes, then to what degree – does indeed also depend on more detailed research studies of economic history.[35] But even if we would like to follow this benevolent line of interpretation, it is surely only partially valid, because the "hinterland" identified by List is so immense that it reaches the religiously and culturally different country of Turkey, including it in the "whole". We can therefore recognize, in List's proposal, the beginnings of German expansionism – at least from the viewpoint of the original inhabitants of the "hinterland" – even though List's original aim was simply to ensure the survival of the impoverished peasants and promote political participation on their part, as well as to balance the industrial and the agricultural sector. List's method was, however, not only highly likely to bring about the oppression of the original inhabitants; it also presupposed a drawing level with other great powers, thus leading to the expansion of the German state as one great power in competition with the others.[36]

## The paradox of List's politico-economic thought

As mentioned above, the remarkable paradox at the heart of List's concept of the political economy emerges, according to Kobayashi, when List writes "The Agricultural Constitution".[37] The paradox is this: whereas Friedrich List as a progressive thinker intended not only to develop the national economy in a balanced way (in *The National System*), but also to improve the socio-political conditions by relieving the impoverished peasants, and to increase democracy by enabling their participation in politics (in "The Agricultural Constitution"), this intention led – either by its result or by its means – to the expansionist policy against France and Russia, making possible further oppression of inhabitants in the Balkans and Turkey. Unfortunately for List, his later quasi expansionist standpoint and his accompanying conversion to a German–English alliance were not broadly accepted, especially not by the British. Deeply disappointed by Peel's negative answer, on his return journey from London to Germany, which continued further south, he committed suicide in 1846 in Kufstein in Austria. Kobayashi therefore says of List, "List, whose thought embodied the deep contradiction and distress of German capitalism".[38]

The aforementioned paradox is an important characteristic of Kobayashi's interpretation of List, which became – and still remains – the standard interpretation of "The Agricultural Constitution" in Japan, and is central to the interpretation of the whole of List's politico-economic concept for Japanese historians of political economy.[39]

## V

However, if we neglect the democratic representative aspect of Friedrich List's thought and only emphasize its expansionist tendency, this could create a partial and unfair image of List as a mere forerunner of National Socialism.[40] It is therefore important to understand that – at least domestically – List was primarily and consistently focused on the democratic aspect, even if we perceive the expansionist aspect as its result or its means. This, precisely, is the work that was undertaken by Kobayashi.[41]

## List as the representative – but corporativist – democrat on the basis of Justus Möser's political thought

Although List's representative democratic thinking is indeed originally based on the modern Enlightenment, it is neither atomistic nor populistic but moderately corporativist, advocated by a variety of intellectuals at that time in Germany, for example the philosopher G.W.F. Hegel. These intellectuals were searching for a political system in which the middle and the lower (but not the lowest) classes could participate, who would not disturb the stable social and political conditions.[42] Friedrich List conceived this kind of representative system, inspired by the politico-economic thought of the Osnabrück-based Justus Möser (1720–1794), whose work also fascinated J.W. Goethe.[43] Möser was influenced by such moderate thinkers of the French Enlightenment as Montesquieu, who accepted varieties of societies originating from their different historical cultural backgrounds[44] and rejected such tendencies of the Enlightenment as the modern uniformity advocated by Voltaire and Friedrich II of Prussia. So, one of the most important features of Möser's political thought is the inclination to respect different municipal self-governments that originate from historical communities.[45]

The name Justus Möser appears right at the beginning of List's article "The Agricultural Constitution".[46] Referring to Möser's book *Osnabrückische Geschichte* (probably its 1780 version),[47] List emphasizes Möser's ideal of the farmer who has his own "estate to defend" (Wehrgut). According to the ideal, this type of farmer is the true national citizen, legitimized to take part responsibly in the politics of the state in the same way as the stockholder in the management of the company. List says, "Justus Möser calls land ownership the state stock [Staatsaktie]".[48]

Möser's ideal had a decisive influence on Friedrich List's political thought. As mentioned above (section IV), in the "The Agricultural Constitution" List mentions the three characteristics of the true national citizen, which would also be expected of the new smaller- and middle-sized farmers. Firstly, the national citizen should be economically independent and should be able to afford to contribute to public welfare; secondly, he should be qualified to take part in political matters and fulfill national obligations, including military defense of the estate; and thirdly, he should be capable of educating children so that they grow up to be true national citizens. List's argument is obviously based on Justus Möser's thought with the idea of the "estate to defend". So, not only in the "The Agricultural Constitution" of 1842 but also in the "Against the Unlimited Division of Agricultural Estate" of 1816, List argues from the standpoint of allowing impoverished peasants to have appropriate land and be true national citizens with political participation. Besides being mentioned in the *Osnabrückische Geschichte*, these same ideas of Möser's are also found in his writings in the book *Patriotic Fantasies (Patriotische Phantasien)* of 1774–1786,[49] which is mentioned by the younger List, citing Möser.[50]

Kobayashi stressed that List's devotion to Möser already appears in List's works from his earlier period, namely from the time when he was active as "a Swabian 'democrat'",[51] campaigning for a representative political system in the "Constitution Dispute" in the territorial state of Württemberg, in the region of Swabia.

In List's lecture of 1818 or 1819 "On Württemberg's Constitution" ("Über die württembergische Verfassung") at the University of Tübingen (he was a professor there), he tried to inspire students with the noble idea of Swabian communities as self-governing, referring to Möser's *Osnabrückische Geschichte*. He says, "*Möser*, the first authority on old German history, says in his History of Osnabrück, page 133, that Germania is an old Swabian association, and that this set up the beginning of the later empire". In Swabian communities with their land systems, according to List, "the original Swabian freedom" still survived in spite of feudalism, and could become "the pillar at which civil freedom could be established again".[52] In this case, "page 133" means the same page of the 1780 version of the *Osnabrückische Geschichte*,[53] where Möser is "perfectly convinced" that "Germania is an old Swabian association". In the same book, Möser says that in the "first and golden" period of Germany, "each German farm was occupied by a land owner or *estate defender* [Wehre][...]. There was nothing but noble and communal *honor* in the nation. [...] The communal head was an *elected* judge".[54] These statements of Möser's also recall Montesquieu's remark, referring to Tacitus, that ancient Germans elected the head of their local governments.[55]

Besides the lecture "On Württemberg's Constitution", we find the younger List's concept of the corporativist representative state system in such works as "Considerations on the State Government of Württemberg" ("Gedanken über die würtembergische Staatsregierung")[56] of 1816, "The System of Municipality Management" ("System der Gemeindewirtschaft") of 1817, "Criticism of the Constitution Draft" ("Kritik des Verfassungsentwurfs")[57] of 1817, "An Outline of Württemberg's State Knowledge and State Practice" ("Die Staatskunde und Staatspraxis Württembergs im Grundriß)[58] of 1818, and "On the Constitution and Administration of Communities" ("Über die Verfassung und Verwaltung der Koporationen") of 1818–1819. Kobayashi explained the younger List's concept of the state on the basis of these works by List.[59]

This concept of the state is not such a radically individualistic one as has emerged since the French Revolution and which is based on each person being separate from any group. List says,

> Furthermore, I think that France cannot exist, in its Enlightenment, in these masses [of people], and that it will find peace and order only if it returns again to the natural, i.e. to the progressively ascending social

union [Gesellschaftsverband], and if its provinces are constructed in accordance with their departments.[60]

(List, 1927–1935, vol. 1, p. 208)

In the aforementioned works, List's explanations of his concept of the state contain some ambiguities and confusions, but Kobayashi attempted to summarize it as proceeding roughly in four stages of construction: the whole of the state is constructed from bottom to top, namely from (1) "municipality" ("Gemeinde") through (2) "canton" ("Kanton") or "larger district" ("Oberamt"), further through (3) "province" ("Provinz"), and lastly to (4) the "state" ("Staat"). The municipality and the canton in particular have their own elective representative assemblies or parliaments.[61] Thus List says:

> After we have deduced the existence of the whole of the state [Gesamtstaat] from its roots, now we stand at the highest point of view and return to the sentence: *the state is the association of several provinces, the province is an association of several cantons, the canton is the association of several municipalities, and the municipality is an association of individuals, all committed to achieving the whole purpose.*[62]
>
> (List, 1927–1935, vol. 1, p. 209)

Incidentally, this corporativist view of the state still remains in his later work "The Agricultural Constitution" of 1842. Here, says List, "the true constitutional order requires [...] a corporative system [Korporationssystem] that ascends from the municipality to the national association [Nationalverband]".[63]

### Möser's influence as the "deepest" influence on Friedrich List

Möser's name is found in the works of the younger List as well as in "The Agricultural Constitution" of his later period (later than the publication of *The National System*) in connection with his main arguments, so his devotion to Möser is indeed quite obvious in these two periods. But in his main work *The National System* (1841) of his middle period, the devotion is not apparent, even though he mentions Möser's name once – but rather lightly – in relation to the decline of the Hanseatic cities,[64] and even though during this period List debated railway issues under the pseudonym of Justus Möser.[65]

Möser's influence on List's thought is therefore often ignored, because most people – even scholars of the history of economic thought – read almost only *The National System* in order to understand List's politico-economic thought. But, as Kobayashi indicates, Möser's influence is very important in understanding List's intentions. Kobayashi says:

> The state should therefore decide the appropriate size of each agricultural land and forbid its further division, as well as allow the

already divided lands to merge again. This is List's assertion. Incidentally, we can say that this argument is certainly the main point of
"The Agricultural Constitution" and, at the same time, the content
most easily able to be connected with the writings of Möser's *Patriotic Fantasies*. We must say that the influence of Möser on List is
therefore the deepest one, insistently extending from his early period
into his later years.

(Kobayashi, 1948, p. 266 and cf. Kobayashi, 1990, pp. 76–77)

Kobayashi translated not only *The National System* but also "The Agricultural Constitution" into Japanese (see section II) in order to enable Japanese
scholars to understand List's thought more precisely. As far as I am aware,
his Japanese translation is the only translation of the latter text available in
any foreign language.

# VI

By way of concluding remarks, I would like to consider a number of points
further.

### List's quasi expansionist politics do not stem from Möser's idea itself but mainly from List's industrialism and the ideal of a balance between the two sectors

List proposes an expansion-oriented world politics in his later period on the
one hand, but at the same time he is also influenced by Möser's thinking on
the corporativist state system, represented by economically independent –
even if not large-scale – farmers across all his periods. But we should not
interpret Möser's influence itself as the cause of List's expansionism.

In comparison with democracy today, which is understood as the direct
representation of each individual within the political system, Möser's ideas
did indeed have conservative aspects, and he inclined toward the cooperation of neighboring German countries on some economic issues.[66] However,
Möser, i.e. the thinker as the statesman of Osnabrück, did not intend to
expand his rather small country even into the other German countries, to
say nothing of expanding into foreign nations. He was inclined to defend
his country with its communities while striving to progress these, and as a
decentralist he was therefore against Prussia's attempt to bring about
German integration. He saw the king of Prussia as an enlightened despot
who was trying to command his own country from top to bottom by
imposing uniformity, and was trying to expand the country further.[67]

Where, then, did List's expansionist tendency come from?

List continually endeavored to industrialize Germany and at the same
time keep the balance between the agricultural and the industrial sectors in
the domestic economy. But the new machine production meant that the

industrial sector alone was increasing its productivity enormously, whereas the agricultural sector was not. He therefore proposed the expansion of the agricultural sector into neighboring countries and regions. This was also a proposal to confront the other countries, which were becoming great powers at that time. This was seen by List as inevitable, especially in terms of the ideal of the state, which was based on the independent farmers as true national citizens, i.e. the ideal influenced by Möser. In this context, the main impulse behind List's quasi expansionism is his industrialism – which Möser had not known in his lifetime – and the ideal of balancing the two economic sectors.

This interpretation suggests that List's expansionist tendency is not a uniquely German one but has many similarities with other countries (especially "latecomer" countries) which were becoming great powers at that time. For example, we can compare the development of the United States of America, even though its state ideal is characterized not by Möser's but by another type of Enlightenment. This country was also – due to its industrialization – expanding into the western regions inhabited by First Nations people, creating its own farmers as sound national citizens, oppressing the First Nations and confronting England and Spain on the North American continent. As a matter of fact, List – who lived from 1825 to 1832 in the United States – not only accepts the influence of American protectionism[68] but also compares his quasi expansionist proposal for Germany to that of the "Americans" in "The Agricultural Constitution".[69]

### Kobayashi's critical standpoint vis à vis industrialism, and his sympathy toward the tragic List

As a historian of economic thought, Noboru Kobayashi did tend to refrain from giving his own opinions about real economic and political issues. But from his critiques and shorter essays on contemporary problems, it is quite clear that he was basically skeptical toward modern industrial powers of production and was especially critical of an optimistic evaluation of the development of modern society on the basis of powers of production. Notwithstanding this, Kobayashi approved of certain aspects of List's thought, such as the idea that the powers of production consist not only of material but also of immaterial – institutional, spiritual, cultural and environmental – elements, and the idea that there should be domestic balance between the industrial and the agricultural sector. In this regard, Kobayashi commented critically on contemporary problems; for example he criticized the market economy, which prioritizes material exchange values over environmental problems, and he criticized the very low rate of self-sufficiency of domestic agricultural products in relation to that of imports in Japan.[70]

Kobayashi was of course against imperialism and expansionism, and he was critical of List's inclination toward these. Nevertheless, Kobayashi did not conceal his sympathy toward List. Moreover, according to Kobayashi, many meaningful things can be learned from List, as he is a very important figure in the history of politico-economic thought. It is often possible to see how a progressive thinker who was endeavoring to modernize his country – one which was able to rise up to become one of the great powers – might end up holding such problematic views. Although this thinker was striving for industrialization and even for democratic representation, his thinking became more expansionist and focused on the oppression of the inhabitants in neighboring regions. This is the dark side to modernization or "modernity" in itself. The more a potentially large and strong nation develops economically and politically, the more it takes on expansionist and colonialist characteristics. Friedrich List had to bear this paradox, and in this sense he could be seen as a tragic sacrifice to the paradox of modernization.

This is why, despite exposing the problematic aspects of List's thought, Kobayashi remained steadily sympathetic toward List. He attempted to reveal the true seriousness of the problem of modern industrial capitalism through his research on List. Kobayashi spoke of "List, who grew from 'a Swabian democrat' into 'an advocate for large industrial capitalists' (Marx), and whose thought embodies the deep contradiction and distress of German capitalism".[71]

I believe Kobayashi compared List, inwardly and indirectly, with his own experiences of the war. It seems it was during the war that he first realized he could contribute to the economic and political development of Japan and East Asia by applying his socio-scientific knowledge appropriately for that period.[72] But he became deeply disappointed, for he became more and more convinced that the war was damaging not only himself mentally and physically, but also the inhabitants of the countries affected; that it was an imperialist war of expansion by Japan, and that it was therefore not justifiable.[73]

Presumably, therefore, Kobayashi arrived at the conclusion that a nation which develops economically as a "latecomer" and has the potential to become a world power often produces progressive thinkers who, at home, demonstrate democratic conviction but tend to contribute to their country's hegemony over a larger area, including other nations. In this sense, Kobayashi takes pains to mention past Japanese emigration to Manchuria on the Chinese continent, comparing this to List's emigration proposal.[74] For example, Ishiguro Tadaatsu (1884–1960), Minister of Agriculture 1940–1941, who strove steadily before and after the war to ensure the survival and independence of the impoverished peasants through land-acquisition, but promoted the Manchuria emigration, i.e. colonization, enthusiastically at the time of the war.[75]

## Further research on the relation between Möser and List

Kobayashi's arguments on the relation between Möser and List tend to be at the level of the political system, even if the role expected of the smaller-

and middle-sized landowners is economically very important. There is still scope for further analysis of the relation between Möser and List in the field of economic thought in the broader sense.

For example, in the writings – other than the aforementioned ones – of the younger List, Möser's name is mentioned on several occasions, as in "How Should the Revenue from a Common German Customs Border be Used?" ("Wozu sollte der Ertrag einer gemeinschaftlichen deutschen Dounanenlinie verwendet werden?")[76] of 1820 and "On a Common Customs Border for the Southern German States" ("Über eine gemeinschaftliche Douane der süddeutschen Staaten")[77] of 1820. In these writings Möser's name is invoked in connection with such economic issues as commerce, tariffs and the economic relations between German countries or regions. Incidentally, we should not ignore the fact that List sometimes wrote under the pseudonym of Justus Möser even in the case of railway systems in his middle period.[78]

Wilhelm Roscher explains Möser's politico-economic thought in his voluminous book *History of Political Economy in Germany* (*Geschichte der National-Oekonomik in Deutschland*) of 1874[79] – which is still outstanding today – devoting more pages to Möser than to List. He presents Möser as no less of a thinker of political economy than List. For example, Möser also wrote about the economic relationship between German-speaking countries in his article "Ideas on Setting Up a District Association to Regulate Spirit Distillation When There is a Concerning Shortage of Grain" ("Vorstellung zu einer Kreisvereinigung, um das Branteweinsbrennen bei dem zu besorgenden Kornmangel einzustellen") of 1770.[80] However, as far as I am aware, there has been very little adequate research – beyond Roscher's work – on Möser's thought as economic thought, neither in Germany nor in Japan. Further research of this kind should focus on a more precise comparison of the two thinkers.[81]

## Notes

\* This contribution is based – even though translated and enlarged – on Harada (2015). Unless otherwise indicated, all translations from Japanese and German are the author's own
1 Cf. Kobayashi (1988), pp. 1–2.
2 Cf. List (1927–1935), *Das nationale System der politischen Ökonomie* (1841), vol. 6, p. 58, pp. 69–70.
3 Cf. Kobayashi (1988), pp. 3–4.
4 Cf. Takashima (1941), pp. 245–342; Harada (1997; 2012).
5 Kobayashi (1988), pp. 4–11.
6 Schefold (2011 and 2016).
7 Wendler (2011), p. 316.
8 Wendler (2011), pp. 317–318.
9 When Kobayashi was a soldier in the Second World War in a military transport ship on the way to south-east Asia, the ship was sunk late in the night by a torpedo from an American submarine, so he had to swim for his life. After he was rescued by another Japanese warship, he was still compelled to go into battle in

Vietnam. Cf. Kobayashi (2002), p. 74. This book is his autobiography. "The City" means Fukushima City, i.e. the capital of the prefecture of the same name, on the coast of which the dreadful disaster at the nuclear power station happened in 2011. Before his Tokyo period (since 1955 at Rikkyo University, Tokyo), Kobayashi had taught for a long time at Fukushima College for Commerce (later renamed Faculty of Economics of Fukushima University – of which the author is an alumnus). As the title of the autobiography shows, he always looked back on his Fukushima period and the city with a sense of nostalgia until in his Tokyo period toward the end of his life. He even wrote his main book on List *Friedrich List's Theory of the Powers of Production* (フリードリッヒ・リストの生産力論) in 1948 during the Fukushima period. Incidentally, he was already critical of the nuclear power plant at the time of its construction. Cf. Noboru Kobayashi (1979), pp. 253–254. This "Recommendation" was first communicated in 1979 as a lecture at the public symposium of "The Society for a Moratorium on the Nuclear Power Plant".

10 Kobayashi often mentioned his admiration for Dr. Paul Schwarz (the head of the Reutlingen City Archive at that time) and his valuable works and kindnesses. Cf. Kobayashi (1964–1965), pp. 338–340 and Kobayashi (1965), pp. 294–302.

11 Kobayashi (1978), p. 461.

12 Morota (2003), p. 320.

13 Schefold (2011 and 2016).

14 Cf. Wendler (2004, 2013).

15 Kobayashi (1948), vol. 6, pp. 101, 103, 175.

16 Kobayashi (1948), pp. 100–101. In quotations, brief supplementary information by the author is in square brackets.

17 Kobayashi (1988), p. 15.

18 List (1927–1935), vol. 6, pp. 53–54, 212. For an English translation of *Das nationale System*, see List (1856, 2011). However, translations in this contribution are not identical to these English editions but are formulated by the author.

19 In quotations, the passages with letters in italics show those with the letters spaced in the originals, or book titles. Cf. Katagiri (2004), *Social Thought* (社会思想), pp. 155–156.

20 List (1927–1935), vol. 6, pp. 210, 212.

21 Cf. Harada (2006), pp. 34–38.

22 List (1927–1935), vol. 1.2, pp. 580–584. Its Japanese translation by Kobayashi and his precise analysis of it are in his essay from 1966. Cf. Kobayashi (1966-1967), esp. pp. 231–254.

23 Lenz (1936), p. 410.

24 List (1927–1935), vol. 5, p. 426. Cf. Kobayashi (1948), pp. 198, 203 and Kobayashi (1990), p. 73.

25 List (1927–1935), vol. 6, p. 219. Cf. Kobayashi (1948), vol. 6, pp. 196–197.

26 List (1927–1935), vol. 5, pp. 435–436. Cf. Kobayashi (1948), p. 203 and Kobayashi (1990), p. 65.

27 List (1927–1935), vol. 5, p. 502.

28 List (1927–1935), vol. 5, p. 499.

29 List (1927–1935), vol. 5, p. 502. In quotations, supplements in round brackets come from original texts.

30 List (1927–1935), vol. 5, p. 500. Cf. Kobayashi (1948), vol. 6, pp. 172–173.

31 Cf. "Die englische Allianz und die deutsche Industrie", 1843, in: List (1927–1935), vol. 7, pp. 250–254,"Die wahren Grundbedingungen einer englisch-deutschen Allianz", 1845, in: List (1927–1935), vol. 7, pp. 263–267; "Über den Wert und die Bedingungen einer Allianz zwischen Großbritannien und Deutschland", 1846, in: List (1927–1935), vol. 7, pp. 167–296; "Sir Robert

Peel an List", 1846, in: List (1927–1935), vol. 8, p. 826. Cf. also, Kobayashi (1948), pp. 50–51 and Morota (2007), pp. 280–288.

32  List (1927–1935), vol. 5, p. 430. Cf. Kobayashi (1948), p. 201 and Kobayashi (1990), p. 73.

33  List (1927–1935), vol. 5, p. 449. Cf. Kobayashi (1948), pp. 209–211 and Kobayashi (1990), p. 67.

34  List (1927–1935), vol. 5, p. 447.

35  The author thanks Mr. Bertram Schefold for the suggestion of taking in comparison an example of the welcome settlement of Germans in Russia under Catherine II. Concerning this question of List's thought, the facts discovered by Kobayashi are very instructive: although List's main work *The National System* had been met with a positive response in Hungary and was already translated into Hungarian by 1843, "The Agricultural Constitution" was met with no such response. Cf. Kobayashi (1974), pp. 287–288.

36  Cf. Kobayashi (1948), pp. 225–226; Kobayashi (1990), p. 75.

37  Cf. N. Kobayashi (1948), pp. 192–217.

38  Kobayashi (1976), p. 354.

39  There are some research studies on the expansionist and imperialist character inherent in List's thought, of which the author became aware during his proof-reading of the previous (shorter) German version of this contribution. Cf. Harada (2015).

In his book *Imperialistisches und kolonialistisches Denken in der politischen Ökonomie Friedrich Lists* (Hamburg, 2009), Rüdiger Gerlach says: "there is no significant secondary literature" (p. 22) that addresses this issue. The only reliable pieces we have are, according to Gerlach, two old articles by Ludwig Sevin: "Die Entwicklung von Friedrich Lists kolonial- und weltpolitischen Ideen bis zum Plane einer englischen Allianz von 1846", In: *Jahrbuch für Gesetzgebung, Verwaltung und Volkswirtschaft im Deutschen Reich*, New Series, vol. 33, 1909; "Die Listsche Idee einer deutsch-englischen Allianz in ihrem Ergebnis für Deutschland", in: the same, *Jahrbuch*, vol. 34, 1910. Gerlach's research is indeed thought-provoking, especially because of his attempt to relate List's idea to research on imperialism today. But it is regrettable that Gerlach does not know Kobayashi's research on List at all, even his German article of 1990. Concerning Sevin's research, see Kobayashi (1948), pp. 153, 173 and 177. However, Sevin's research has some major weaknesses in comparison with that of Kobayashi. Firstly, Sevin did not use the complete version of "The Agricultural Constitution" (List 1927–1935, vol. 5) but the shorter version without the key concept of the "hinterland" (because he used Ludwig Häusser (Ed.): *Friedrich List's gesammelte Schriften*, vol. 2, Stuttgart and Tübingen 1850–1851), so Sevin's analysis of "The Agricultural Constitution" is inadequate (Cf. "Kommentar", in: List (1927–1935), vol. 5, pp. 643–645). Secondly, in Sevin's research we find barely any explanation of List's idea of representative self-government as influenced by Justus Möser's political thought. The latter weakness is also apparent in Gerlach's research.

Klaus Thörner's book *"Der ganze Südosten ist unser Hinterland": Deutsche Südostpläne von 1840 bis 1945*, Freiburg, 2008, is also quite thought-provoking as an ambitious attempt to trace German expansionism and colonialism from Friedrich List to the first half of the 1940s and further. However, in his chapter on List there are many crude arguments which could lead to a misunderstanding of List. Although Thörner obviously adopts the book title "Der ganze Südosten ist unser Hinterland" from the phrase "der ganze Südosten jenseits Ungarn ist unser Hinterland" ("the whole of the south east beyond Hungary is our hinterland") from

List's "The Agricultural Constitution" (List 1927–1935, vol. 5, p. 502), he spends only a few pages on this (pp. 27–29) out of a total of over 500 pages of the book! Thörner's chapter on List therefore does not have enough explanation of Friedrich List's original aims, namely the domestically balanced development of the national economy, and ensuring the survival and political participation of the impoverished peasants. Thörner's chapter on List therefore barely addresses the aspect of List as a proponent of democratic representation. These inadequacies mean Thörner could potentially give a false impression of List as a mere forerunner of the later dictatorial National Socialism.

40  For example, the case of Thörner (2008). Cf. the older case of Wiskemann (1937), pp. 11–12.

Kobayashi briefly suggests the possible interpretation that List's concept of the agricultural constitution extends through the agrarian historian and economist Georg Hanssen (1809–1894) to Walther Darré (1895–1953), the agrarian minister in the Hitler regime. However, Kobayashi's discussion on this point is very brief, whereas he writes much more about List's ideas on democratic representation. Incidentally, Hanssen was already mentioned positively by List in "The Agricultural Constitution", cf. List (1927–1935), vol. 5, pp. 439, 491. Cf. Kobayashi (1948), vol. 6, p. 271.

Carelessly attempting to connect List's politico-economic thought with such nationalistic, dictatorial Nazism would be a serious mistake. Even if it is perhaps possible to trace the misuse of this idea from Möser through List and Hanssen to Darré, the result of the misuse or the modification would normally be quite different from the original idea.

41  Cf. Kobayashi (1948), pp. 239–267.

42  Cf. Harada (1989).

43  Cf. Goethe (1955 and 1959), vol. 9, pp. 596–597; vol. 10, pp. 52–53.

44  Cf. Vierhaus (1994), pp. 12–13, about Montesqieu's influence on Möser. Here Vierhaus says pointedly that Möser was one of the "conservative Enlightenment thinkers" in Germany at that time.

45  Cf. Möser (1772a), pp. 22–27 and Möser (1777), pp. 64–68.

46  Cf. List (1927–1935), vol. 5, p. 418.

47  List himself writes only "Osnabrückische Geschichte, S. 43" in his own footnote. But we can identify this noted page with page 43 (§ 24) of Möser's *Osnabrückische Geschichte: Erster Theil, mit Urkunden: Neue vermehrte und verbesserte Auflage*, Berlin, Stettin 1780, because Möser's description of "estate to defend" can only be found here, not on page 43 of its first version *Osnabrückische Geschichte: allgemeine Einleitung*, Osnabrück 1768, although List had been able to read both these versions of the *Osnabrückische Geschichte* in chronological order before writing "The Agricultural Constitution". This is quite important from the point of view of searching for the precise content List had taken from Möser, particularly since Möser's book has different content in its different versions due to his own revisions. Unfortunately, the editors of *List Schriften/Reden/Briefe* did not identify this (see vol 5 of List (1927–1935), p. 645).

48  List (1927–1935), vol. 5, p. 418. The key concept of "state stock" (Staatsactie) addressed by List is also found in § 24 (p. 43) of the 1780 version, but not in its corresponding section § 29 (p. 53) of the 1768 version . Cf. Göttsching (1965) p. 13, 29. Cf. also § 13, esp. its footnote "g", in the 1768 version about the "estate to defend" (Wehrgut); and Möser (1774), pp. 255–270 on Möser's concept of "stock" (Aktie).

We can therefore assume that Möser added the concept of "stock" (lacking in the first version of the *Osnabrückische Geschichte* 1768) to the 1780 version of the *Osnabrückische Geschichte* on the basis of his setting up the concept in his text "Der Bauernhof als eine Aktie betrachtet" of 1774.

49  Cf. Kobayashi (1948), pp. 263–266. Here Kobayashi refers to three writings of Möser, namely Möser (1772b), Möser (1774) and Möser (1777–1778).

50  "Die Staatskunde und Staatspraxis Württembergs in Grundriß", 1818, in: List (1927–1935), vol. 1, p. 288.

51  Lenz (1936), p. 410.

52  "Über die württembergische Verfassung", 1818 or 1819, in: List (1927–1935), vol. 1, pp. 428, 429. Cf. the same vol., pp. 15–16, about the year the draft of this lecture was written. Passages in italics in quotations are already accentuated in originals. Cf. Kobayashi (1948), pp. 255–257.

53  Again, this confirms that List read the 1780 version of the *Osnabrückische Geschichte*. Its "page 133" corresponds to p. 162, *Mösers Sämtliche Werke*, vol. 12, 2, p. 162.

54  Möser (1780), p. 49. Cf. also Möser (1768), p. 35.

55  Cf. Montesquieu (1748), p. 409 (Livre 11, Ch. 8), p. 946 (Livre 31, Ch. 4).

56  List (1927–1935), vol. 1, pp. 87–148.

57  List (1927–1935), vol. 1, pp. 205–283.

58  List (1927–1935), vol. 1, pp. 284–307.

59  Cf. Kobayashi (1948), pp. 242–249.

60  "Kritik des Verfassungsentwurfs", 1817, in List (1927–1935), vol. 1, p. 208. Cf. Kobayashi (1948), pp. 242–243.

61  Cf. Kobayashi (1948), vol. 6, pp. 246–248.

62  "Kritik des Verfassungsentwurfs", in List (1927–1935), vol. 1, p. 209. Cf. Kobayashi (1948), p. 243.

63  List (1927–1935), vol. 5, p. 485.

64  Cf. List (1927–1935), vol. 6, p. 79. According to its editor, this passage is related to Möser (1769).

65  Cf. "Kommentar", in: List (1927–1935), vol. 3, p. 923.

66  Cf. Möser (1770), pp. 300–303.

67  Cf. Möser (1772a), pp. 22–27 and Möser (1777), pp. 64–68.

68  Cf. "*Outlines of American Political Economy*", 1827, in: List (1927–1935), vol. 2, pp. 97–156 and Morota (2003), pp. 188–191.

69  List (1927–1935), vol. 5, p. 502.

70  Cf. Kobayashi (1975).

71  Kobayashi (1976), p. 354. Cf. Marx (1847), p. 296.

72  Cf. Kobayashi (1942), pp. 799, 807. During the Second World War, but just before his conscription, Kobayashi had been professor for colonial policy at the Fukushima College for Commerce. Cf. also Kobayashi (2002) pp. 7–8, 25, 57.

73  Cf. Kobayashi (1984), pp. 44–72.

74  Cf. Kobayashi (1976), vol. 8, p. 354. Cf. also Kobayashi (1942), p. 799.

75  Cf. Otake (1984), pp. 189–377.

76  List (1927–1937), vol. 1, pp. 593–594.

77  List (1927–1937), vol. 1, p. 652.

78  Cf. "Namenverzeichnis A", in: List (1927–1935), vol. 10, p. 222.

79  Roscher (1874), pp. 500–527 for Möser and pp. 970–991 for List.

80  Möser (1770).

81  For important research on the relation between the two thinkers from the point of view of Möser research, see Grywatsch (1994), pp. 287–292. At the end of the paper, Grywatsch also writes that precise research on Möser's influence on List "is lacking". It is a pity that Roscher's research is not mentioned by Grywatsch here.

# References

Gerlach, R. (2009), *Imperialistisches und kolonialistisches Denken in der politischen Ökonomie Friedrich Lists*, Hamburg: Dr. Kovač.

Goethe, J.W. (1955 and 1959), "Aus meinem Leben: Dichtung und Wahrheit (1811–1831)", in: L. Blumenthal and W. Loos (Eds.): *Goethes Werke: Hamburger Ausgabe in 14 Bänden*, vol. 9–10, Hamburg: Christian Wegener.

Göttsching, P. (1965), "Vorrede", in: *Justus Mösers Sämtliche Werke: Historisch-kritische Ausgabe in 14 Bänden*, Oldenburg, Berlin etc. 1943–1990: G. Stalling, H. Th. Wennr, vol. 12 (2).

Grywatsch, J. (1994), "'Der Ihrige ergebenst Justus Möser der Jüngere, Doctor der unexacten Wissenschaften'. Möser-Rezeption bei Friedrich List", in: *Möser-Forum*, 2, pp. 287–292.

Harada, T. (1989), *Politische Ökonomie des Idealismus und der Romantik: Korporatismus von Fichte, Müller und Hegel*, Berlin: Duncker & Humblot.

Harada, T. (1997), "Two Developments of the Concept of Anschauliche Theorie (Concrete Theory) in Germany and Japan", in: P. Koslowski (Ed.): *Methodology of Social Sciences, Ethics, and Economics in the Newer Historical School*, Berlin and Heidelberg: Springer.

Harada, T. (原田哲史) (2006), "F. List: Protectionism for Large Countries of the Temperate Zone" (F.リスト: 温帯の大国民のための保護貿易論), in Japanese, in: K. Yagi (八木紀一郎) (Ed.): *The German Tradition of Economic Thought* (経済思想のドイツ的伝統), Tokyo: Nihon Keizai Hyoronsha.

Harada, T. (2012), "Die modifizierende Aufnahme der 'Anschaulichen Theorie' bei Z. Takashima und ihre Nachwirkungen: Ein Stammbaum der ideengeschichtlichen Wirtschaftsforschungen in Japan", in: H.D. Kurz (Ed.): *Studien zur Entwicklung der ökonomischen Theorie*, vol. 26, Berlin: Duncker & Humblot.

Harada, T. (2015), "Über die Beschäftigung Noboru Kobayashis mit Friedrich List: Ein Beitrag zur List-Rezeption in Japan", in: *Reutlinger Geschichtsblätter*, 2014, New Series, 53, pp. 115–131.

Häusser, L. (Ed.) (1850–1851), *Friedrich List's gesammelte Schriften*, vol. 1–3, Stuttgart and Tübingen: J.G. Cotta.

Katagiri, T. (片桐稔晴) (2004), *Social Thought* (社会思想), in Japanese, Tokyo: Chuo University.

Kobayashi, N. (1942), "The Establishment of the Large-Area Economy and Colonialogy: Outline of a General Theory of the Nature of Colonial Phenomena" (広域経済圏の成立と植民学: 植民現象の本質に関する一般理論の素描), in: *Studies of International Economy* (国際経済研究), Tokyo, 3 (6), pp. 35–53.

Kobayashi, N. (1948), *Friedrich List's Theory of the Powers of Production* (フリードリッヒ・リストの生産力論), in Japanese, 1st ed., Tokyo: Tokyo Keizai Shimposha . Republished, in: *Works of Noboru Kobayashi on the History of Political Economy* (小林昇経済学史著作集), in Japanese, 11 vols., Tokyo: Miraisha, 1976–1989, vol. 6.

Kobayashi, N. (1964–1965), "The Traces of List" (リストの跡), in: N. Kobayashi (Ed.): *Works of Noboru Kobayashi on the History of Political Economy* (小林昇経済学史著作集), in Japanese, 11 vols., Tokyo: Miraisha, 1976–1989, vol. 8.

Kobayashi, N. (1965), "Literature on List, and the List Archive" (リスト文献とリスト文庫), in: N. Kobayashi (Ed.): *Works of Noboru Kobayashi on the History of Political Economy* (小林昇経済学史著作集), in Japanese, 11 vols., Tokyo: Miraisha, 1976–1989, vol. 8.

Kobayashi, N. (1966–1967), "The Prehistory and Context of List's 'The Agricultural Constitution'" (リスト『農地制度論』の前史と周辺), in Japanese, in: N. Kobayashi (Ed.): *Works of Noboru Kobayashi on the History of Political Economy* (小林昇経済学史著作集), in Japanese, 11 vols., Tokyo: Miraisha 1976–1989, vol. 7.

Kobayashi, N. (1974), "Translator's Commentary" (訳者解説), in Japanese, in: F. List (Ed.) (trans. by Noboru Kobayashi): *Die Ackerverfassung, die Zwergwirtschaft und die Auswanderung* (農地制度論), in Japanese, Tokyo: Iwanami Shoten.

Kobayashi, N. (1975), "On the Problem of Establishing National Economies: Smith, List and Solzhenitsïn" (国民経済形成の問題に寄せて: スミス、リスト、ソルジェニツィン), in: S. Suzuki (鈴木成高), M. Shiro (増田四郎) et al. (Eds.): *The Breakdown of History: Culture, Economy and State* (歴史の破綻＝文化・経済・国家), Tokyo: Nigensha.

Kobayashi, N. (1976), "List in 'List and Weber': On the Character of List in Kazuo Sumiya's Book 'List and Weber'", in: N. Kobayashi (Ed.): *Works of Noboru Kobayashi on the History of Political Economy* (小林昇経済学史著作集), in Japanese, 11 vols., Tokyo: Miraisha, 1976–1989, vol. 8.

Kobayashi, N. (1978), "Postscript" (あとがき), in: N. Kobayashi (Ed.): *Works of Noboru Kobayashi on the History of Political Economy* (小林昇経済学史著作集), in Japanese, 11 vols., Tokyo: Miraisha, 1976–1989, vol. 6.

Kobayashi, N. (1979), "Recommendation for Minus Growth" (マイナス成長のすすめ), in: N. Kobayashi (Ed.) (1984), *Stroll of a Returned Soldier* (帰還兵の散歩), in Japanese, Tokyo: Miraisha.

Kobayashi, N. (1984), "Rooted in Vietnam" (ヴェトナムに根ざす), in: N. Kobayashi (Ed.), *Stroll of a Returned Soldier* (帰還兵の散歩), in Japanese, Tokyo: Miraisha.

Kobayashi, N. (1988), "Forschungen über Friedrich List in Japan", in: *Economic Journal* (経済学論集), Tokyo: Daito Bunka University (大東文化大学), 46, pp. 1–21.

Kobayashi, N. (1990), "Friedrich Lists System der Sozialwissenschaft – von einem japanischen Forscher betrachtet", in: B. Schefold (Ed.): *Studien zur Entwicklung der ökonomischen Theorie*, 10, Berlin: Duncker & Humblot.

Kobayashi, N. (2002), *The City unto the Mountain* (山までの街), in Japanese, Tokyo: Hassakusha.

Lenz, F. (1936), *Friedrich List: Der Mann und das Werk*, Munich and Berlin: R. Oldenbourg.

List, F. (1856), *National System of Political Economy*, trans. by G.A. Matile, Philadelphia: J.B. Lippincott.

List, F. (1927–1935), *Schriften/Reden/Briefe*, E. von Beckerath, K. Goeser, F. Lenz, E. Salin et al. (Eds.), Vol. 1–10, Berlin: Reimar Hobbing.

List, F. (2011), *National System of Political Economy*, without translator's name, New York: Cosimo.

Marx, K. (1847), "Die Schutzzöllner, die Freihandelsmänner und die arbeitende Klasse", in: *Karl Marx, Friedrich Engels Werke*, Berlin: Dietz, Bd. 4, 1959.

Montesquieu (1748), *"De L'Esprit des Lois"*, in: R. Caillois (Ed.): *Montesquieu Œuvres Complètes*, II, Paris: Éditions Gallimard, 1951.

Morota, N. (諸田實) (2003), *Friedrich List and his Time: The Emergence of the Political Economy* (フリードリッヒ・リストと彼の時代: 国民経済学の成立), in Japanese, Tokyo: Yuhikaku.

Morota, N. (諸田實) (2007), *Friedrich List in His Later Years: The Course of the German Tariff Union* (晩年のフリードリッヒ・リスト：ドイツ関税同盟の進路), in Japanese, Tokyo: Yuhikaku.

Möser, J. (1768), Osnabrückische Geschichte: allgemeine Einleitung, in: *Justus Mösers Sämtliche Werke: Historisch-kritische Ausgabe in 14 Bänden*, Oldenburg, Berlin et al: G. Stalling, H.Th. Wennr, 1943–1990, vol. 12, (1).

Möser, J. (1769), "Von den wahren Ursachen des Steigens und Fallens der Hanseatischen Handlung", in: *Justus Mösers Sämtliche Werke: Historisch-kritische Ausgabe in 14 Bänden*, Oldenburg, Berlin et al: G. Stalling, H.Th. Wennr, 1943–1990, vol. 4 (Patriotische Phantasien I).

Möser, J. (1770), "Vorstellung zu einer Kreisvereinigung, um das Branntweinsbrennen bei dem zu besorgenden Kornmangel einzustellen", in: *Justus Mösers Sämtliche Werke: Historisch-kritische Ausgabe in 14 Bänden*, Oldenburg, Berlin et al: G. Stalling, H.Th. Wennr, 1943–1990, vol. 4 (=Patriotische Phantasien I).

Möser, J. (1772a), "Der jetzige Hang zu allgemeinen Gesetzen und Verordnungen ist der gemeinen Freiheit gefährlich", in: *Justus Mösers Sämtliche Werke: Historisch-kritische Ausgabe in 14 Bänden*, Oldenburg, Berlin et al: G. Stalling, H.Th. Wennr, 1943–1990, vol. 5 (Patriotische Phantasien II).

Möser, J. (1772b), "Nichts ist schädlicher als die überhandnehmende Ausheurung der Bauernhöfe", in: *Justus Mösers Sämtliche Werke: Historisch-kritische Ausgabe in 14 Bänden*, Oldenburg, Berlin et al: G. Stalling, H.Th. Wennr, 1943–1990, vol. 6 (Patriotische Phantasien III).

Möser, J. (1774), "Der Bauernhof als eine Aktie betrachtet", in: *Justus Mösers Sämtliche Werke: Historisch-kritische Ausgabe in 14 Bänden*, Oldenburg, Berlin et al: G. Stalling, H.Th. Wennr, 1943–1990, vol. 6 (Patriotische Phantasien III).

Möser, J. (1777), "Sollte man nicht jedem Städtgen seine besondere politische Verfassung geben?", in: *Justus Mösers Sämtliche Werke: Historisch-kritische Ausgabe in 14 Bänden*, Oldenburg, Berlin et al: G. Stalling, H.Th. Wennr, 1943–1990, vol. 6 (Patriotische Phantasien III).

Möser, J. (1777–1778), "Über die Absteuer der Töchter der Landbesitzers", in: *Justus Mösers Sämtliche Werke: Historisch-kritische Ausgabe in 14 Bänden*, Oldenburg, Berlin et al: G. Stalling, H.Th. Wennr, 1943–1990, vol. 7 (=Patriotische Phantasien IV).

Möser, J. (1780), "Osnabrückische Geschichte: Erster Theil, mit Urkunden: Neue vermehrte und verbesserte Auflage, Berlin, Stettin", in: *Justus Mösers Sämtliche Werke: Historisch-kritische Ausgabe in 14 Bänden*, Oldenburg, Berlin et al: G. Stalling, H.Th. Wennr, 1943–1990, vol. 12 (2).

Otake, K. (大竹啓介) (Ed.). (1984), *Tadaatsu Ishiguro's Thought of Agricultural Politics* (石黒忠篤の農政思想), Tokyo: Nosanson Nunkakyokai.

Roscher, W. (1874), *Geschichte der National-Oekonomik in Deutschland*, Munich: R. Oldenbourg.

Schefold, B. (2011 and 2016), "Über Herrn Noboru Kobayashi (1916–2010) und seine Friedrich-List-Forschung", the German manuscript in the anthology, in: M. Hattori (服部正治) and H. Takemoto (竹本洋) (Eds.): *Reminiscences of Noboru Kobayashi* (回想 小林昇), in Japanese, Tokyo: Nihon Keizai Hyoronsha, 2011. Original German version published as "Nachruf auf Noboru Kobayashi (1916–2010)", in: H.-M. Trautwein (ed.): *Studien zur Entwicklung der ökonomischen Theorie*, 30, Berlin: Duncker & Humblot, 2016.

Sevin, L. (1909), "Die Entwicklung von Friedrich Lists kolonial- und weltpolitischen Ideen bis zum Plane einer englischen Allianz von 1846", in: *Jahrbuch für Gesetzgebung, Verwaltung und Volkswirtschaft im Deutschen Reich*, New Series, 33, pp. 299–341.

Sevin, L. (1910), "Die Listsche Idee einer deutsch-englischen Allianz in ihrem Ergebnis für Deutschland", in: *Jahrbuch für Gesetzgebung, Verwaltung und Volkswirtschaft im Deutschen Reich*, New Series, 34, pp. 173–222.

Takashima, Z. (1941), (高島善哉), *Fundamental Problems of Economic Sociology: Smith and List as Economic Sociologists* (経済社会学の根本問題: 経済社会学者としてのスミスとリスト), in Japanese, Tokyo.

Thörner, K. (2008), *Der ganze Südosten ist unser Hinterland: Deutsche Südostpläne von 1840 bis 1945*, Freiburg: ça ira.

Vierhaus, R. (1994), "Justus Möser und die Aufklärung", in: *Möser-Forum*, 2, pp. 3–20.

Wendler, E. (2004), *Durch Wohlstand zur Freiheit: Neues zum Leben und Werk von Friedrich List*, Baden-Baden: Nomos.

Wendler, E. (2011), "Prof. Dr. Noboru Kobayashi (1916–2010) – Erinnerungen an einen Freund und ehrwürdigen Gelehrten", in: M. Hattori (服部正治) and H. Takemoto (竹本洋) (Eds.): *Reminiscences of Noboru Kobayashi* (回想 小林昇), in Japanese, Tokyo: Nihon Keizai Hyoronsha.

Wendler, E. (2013), *Friedrich List (1789–1846): Ein Ökonom mit Weitblick und sozialer Verantwortung*, Wiesbaden: Springer.

Wiskemann, E. (1937), "Der Nationalsozialismus und die Volkswirtschaftslehre", in: E. Wiskemann and H. Lütke (Ed.): *Der Weg der deutschen Volkswirtschaftslehre: Ihre Schöpfer und Gestalter im 19. Jahrhundert*, Berlin: Junker und Dünnhaupt.

# 12 Friedrich List and the American system of innovation

*Mark Knell*

## 12.1. Introduction[1]

Georg Friedrich List provided the economic rationale for infant industry protection and export subsidies. In doing so, he also offered a convincing story about how international trade, accumulation, and uneven development were related to the twin issues of technical change and technological learning. List raised several concerns about the nature of political economy and the cosmopolitan ideal in the works of Adam Smith and Jean-Baptiste Say through a series of letters addressed to Charles J. Ingersoll, first published in Philadelphia in the newspaper *The National Gazette,* in July 1827, and re-published later that year as *Outlines of American Political Economy* (Wendler 2015). In these letters, List suggested that Smith's system was about self-interested individuals living in an ideal global free market and how the accumulation of wealth might influence them. He used the expression *cosmopolitical economy,* which originated in the American policy discourse, to differentiate Smith and Say from what he believed to be true political economy, as they did not adequately consider the institutional arrangements of the national economy. List (1827: 10) believed that "power secures wealth, and wealth increases power" and that the object of national policy should be to put agriculture and industry, tangible and intangible capital, and domestic and foreign trade on a balanced path of economic growth.

This chapter pulls together those aspects of List's analysis that relate to the American system of political economy, as he would have experienced it after settling in the United States in 1825, and as it unfolded in the two centuries that followed. In the letters to Ingersoll, List considers the systemic nature of manufacturing production, which Freeman (1982, 1995) interpreted as the "national systems of innovation". List believed that building a national technological infrastructure and a strong national knowledge base was essential to the American system. Freeman and Perez (1988) wrote about new technology systems and changes in the techno-economic paradigm, which fits very well with the American system and subsequent elaborations by List on various European systems in 1837 and 1841. Freeman et al. (1982) had described how the birth, growth, maturity, and decline of industries and technologies evolved during the course of the second industrial revolution (long-wave) that List observed as the pervasiveness of steam engines and emergence of the national system of railways.

A second unifying theme in this chapter is that true political economy should start from the point of view of the interests of nations and not individuals. But List never provides a convincing refutation of Smith's ideas in his writings. Tribe (1995) even suggested they were "superficial and misleading", but they "possess a general coherence that transcends its flawed detail". Although List was largely a derivative of Smith, he assigned social and mental capital an important role in the classical method and he gave the twin issues of technical change and technological learning greater prominence in his historical analysis. More importantly, he created a novel combination of policy and polemic through his journalism, which is what may have prompted List to write his letters to *The National Gazette* in 1827. In the third letter, List (1827: 13) described himself as a "faithful disciple" of Smith and Say up until the collapse of the continental system, which led to a flood of cheap British goods into the German market (Henderson 1983). List quipped, "those who venture to oppose [Smith], or even to question its infallibility, expose themselves to be called idiots". List subsequently revised and extended his ideas and published these letters as *The Natural System of Political Economy* in 1837, and further developed them in his best-known book, the *National System of Political Economy*, published in 1841.

The following section considers the cosmopolitan ideal in enlightenment thought and contrasts this ideal with political economy. Section three then considers the importance of intellectual capital and technological learning in Adam Smith and Friedrich List. Changes in the techno-economic paradigm and new technology systems are then described from the origin of the American system of innovation to the present day in section four. Although inspired by List, the idea originates in Schumpeter's interpretation of the Kondratieff wave, which is then carried over to the idea of technological revolutions by Freeman and Perez (1988). Freeman and Perez identify five successive technological revolutions, in which List can be placed in the first half of the second revolution. The American story continues with the transition from a catching-up economy to becoming the technological leader and no longer reliant on protectionist measures. Section five associates the national systems of innovation perspective with List's national systems of political economy perspective. Some final remarks then are added at the end of section six.

## 12.2. Friedrich List and cosmopolitical economy

Friedrich List initiated his criticism of the American system of national economy in his first letter to *The National Gazette*. In this letter he emphasized the importance of the national economy, downplaying the importance of the individual economy and economy of humankind found in the writings of Adam Smith. List (1827: 8) contended that Smith was mainly concerned with the "means [by which] an individual creates, increases and consumes wealth in society with other individuals, and how the industry and wealth of mankind influence the industry and wealth of individuals". Instead focus should be on the national economy or

> by what means a certain nation, in her particular situation, may direct and regulate the economy of individuals, and restrict the economy of mankind, either to prevent foreign restrictions and foreign power, or to increase the productive powers within herself.
>
> (List 1827: 8)

He believed that the sum of individual interests did not necessarily equal to the national interest. List was critical of the free trade, laissez-faire "British System" and in favour of the "American system" advocated by Alexander Hamilton (1791) and Henry Clay (1959).[2]

In the second letter, List used the expression "*cosmopolitical economy*" to differentiate Smith and Say from what he described as true political economy.[3] Every country has its own unique set of institutional arrangements, which List illustrated as differences in the American system and the British system. He basically placed national interests and political discourse over the cosmopolitical economy of Adam Smith. List reasoned that the "individual economy is not political economy" and that "political economy is not cosmopolitical economy". He devoted chapter four to the issue of Smith's confusion of private vs. national economic interest. And in his fifth letter, List (1827: 24) emphasized, "Every nation must follow its own course in developing its productive powers; or, in other words, every nation has its particular political economy".

The idea of cosmopolitanism dates back to ancient stoic philosophy (Zeno of Citium), but it took on a completely new meaning at the time of the Enlightenment. The basic philosophy of the stoics was about "living in accordance with nature". Adam Smith departed from the ethical stoicism of the ancient stoics in his essay on *The History of Ancient Physics* and in the *Theory of Moral Sentiments* (Clarke 2002) and moved progressively toward the idea of commercial cosmopolitanism. The ancient stoics were still important to his thoughts and beliefs, mainly through the thinking of his mentor, Francis Hutcheson, who also had an important influence on the moral philosophy of David Hume and Immanuel Kant.[4] Although Smith never used the words *cosmos, cosmopolitan,* or *cosmopolitical* in any of his writings, he did have a cosmopolitan attitude reminiscent of Hume, Franklin, and Say and he repeatedly emphasized their view of free international trade and economic liberalism (Schlereth 1977: 97).[5] The experimental method of Newton and its application to moral philosophy formed the basis of the cosmopolitan ideal.

At the time List wrote his letters to Ingersoll, the idea of a cosmopolitical economy was prominent in the American policy discourse, and not the German discourse (Tribe 1995). List was being polemical in his characterization of the classical political economy. Tribe (1995: 34) suggested that use of the term "cosmopolitical" was part of "a long tradition of popular economic writing that deliberately sets itself in opposition to the assumptions and policy implications of a prevailing theoretical tradition". List made the American system of national economy more accessible to popular understanding. Shortly after his arrival in the United States in 1825, List developed his theory and policy for protection.[6] His policy proposals became part of the prevailing discourse that coincided with the presidency of John Quincy Adams (National Republican) in 1825, and Andrew Jackson (Democrat) in 1828. After he returned to Germany in the 1830s, he had developed his ideas further, but continued to use the same polemical style of reasoning. Tribe (1995: 44) claimed that it would be misleading to think of List as a German economist, as he played an active role in the American economic discourse in the Antebellum period.

## 12.3. Friedrich List and Adam Smith on technological learning

Adam Smith ([1776] 1976) began the *Wealth of Nations* by describing how the interaction between market demand and the specialization of tasks triggered innovation and economic growth. In the first three chapters, he recognized that an increasing division of labour could increase the dexterity of workers, save time lost in switching between different tasks, and lead to the invention of new methods of production and types of organization that facilitates work. Smith knew that an ever more sophisticated division of labour was the main source of productivity growth, provided that the skills of the labour force were complementary with the machinery and equipment, and that this implied an increasing heterogeneity and fragmentation of knowledge across the many different tasks, whether achieved within the same enterprise or between ones.[7] An increase in market demand, whether coming from domestic or international sources, encourages the further specialization of tasks, which then led to the creation of new differentiated knowledge. For Smith, the interaction between market demand and the specialization of tasks drives technical change and technological learning.[8]

Smith also described how machines could increase productivity through the use of new technology, such as wind or water mills, or the condensing engine. These machines, "which were the inventions of such workmen", where also used to "facilitate and quicken their own particular part of the work" Smith ([1776] 1976: 20). Smith also makes a point that scientists and engineers can also be an important source of innovation. In this context innovation appears to be science-driven in that the inventor may continue to improve on the original invention new machine, or it could be supply-driven in that the financier may facilitate the innovation process by providing necessary capital and reducing the risk. In these three chapters, Smith anticipated the concepts of induced and embodied technological change, learning by doing, and learning using, and over the course of the book, he provides the foundation for the classical theory of endogenous growth and capital accumulation.[9]

Subsequent chapters of book one were devoted to the theory of value and distribution in a competitive economy from a long-period perspective. In the classical approach, the prices of production reflect the conditions of reproduction of the economy as a whole; that is, the cost of production plus profits at an *ordinary* rate of return. They were not based purely on accounting practices as suggested by List, but on the idea that self-interested individuals would search for the most profitable opportunities and minimize the costs of production. The outcome of this process of competition and selection is a cost-minimizing system with a uniform rate of profit and uniform rates of remuneration for each particular kind of input in the process of production, such as the different kinds of labour and materials used in production (Kurz and Salvadori 1995). This process of search and selection explains movements of capital (circulating capital) and labour (or human effort) across industries in the absence of significant barriers to entry and exit.

Smith did not write explicitly on intellectual capital, but the idea was implied in his writings on dexterity and skill of the workforce. He distinguished between a new process innovation and the machinery that realizes the process, which differentiates between mental and manual labour. Smith ([1776] 1976: 118) also recognized that technological learning should result in higher than average wages, and that the expenses of education should be included "with at least the ordinary profits of an equally valuable capital". Say (1803 [1971]: 92) referred not only to the dexterity of the workforce, but also differentiates between "corporeal and intellectual" activities. In a similar way, List makes a specific point about building up productive power through the development of social and mental capital in *the American system*. In the fourth letter, List (1827: 19) asserts that the productivity of capital depends on "means afforded by nature" and "the intellectual and social conditions of nation". He attributes the capital stock to being either from nature, mind, or productive matter, and asserts that the productive powers of a nation depend mainly on the first two sorts of capital. This reference to intellectual-social capital is reminiscent of the twin conceptions of human capital and social capital, but strongly suggests that the institutional arrangements of the national economy are the main issue.[10]

List raised a specific objection to Smith's definition of capital in *National System of Political Economy*. Here he wrote,

> Adam Smith has merely taken the word capital in that sense in which it
> is necessarily taken by rentiers or merchants in their book-keeping and

their balance-sheets, namely, as the grand total of their values of exchange in contradistinction to the income accruing therefrom.[11]

(List (1841 [1991]: 181)

Smith effectively disregards the mental and bodily abilities of producers in his definition of capital.[12] List 1841 [1991]: 113) considered "the mind and capabilities of production" as a kind of fixed intellectual or mental capital that "is the result of the accumulation of all discoveries, inventions, improvements, perfections, and exertions of all generations which have lived before us". He never used the terms "intangible assets" or "intellectual capital", but they could have been synonyms. Smith was more concerned about exchange value, rather than the different component parts of productive power.[13] List believed that national wealth is created by intellectual capital.

## 12.4. Technological revolutions and the American system of innovation[14]

Friedrich List wrote his letters on *the American system* at a time when the first technological revolution was reaching maturity and steam power and railways were about to emerge as a new paradigm. Some 55 years earlier Arkwright had pioneered the first mechanical spinning machine, placing it into a Cromford water-powered mill in 1771 (Freeman and Perez 1988; Freeman and Louçã 2001; Perez 2002). Subsequent refinements in milling and spinning technologies encouraged the development of the machine tool industry. Falling prices of wrought iron and universal availability stimulated multiple applications of the "puddling" and rolling process in the iron industry. By the turn of the century, the use of wrought iron was prevalent in virtually every industry as new machinery and equipment replaced older wooden ones. Iron, raw cotton, and coal became the key inputs, or *general purpose technologies* in the production system. Improved waterwheels and the development of turnpike roads, canals, and other waterways facilitated a new transport and communications infrastructure. Labour productivity growth also began to take off in the United Kingdom, with much of it attributed to large-scale factory manufacturing with mechanized production and specialization in tasks (Von Tunzelmann 1995).

The United States was a relatively backward country when List wrote his American Letters to *The National Gazette* in 1827. But there were important signs that the United States was catching-up with the United Kingdom. During the first technological revolution the US had internalized and improved upon much of the new technology in textiles, engines, and printing transferred from the UK. There were also important improvements made to clocks, woodworking, and firearms that relied on European technology (Thomson 2009: 59). Writing about the same time as List, Alexis de

Tocqueville remarked, "no people in the world have made such rapid progress in trade and manufactures as the Americans".[15]

Steam engines based on James Watt's designs were already being used during the first technological revolution, but they were not widely adopted because of high costs and the lack of technical feasibility. The Rainhill Locomotive trials and the opening of the Liverpool–Manchester line between 1829 and 1831 marked the beginning of the second technological revolution. Innovations in the machine tool industry and in precision engineering from 1800 to 1830 made it possible to design and construct high-pressure engines. Steam made it possible to provide energy anywhere, and railways, telegraphs, transatlantic steamship navigation, and a universal postal service made it possible to network the economy. While coal and iron remained key inputs into the production system, steam-powered mechanization of industry now became the main driver of industry. Agglomeration, standard parts, construction, and steam engines and specialized machinery emerged as key inputs during this period, as did the appearance of large joint stock companies. Labour productivity rapidly increased in Britain, much of which was attributed to timesaving management and specialization in tasks within the enterprise (Von Tunzelmann 1995).

At the time List published the *National System of Political Economy* in 1841, Victorian prosperity realized low-cost coal and steam-powered transport. List's story ends in late 1846, just before a speculative frenzy in the British railway industry in the 1840s culminated in financial panic, which was followed by the 1848 revolutions in Europe and increased poverty.[16] He was writing at a time when Britain's industrial revolution was enabling its capitalist class to dominate world markets, and he understood the role that public roads, canals, and railways played in enabling the economic environment. In the years that followed his death, many countries experienced significant nationwide economies of scale, including Germany and the United States. Perhaps most importantly, List recognized the importance of steam power, machinery, machine tools, and the telegraph in facilitating technical change and technological learning. And he cofounded one of the first railways in the United States, completed in 1831, but without a locomotive until the winter of 1833 (Wendler 2015: 119).[17] List believed that new means of transport and communications were essential to each technological revolution. (Wendler 2015: 194). In *Natural System of Political Economy*, List provided a concise description of the first industrial revolution:

> Nothing is more important for industrialists than the availability of cheap fuel and also easy, speedy, and regular transport at a low cost for all the products and raw materials, which they need to build factories and to produce manufactured goods. Consequently industrialists hasten to promote the expansion of communications within a country. They foster the construction of highways, canals, and railways and the

improvement of navigable rivers. Moreover they turn these improvements into lucrative industrial undertakings.

(List 1837 [1983]: 61)

List had essentially identified what Schumpeter (1939), and Freeman and Perez (1988) would later describe as a Kondratieff Wave. Schumpeter (1939) had observed that major or radical innovations initiate a fundamental change in the way things are produced, the types of products being produced, how a firm is organized, how networks are formed, and the way people transport things and communicate.[18] Freeman and Perez (1988) identified a series of five successive technological transformations or techno-economic paradigms, each lasting between 50 and 75 years. Each paradigm is a technology system, which involves extensive changes to certain key factor industries that offer abundant supply at declining relative prices.[19] A paradigm may contain several interrelated radical breakthroughs, such as electricity and microprocessors that form a major constellation of interdependent technologies. The technologies affect the entire global economy, and are used either directly or indirectly in the production of virtually every other product. Following Schumpeter, the radical innovations underlying a technological revolution will spread far beyond the original sector and geographic location where it was first developed, creating the potential for long-term productivity growth and catching up over the course of the cycle.

There are six phases within each technology revolution Freeman and Louçã (2001). The first and last phases typically overlap as both the new and old technology systems coexist during the transition. A new technology system will begin a laboratory-invention phase, with prototypes, patents, and early applications. This phase is the gestation period of the new technology and may challenge the dominant technology system by demonstrating its feasibility and potential application to other industries. It is followed by a third phase, which is marked by significant and sometimes turbulent changes to industrial structure and the regulatory regime. In the fourth phase, stable long-term growth occurs as the new technology system asserts itself as the dominant system in the countries on the technological frontier. The technology system then enters a period of maturity, when it first experiences a slowdown and erosion of profitability and then becomes increasingly challenged by the new technologies that will drive the next technology system.

The American economy evolved in three phases since its independence, the first of which corresponds roughly to the first two technology revolutions, with the transition to the age of steel, electricity, and heavy engineering. In these years the United States was a relatively backward country that required technical change and technological learning. Initially, the United States was made up of small markets, scarce capital and labour, and limited technological knowledge, and it could not match European knowledge of crafts, machinery, or applied science (Thomson 2009: 17).

Technical knowledge was introduced from abroad, and then coupled with local technological learning. It was against this backdrop that political economists such as Alexander Hamilton, Daniel Raymond, John Rae, and Henry Carey promoted protectionist policies.[20] Entrepreneurs sought to gain access to knowledge from abroad, but they still required the "ability to recognize the value of new information, assimilate it, and apply it to commercial ends" (Cohen and Levinthal 1990). The United States would follow a relatively slow and uneven growth path during the first revolution.

Steam power and technological diffusion exemplified the United States, as Britain was moving into the second technological revolution. The application of steam engine technology was universal, but it still involved extensive learning costs to acquire it. Engine builders were organized around networks, engine users, and blacksmiths and they improved machine tools, casting, and measurement techniques from other sectors (Thomson 2009:87). American firms became increasingly adept in acquiring new knowledge and using it profitably, and they knew how to adapt it to American conditions. Successful innovation in the machine tool industry required the capability to identify, conceive, and solve technological problems, and it increasingly became dependent on local knowledge from skilled immigrants (Thomson 2009: 28).

The flexibility of steam power made it possible to provide energy anywhere, and the railroad and telegraph made it possible to create a national network that could connect the most important industrial cities, creating a truly national market (Chandler 1977). Large joint stock companies were also formed during this time, creating a need for principled management. The expansion of markets, both local and global, saw international trade rise in the second revolution, further encouraging productivity growth.[21] Although List died before the second revolution fully played out, he understood the potential that these technologies had for the United States, but he did not fully comprehend the implications this had for the agglomeration of its various markets, and its potential to become the new technological leader. At the Paris Universal Exposition of 1867, the United States had received several top awards for machine tools, steam engines, telegraphs, and locomotives, among others.

Three more technological revolutions took place in the years that followed. The discovery of electricity, inexpensive steel, and heavy chemical and civil engineering triggered the third technological revolution, which began around 1875. New industries included the electrical equipment industry, packaging, especially foods, as well as the birth of the professional research and development (R&D) laboratory. The infrastructure also became globalized, which not only included development of a worldwide telegraph and telephone network, but also the further development of shipping (steamships), railways, and great bridges and tunnels. This encouraged international trade, but economies of scale tended to be located mainly within the plant, as enterprises became larger. Motorized vehicles and oil appeared in the second half of this revolution, but became core inputs in the fourth technological revolution, which was triggered by Henry Ford when he introduced the moving assembly line in 1913 to build the Model T. This application of mass production techniques, including making use of machines and presses to stamp out parts and ensure interchangeability, led to the relative cheapness of large-scale production and the emergence of mass consumption (Hounshell 1984). Oil also became a key factor because of its abundance and declining prices. Science became a productive force in 1876 when Edison set up the first research laboratory with the specific purpose of producing a steady stream of new products for the market, including the phonograph, microphones, electric lighting, and a system for electrical distribution, as well as other goods (Israel 1998). Many other industries emerged using mass production techniques, including automotive components, tractors, aircraft, consumer durables, and synthetic materials, and to ensure that mass consumption continued, consumer credit was introduced (Freeman and Louçã 2001).

The rapid growth of the consumer markets generated large economies of scale, but it also created even larger corporations that required new ways of managing diverse operations (Chandler 1977). Speculation leading to the financial crash of 1929 and the subsequent (Great) depression triggered the global war.

A new dynamism reignited mass production and consumption after World War II. Transistors, a fundamental building block of the microprocessor, first appeared in 1947 when Bell Labs demonstrated the point-contact transistor amplifier. Over the next 13 years, Bell Labs developed several different types of transistors, mainly for the telephone, and led to the emergence of a vibrant electronics cluster in the Santa Clara (Silicon) Valley (Isaacson 2014). Then in 1971, Intel made the first commercially viable microprocessor, which made it possible to incorporate the functions of a central processing unit into a single integrated circuit. This was the event that triggered the Information and Communications Technology (ICT) revolution and what led to the development of personal computers, digital control instruments, software, and the application of integrated circuits in a wide variety of products and services. Semiconductors also made it possible to develop a global digital telecommunications network, and the internet, together with electronic mail and other e-services, emerged as a new way to communicate and network the economy. Many small entrepreneurial enterprises that emerged during the early part of this period became large corporations in a relatively short period of time, including Apple, Cisco Systems, and Microsoft. The number of transistors per integrated circuit has increased from 29,000 transistors on the Intel 8086 microprocessors introduced in the late 1970s, to over 10 billion transistors on the Intel Ice Lake 18-core CPU microarchitecture expected in 2018.

## 12.5. The national systems of political economy to national systems of innovation

Soete et al. (2010) remarked that List was "one of the first economists to recognize the crucial role of the 'systemic' interactions between science, technology and skills in the growth of nations". He was a forerunner of the German historical school of economics and he had anticipated the *national* innovation systems approach to technical change and technological learning. List 1841 [1991]: 157) begins chapter 16 of *National System*, by describing the economy as the set of "institutions, regulations, laws, and conditions on which the economy of the individual subjects of a State is dependent, and by which it is regulated". Moreover, List 1841 [1991]: 113) thought that capabilities and competencies represent the accumulated knowledge of a nation and "is productive only in the proportion" to the nation's ability "to appropriate those attainments of former generations and to increase them by its own acquirements". List 1841 [1991]: 162) also suggested that the accumulation of mental capital represents "progress over the last thousand years in sciences and arts, domestic and public regulations, cultivation of the mind and capabilities of production". Freeman (1995: 7) also included "education and training institutions, science, technical institutes, user-producer interactive learning, knowledge accumulation, adapting imported technology, promotion of strategic industries, etc."

The first use of the concept of a national system of innovation in its modern context appeared in an OECD document written by Freeman ([1982] 2004). Freeman (1987) defined the systemic methodology as "the network of institutions in the public and private sectors whose activities and interactions initiate, import, modify and diffuse new technologies".[22] It is a complex and changing network of interactions and cooperation among many different agents contributing to the innovation process that contains the flow of knowledge and technology among people, enterprises, and institutions. The institutional arrangements of the national innovation system set the rules of the game for each location, or node, within the global innovation network. These networks, the OECD (2010) contends, "govern the transfer of various types of knowledge, such as intellectual property, know-how, software code or databases, between independent parties". Innovation networks often form because enterprises need certain kinds of technical knowledge they are unable to generate themselves, but they also reflect existing relationships and network capabilities. The OECD (1997) points to evidence suggesting that the "most innovative firms are those with the ability to access outside knowledge and to link into knowledge networks, including informal contacts, user-supplier relations and technical co-operation", but they also emphasize that these firms "also need the ability to adapt the technology and knowledge to their own needs". Over the past decade the creation, use, and diffusion of new knowledge has increasingly become more of a collective endeavour, shaped by a combination of institutional arrangements and knowledge-sharing systems.

Godin (2015) identified two general perspectives in the national systems of innovation approach, one based on Lundvall (1988), which focuses on knowledge and the processes of learning, and the other based on Nelson (1993), which describes the ways that nations organize their innovation systems.[23] Lundvall (1988) developed an interactive learning perspective to innovation systems, which considers the interrelationships between actors involved in the creation and use of technical knowledge to be central to the innovation process. Recurrent interactions generate dynamic capabilities and the kind of knowledge necessary for creating new products and processes. Continuous interactive innovation necessarily involves non-market relationships of a network type. Lundvall and Johnson (1994), broadened the approach to include individual, organizational, and inter-organizational learning so that it can be more easily linked to issues related to growth and catching-up – issues that are directly relevant to the policies advocated by List. Because knowledge is different from information and learning is different from technical change, these authors suggest focusing attention on the processes by which different kinds of knowledge are created and used in the process of innovation, or what they call the "learning economy".

Nelson (1993) focuses more on the evolutionary basis of institutional change by showing how systemic differences affect the selection process and the generation of diversity. The creation of new knowledge at the firm level leads to new product variety, including incremental improvements in existing products, and an increase in uncertainty. To reduce the uncertainty, firms will develop new varieties of organization and find ways to increase its share of the market. The market then selects through competition which products the firm will offer and the methods of production it will use. Sustainable growth depends therefore on the coevolution of technology and institutions and the role given to institutions and public policy (Nelson 1994). This idea of national systems of production is considered to be at the centre of a wider set of supporting national institutions, which includes education, training, infrastructures, and networks of transportation of commodities and people.

An alternative way to think about national systems of innovation would be to take a more institutional perspective, where firms and organizations are embedded in a social structure composed of formal and informal institutions, and knowledge flows can be both tacit and codified.[24] Nation-states provide the institutional arrangement around which agents interact with one another to provide new knowledge, and utilize existing knowledge. North (1990) describes them as "the rules of the game in a society" or "the humanly devised constraints that shape human interaction". This idea is similar to the technology systems approach taken by Carlsson and Stankiewicz (1991), but it more clearly recognizes the role of the nation-state in providing the arrangements, as List 1841 [1991]), Freeman (1995) and Lundvall (1988) contend. Evolutionary economics and agent-based models (Pyka and Scharnhorst 2009) would then provide the theoretical framework for why innovation networks arise.

## 12.6. Concluding comments

This chapter tells a story about the systemic nature of national economies and how they evolved through history. List's story was partly polemical, especially in the way he presented Smith's ideas about "cosmopolitanism". Although individuals can be forward looking in a liberal society, they can be selfish and often neglect the role of the nation-state. In Smith's system, individuals were "mere producers and consumers" who "do not concern themselves for the prosperity of future generations". List believed that one should not rely on the self-regulating mechanism of the free market, but on the productive powers of the nation. This requires building "the capacity to assimilate and use all the discoveries, inventions and improvements which had been made in any part of the world *and* to improve upon them", as Freeman ([1982] 2004: 16) also stressed.

Writing in the same year as the US Declaration of Independence, Adam Smith [1776] 1976: 376) expressed deep concerned about the use of protectionist policies by the United States, but he acknowledged that the country was based on agriculture and relatively backward at the time. List 1841 [1991]) believed that this view of the United States was not very "flattering", but he knew the country was catching-up in some sectors and even taking the lead in some instances. Public policy was essential to this process. Britain was the first to use such protectionist policies, but as British technology pulled ahead, it advocated free-market and free-trade policies. List reasoned,

> It is a very common clever device that when anyone has attained the summit of greatness, he kicks away the ladder by which he has climbed up, in order to deprive others of the means of climbing up after him.[25]
>
> (List 1841 [1991]: 295)

And, "In this lies the secret of the cosmopolitical doctrine of Adam Smith".[26]

List advocated a policy of technology upgrading and the catching-up of American and German enterprises.[27] He supported the protection of infant industries, but endorsed a broad range of policies designed to accelerate economic growth and development. List also agreed that free trade is beneficial to some nations in some circumstances.[28] In his writings, List contrasted the systems of protectionism in America and Germany against the system of free trade advocated by the British. He was very sympathetic to the American tradition of promoting such policies by the early political economists, including

Alexander Hamilton. A country's capabilities and assets can be a source of competitive advantage, provided they are developed, deployed, and protected in order to maintain a competitive edge. Over time the United States developed its capacity to create, acquire, use, and transform knowledge (mental capital), and to build its productive structure (material capital).

List understood the importance of *national* industrial development and how the creation, diffusion, and assimilation of new technology can facilitate productivity growth. As Joan Robinson (1962: 124) put it more directly, "The very nature of economics is rooted in nationalism". Without it economic policy has no national purpose and direction, much the same as the literature on the developmental state might argue. List believed that having a shared national identity engenders national community. The idea of the developmental (Chang 2002) or entrepreneurial state (Mazzucato 2013) captures the kind of nationalism that closely intertwined with the imperative of technical change and technological learning. List was both a nationalist and a populist in his understanding of economic and political theory; he wrote about the nation-state and economic nationalism, and he was influential in both American and German policy discourse. Still, List was not a nationalist of the German romantic school, as he easily transformed himself into an American nationalist almost overnight, and then swiftly moved back to being German several years later (Szporluk 1988). He was a true cosmopolitan in the sense that he was a world citizen, but he did not believe that the cosmopolitical economy of Adam Smith was true political economy.

## Notes

1 Georg Friedrich List was born on 6 August 1789 in Reutlingen, Württemberg, Germany and died 30 November 1846 in Kufstein, Austria. In between he had lost his chair in political economy in Tubingen, been jailed, emigrated to the United States, settling in Pennsylvania, returned as US consul to Leipzig, and worked as an activist and pamphleteer for the new railroad companies and other causes of industrial progress. List was one of the forerunners of the German historical school.

2 Alexander Hamilton (1791) espoused the idea that the United States should become economically independent and nationally self-sufficient in all necessary goods in three reports of the Secretary of the Treasury of the United States: on Public Credit (1790); on National Bank (1790); and on Manufacturers (1791). After the War of 1812, Henry Clay (1959) called for an increase in tariffs to foster American industry, the use of federal funds to build and maintain an infrastructure (transportation network), and a national bank. Embedded in the ideas of Hamilton, Clay was the first to refer to it as the "American System".

3 List also criticized Smith for continuing the physiocratic system and neglecting the nation-state. Here List highlighted the differences between agriculture and manufacturing, but reasoned that political economy should be seen from the perspective of the nation.

4 Enlightenment cosmopolitanism continued to be a source of debate in the in the 19th and 20th centuries. Following the philosophy of Newton, Smith used the

idea of an imaginary construct to develop different counterfactuals. Kant (2006: 13) considered the cosmos to be constructed as a system, depending partly on observation, but held that it could be reliably grounded in reality. He also introduced the idea of "cosmopolitan law", which allows that both states and individuals have rights, and the possibility of being a global citizen, rather than from a particular nation.

5 Leonard (2013) suggested that the *Wealth of Nations* "is not a product of the Scottish Enlightenment but of the cosmopolitan radical Enlightenment, stretching from the coffeehouses of Rotterdam to the meeting rooms of Calcutta". Forman-Barzilai (2010) proposed using the term "commercial cosmopolitanism" to capture Smith's suggestion that there are "unintended consequences" of national self-interest.

6 List devoted the first third his book, *National System of Political Economy*, to history. There he generalizes his argument for protectionist policies by showing that Britain was the first country to use infant industry promotion.

7 List (1827: 21) remarked,

> Suppose now the ten manufacturers unite their capital and their labour, they invent a spinning machine, a more perfect weaving machine, they are instructed in the art of dyeing, they, divide the labour amongst them, and in this way they are enabled to manufacture.

List 1841 [1991]: 280) also remarks that Smith does not perceive "the effect of the division of labour as affecting a whole nation".

8 Hamilton applied Adam Smith's arguments for the diversion of labour on a national scale in his *Report on Manufactures*.

9 List suggests that Smith did not consider innovation and competence building as independent and systemic. Although Smith mentions the supply side, List 1841 [1991]: 162) argues that the specialized services of scientists are neglected: "There scarcely exits a manufacturing business which has no relation to physics, mechanics, chemistry, mathematics or to the art of design, etc."

10 Wendler (2015: 124) proposes List's intellectual-social capital to include "ambition, education, entrepreneurial spirit, exchange of ideas, patents and inventions of a nation's citizenry". See also Winch (1998).

11 Note that Sraffa (1960) believed out that Smith's approach resembled an "adding-up theory of prices".

12 In discussing the nature of services, Hill (1977) makes a distinction between services affecting persons and services affecting goods, "a service affecting a person is some change in the physical or mental condition of a person resulting from the activity of the producer unit, whereas a service affecting a good is a change in the state of some good". Smith believed that services "generally perish in the very instant of their performance", which implies the distinction between productive and unproductive labour.

13 List elaborates further on these issues in the *National System of Political Economy*, especially Chapter 31 on Adam Smith and his views of exchange value.

14 A variation of this argument is found in Knell (2010; 2013). But unlike in the previous papers, this section focuses on issues associated with building a national technological infrastructure and the American system.

15 Quoted in Thomson (2009: 59). From Alexis de Tocqueville, *Democracy in America*, 2 vols. (New York: Knopf, 1945), 2:165.

16 Reinert (2013) observed, "Contrary to the predictions of Ricardian economics, what was then called 'the social question' shattered Europe and led to revolutions in all large European countries with the exception of England and Russia".

17 List was actively involved in the management of the Little Schuylkill Navigation, Railroad and Canal Company from December 1828. His plan was to extend the short Little Schuylkill line to Reading and then to Philadelphia. This line was to be part of a comprehensive American railroad system. See also Wendler (2016).
18 The cycle does not appear smooth and continuous, but may contain many upheavals as new enterprises, industries, and technologies displace the old and mature ones, in a similar way as Schumpeter (1942) described the process of creative destruction.
19 Freeman and Louçã (2001: 146) used the term "technology system" to describe how Schumpeterian clusters are formed and the dynamic interrelatedness that develops within them.
20 Hamilton argued for subsidies to industry (to protect infant American industry) and regulation of trade with moderate tariffs (to encourage mechanization through technical change and technological learning) in the *Report on Manufactures*.
21 List (1837 [1983]: 116) remarked in the late 1830s that the United States "would be well advised to foster the establishment of joint stock companies to set up model engineering workshops for the construction of machinery".
22 Freeman (1991) also used the term "networks of innovators" to describe the kinds of networks that are most relevant to the innovation system. Innovation networks represent knowledge flows both within and between enterprises and organizations, irrespective of national borders, but they are also part of the institutional arrangements underlying the innovation system.
23 Edquist (1997: 14) provides a more general definition that includes, "all important economic, social, political, organizational, institutional and other factors that influence the development, diffusion and use of innovations".
24 This idea of knowledge fits very closely to Polanyi's (1958) distinction between tacit and codified knowledge and Nelson's (1991) distinction between generic and specific knowledge.
25 List also maintained that the German confederation of states should have engaged in protectionist countermeasures to offset the more competitive British industrial exports. Chang (2002) used this quote as the basis for his book on development strategy titled *Kicking Away the Ladder*.
26 Bhagwati (2007) also made a distinction between the national national-efficiency argument and the cosmopolitan-efficiency argument. He distinguished between free trade for oneself versus free trade for all. Bhagwati maintained that the national-efficiency case for free trade concerns national trade policies as in Adam Smith's case for free trade.
27 Wendler (2015) observed, "List wanted to open a technical research office in the USA with the purpose of determining the potential utility of American inventions and technical procedures. The project demonstrates how eager he was to promote technological progress in the German territorial states and to avail the inventions and experience of other nations".
28 John Stuart Mill believed that industries should be protected only temporarily; that is, while they are learning new technologies.

# References

Bhagwati, J. (2007), Protectionism. In D.R. Henderson, eds., *The Concise Encyclopedia of Economics*, Indianapolis: Liberty Fund.
Carlsson, B., and R. Stankiewicz (1991), On the nature, function and composition of technological systems, *Journal of Evolutionary Economics*, 1: 93–118.

Chandler, A.D., Jr. (1977), *The Visible Hand*, Cambridge: Harvard University Press.

Chang, H.-J. (2002), *Kicking Away the Ladder: Development Strategy in Historical Perspective*, London: Anthem Press.

Clarke, P.H. (2002), Unity in the influences on Adam Smith, *History of Economics Review*, 36: 10–25.

Clay, H. (1959), *The Papers of Henry Clay*, J.F. Hopkins, eds., Vol. 10, Lexington: University of Kentucky Press.

Cohen, W.M., and D.A. Levinthal (1990), Absorptive capacity: A new perspective on learning and innovation, *Administrative Science Quarterly*, 35: 128–152.

Edquist, C., ed. (1997), *Systems of Innovation: Technologies, Institutions and Organizations*, London: Pinter.

Forman-Barzilai, F. (2010), *Adam Smith and the Circles of Sympathy: Cosmopolitanism and Moral Theory*, Cambridge: Cambridge University Press.

Freeman, C. ([1982] 2004), Technological infrastructure and international competitiveness, *Industrial and Corporate Change*, 13: 540–552.

Freeman, C. (1987), *Technology Policy and Economic Performance: Lessons from Japan*, London: Pinter.

Freeman, C. (1991), Networks of innovators: A synthesis of research issues, *Research Policy*, 20: 499–514.

Freeman, C. (1995), The "national system of innovation" in historical perspective, *Cambridge Journal of Economics*, 19: 5–24.

Freeman, C., J. Clark, and L. Soete (1982), *Unemployment and Technical Innovation: A Study of Long Waves and Economic Development*, London: Pinter.

Freeman, C., and F. Louçã (2001), *As Time Goes by. From the Industrial Revolutions to the Information Revolution*, Oxford: Oxford University Press.

Freeman, C., and C. Perez (1988), Structural crisis of adjustment, business cycles and investment behavior. In G. Dosi, C. Freeman, R. Nelson, G. Silverberg, and L. Soete, eds., *Technical Change and Economic Theory*, London: Pinter, pp. 38–66.

Godin, B. (2015), *Innovation Contested: The Idea of Innovation Over the Centuries*, London: Routledge.

Hamilton, A. (1791), Alexander Hamilton's Final Version of the Report on the Subject of Manufactures, [5 December 1791]. In H.C. Syrett, ed., *The Papers of Alexander Hamilton*, vol. 10, December 1791 – January 1792, New York: Columbia University Press, 1966, pp. 230–340.

Henderson, W.O. (1983), *Friedrich List: Economist and Visionary 1789–1846*, London: Routledge.

Hill, T.P. (1977), On goods and services, *Review of Income and Wealth*, 23: 315–339.

Hounshell, D.A. (1984), *From the American System to Mass Production, 1800 to 1932*, Baltimore: Johns Hopkins University Press.

Isaacson, W. (2014), *The Innovators*, New York: Simon and Schuster.

Isreal P. (1998), *Edison: A Life of Invention*, New York: John Wiley and Sons.

Kant, I. (2006), *Toward Perpetual Peace and Other Writings on Politics, Peace, and History*, New Haven: Yale University Press.

Knell, M. (2010), Nanotechnology and the sixth technological revolution. In S.E. Cozzens & J. Wetmore, eds., *The Yearbook of Nanotechnology in Society*, Vol. 2, New York: Springer, pp. 127–143.

Knell, M. (2013), Multi-source energy networks and the ICT revolution, *European Planning Studies*, 21: 1838–1852.

Kurz, H.D., and N. Salvadori (1995), *Theory of Production. A Long-Period Analysis*, Cambridge: Cambridge University Press.

Leonard, S.A. (2013), Adam Smith, revolutionary, *Platypus Review*, 61: November.

List, F. (1827), *Outlines of American Political Economy*, Philadelphia: Samuel Parker.

List, F. (1837 [1983]), *The Natural System of Political Economy*, Translated and edited by W.O. Henderson, London: Frank Cass.

List, F. (1841 [1991]), *The National System of Political Economy*, Translated by Sampson S. Lloyd, New Jersey: Augustus M. Kelley.

Lundvall, B.-Å. (1988), Innovation as an interactive process: From user-producer interaction to the national innovation systems. In G. Dosi, C. Freeman, R.R. Nelson, G. Silverberg, and L. Soete, eds., *Technical Change and Economic Theory*, London: Pinter.

Lundvall, B.-Å., and B. Johnson (1994), The learning economy, *Journal of Industry Studies*, 1: 23–42.

Mazzucato, M. (2013), *The Entrepreneurial State: Debunking the Public vs. Private Myth in Risk and Innovation*, London: Anthem Press.

Nelson, R.R. (1991), Why do firms differ and how does it matter? *Strategic Management Journal*, 12: 61–74.

Nelson, R.R., ed. (1993), *National Innovation Systems: A Comparative Analysis*, Oxford: Oxford University Press.

Nelson, R.R. (1994), Economic growth via the coevolution of technology and institutions. In L. Leydesdorff and P. Van Den Besselarr, eds., *Evolutinary Economics and Chaos Theory*, London: Pinter.

North, D. (1990), *Institutions, Institutional Change and Economic Performance*, Cambridge: Cambridge University Press.

OECD. (1997), *National Innovation Systems*, Paris: OECD.

OECD. (2010), *The OECD Innovation Strategy: Getting a Head Start on Tomorrow*, Paris: OECD.

Perez, C. (2002), *Technological Revolutions and Finance Capital: The Dynamics of Bubbles and Golden Ages*, Cheltenham: Edward Elgar.

Polanyi, M. (1958), *Personal Knowledge*, Chicago: University of Chicago Press.

Pyka, A. and A. Scharnhorst, eds. (2009), *Innovation Networks, New Approaches in Modelling and Analyzing*, Heidelberg: Springer Verlag.

Reinert, E.S. (2013), Primitivization of the EU periphery: The loss of relevant knowledge, Working Papers in Technology Governance and Economic Dynamics no. 48.

Robinson, J. (1962), *Economic Philosophy*, London: C.A. Watts.

Say, J.B. (1803 [1971]), *Traité d'économie politique, ou simple exposition de la manière dont se forment, se distribuent, et se composent les richesses* (English translation: A treatise on political economy, or the production, distribution and consumption of wealth), New York: A.M. Kelley.

Schlereth, T.J. (1977), *The Cosmopolitan Ideal in Enlightenment Thought: Its Form and Function in the ideas of Franklin, Hume, and Voltaire, 1694–1790*, London: University of Notre Dame Press.

Schumpeter, J.A. (1939), *Business Cycles: A Theoretical, Historical, and Statistical Analysis of the Capitalist Process*, New York: McGraw-Hill.

Schumpeter, J.A. (1942), *Capitalism, Socialism and Democracy*, New York: Harper and Row.

Smith, A. ([1776] 1976), An inquiry into the nature and causes of the wealth of nations. In R.H. Campbell and A.S. Skinner, eds., *Glasgow Edition of the Works and Correspondence of Adam Smith*, Oxford: Oxford University Press.

Soete, L., B. Verspagen, and B.R. Weel (2010), Systems of innovation. In B.H. Hall and N. Rosenberg, eds., *Handbook of the Economics of Innovation*, Vol. 2, Amsterdam: North-Holland, pp. 1159–1180.

Sraffa, P. (1960), *Production of Commodities By Means of Commodities. Prelude to a Critique of Economic Theory*, Cambridge: Cambridge University Press.

Szporluk, R. (1988), *Communism and Nationalism: Karl Marx versus Friedrich List*, Oxford: Oxford University Press.

Thomson, R. (2009), *Structures of Change in the Mechanical Age: Technological Innovation in the United States 1790–1865*, Baltimore: Johns Hopkins University Press.

Tribe, K. (1995), *Strategies of Economic Order German Economic Discourse, 1750–1950*, Cambridge: Cambridge University Press.

Von Tunzelmann, G.N. (1995), *Technology and Industrial Progress: The Foundations of Economic Growth*, Cheltenham: Edward Elgar.

Wendler, E. (2015), *Friedrich List (1789–1846): A Visionary Economist with Social Responsibility*, Heidelberg: Springer.

Wendler, E. (2016), *Friedrich List's Exile in the United States New Findings*, Heidelberg: Springer.

Winch, C. (1998), Two rival conceptions of vocational education: Adam Smith and Friedrich List, *Oxford Review of Education*, 24: 365–378.

# 13  List and Russia

*Vladimir Avtonomov and Elizaveta Burina*

## 13.1. Which aspects of List's works were used by his Russian colleagues

The history of List's reception in Russia resembles the history of Russia itself. It went through great changes following radical reforms not only in Russian foreign trade policy but also in the Russian economic and political systems. We can also conclude that there are different aspects to List's ideas that came to the fore in different periods of Russian history. List faced the Russian public in four main qualities:

1) as a prophet of industry, railways and manufacturing capitalism in general;
2) as a protectionist in foreign trade;
3) as a non-materialist underlining the importance of cultural and mental productive forces; and
4) as a staunch nationalist, caring only about the geopolitical interests of Germany.

But there is another capacity in which List was not and still is not received in Russia. This is List as a political liberal. He received his republican ideals in his native, old imperial, city of Reutlingen, which lost its independence and democratic institutions only in 1802,[1] and then learnt them in Tübingen as a law student (Montesquieu and his ideal of separation and division of powers was probably the main influence he encountered at the university). Democratic institutions plus the basic rights of man: physical freedom, the right to equality, the right to develop and use one's own mental capacity, the right to private property, to physical integrity, to the recognition of human dignity were a very important component of productive forces – his main theoretical concept. But this component was easily overlooked by his Russian admirers. The only person who mentioned List's ideas of civil liberties was Sergey Witte but, as we'll see, his position did not coincide with List's.

## 13.2. List's predecessors in Russia

The topic "List and Russia" is not limited to the reception of List's ideas by Russian readers. First, List used Russia as one of his historical examples of the benefits of the return to protectionist tariffs in 1822, after the short period of free-trade policy inspired by Heinrich Storch's ideas after the Napoleonic wars (from 1819). This rapid change could be a good example for German states. At the same time as stressing the positive results of newly introduced tariffs, List used the opportunity to warn Russia about future barriers that the country will face on the way to progress: serfdom, and a lack of reasonable municipal institutions, education and transportation means.

Russian foreign trade policy during the 19th century underwent several radical changes. Since 1793, Russia had prohibitive tariffs against revolutionary France, and also against some English industrial goods. Thereafter, under the influence of Smith, Say and Storch, liberal tariffs were introduced in 1819. Since the late 1820s, foreign trade affairs had depended on the protectionist views of Mordvinov and Kankrin. A relatively liberal policy was imposed on Russia after the defeat in the Crimea war, in 1857–1868, but after 1882, as Nikolay Bunge became a minister of finance, the decisive turn to protectionism occurred. In 1891 the protectionist tariff was introduced by minister of finance Vyshnegradsky.

The second issue connecting List with Russia, even before the publication of the "National System" is connected with the figure of Admiral Count Nikolay Mordvinov. Russian historians of economic thought, beginning probably with Tugan-Baranovsky in 1898 (Pokidchenko, Kalmychkova 2003: 257), tend to find parallels between Friedrich List and the Russian Navy Minister. They called Mordvinov the "Russian List" and underlined the fact that Mordvinov preceded List by a quarter of a century. The parallels are really impressive, though Mordvinov never expressed his views in a systematic scientific manner and wrote mostly notes for Russian Tsars Alexander I and Nicholas I.[2] List, on the other hand, deduced his protectionist policy from his theory of productive forces (Zweynert 2008b: 105) (though the theory was not of the Ricardian kind, of course). But the very fact that this comparison is repeated many times proves that List's name was popular among Russian economists at the end of the 19th century. In fact, Mordvinov was a follower of British economists and philosophers Smith and Bentham, and at the same time supported protectionism for young industries and fought against the liberal tariffs introduced in Russia in 1819. He resembled List also in other respects. He wrote that freedom, enlightenment, property and law are the only sources of a nation's wealth. He opposed the liberation of serfs in Russia as an untimely measure, but so too did List when he recommended a gradual liberation of slaves in America (Zweynert 2008b: 103). Thus, Mordvinov was liberal, protectionist and pragmatic, and these qualities remind us of List. The "Russian List" wrote about the necessity of railroad construction in Russia and advised financing it from the state military budget (Bogomazov and Blagikh 2010: 260).

He emphasized the prior importance of the industrial sector as well as List did, and explained the economic backwardness of Russia with reference to excessive specialization in the production of agricultural goods.

It is highly improbable that List was influenced by the "Russian List" Mordvinov. However, in the case of the other great Russian economist Heinrich (Andrey) von Storch, who was German by nationality and wrote in French, the influence can be asserted with great certainty. The central element of List's thought, i.e. the theory of productive forces, was in all likelihood formed under the influence of Storch's concept of non-material internal goods, which are required for material well-being.[3] Nevertheless, List's political conclusions were completely opposite to Storch's, as the latter was a free-trader.

Another connection between List and Russia is personified by Count Yegor (Georg) Cancrin, who was the Russian minister of finance from 1823 to 1844 and wrote some partly theoretical books. He introduced the silver rouble as the national currency, which was considered his main achievement. He was a protectionist (and was mentioned approvingly by List in "National System") but not on the same grounds as List – he wanted to keep Russia isolated from the dangers of economic and social crises in Europe. The causes of the latter Cancrin saw in industrial development, railroad construction and joint-stock companies, and he tried to prevent such phenomena in Russia. In general, his views were radically different from those of List, but he was impressed by List's protectionist position and cited him in his main book, *Die Oekonomie der menschlichen Gesellschaften und das Finanzwesen: von einem ehemaligen Finanzminister [Graf Georg Cancrin]* published in 1845 in Stuttgart (Zweynert 2008b: 165–166). He was probably the sole admirer of List in Russia, liking protectionism but not accepting the need for industrialization. However, it is well-known that in 1843 Cancrin met List in Munich, and after a long (five-hour) conversation invited him to Russia, promising him an important position (Wendler 2015: 475). But soon thereafter Cancrin died and the invitation was not enacted.

## 13.3. The first reactions on "The National System" in Russia

One of the first Russian reactions to List was that of Stepan Maslov (1793–1879), the founder of the Imperial Moscow Agricultural Society and the editor of *Agricultural Journal*. Maslov was a famous figure in the realm of agriculture and practically introduced the sugar-producing industry in Russia. In one of the issues of the *Agricultural Journal* in 1852, Maslov reviewed List's "National System" and his speech at the congress of German agricultural and forestry economists, which had taken place ten years previously and where Maslov had attended as a guest. It was a lengthy (38 pages) and, as far as we can judge, laudatory review. (Wendler 1996: 477).

Some ideas of Friedrich List, more precisely the idealist, ethical non-materialist components, were attractive to Russian thinkers of the Slavophile direction and considered as a part of the German historical school which became popular in Russia (especially in the 1870s and 1880s). In the 1850s the ideas of Friedrich List and the older German historical school made their way to Russia (Zweynert 2008a: 58). The influence of the German romantics (first of all, the natural philosophy of Schelling) may have contributed to this similarity. The majority of Russian Slavophiles were not interested in economic problems but Yuri Samarin, who was the best educated in political economy among them, quoted List's "National System Of Political Economy" in support of his argument for inherent diversity of national economic institutions (Avtonomov, Gloveli 2015: 186). Samarin referred to List in polemics on Russian *obshchina*, stressing the incorrect transfer of individual fairness and utility to social and national issues. Moreover he considered List's "National System of Political Economy" as a possible foundation of a methodologically alternative approach to economic science.[4]

The first Russian historian of political economy worth mentioning, Ivan Vernadsky, mentioned List in his essay on the history of political economy[5] in an unusual context. He divided the economic science into two main directions: positive and negative. The first was characterized by the recognition of the important role of the state in economic development, and included mercantilism, protectionism and socialism. The second relied on natural laws of development, proposed the limitation of state interference in economic life and included physiocracy and the school of Smith. Vernadsky himself was a follower of the negative branch and characterized so-called "protectionism" including List, of course, as an attempt (albeit a failed one) to find a compromise between these directions (Zweynert 2008a: 152).

The German historical school was rather popular in Russia in the second half of the 19th century (Avtonomov, Gloveli 2015: 201). Friedrich List was generally recognized as a forerunner, if not the founder, of the historical school and treated accordingly. Alexander Chuprov, who was the leading Russian economist in 1870–1880,[6] studied in Leipzig and Vienna and later received the chair of political economy at Moscow university. He gave List a favorable estimation in his "History of Political Economy" published in 1892. Chuprov's views in economics were rather eclectic, but he appreciated List's ideas about the nation as an integer organism and an intermediary between individuals and humankind. It is interesting to mention that Chuprov, as well as List, was a great enthusiast of railways and was a member of the Russian Special Higher Commission on Railways, which developed a "Statute of Russian Railways" and acquired private railways for state ownership (Avtonomov, Gloveli 2015: 190). Describing productive forces in agriculture, manufacturing and trade Chuprov, like other Russian admirers of List, did not mention productive forces connected with democratic freedoms.

## 13.4. Sergey Witte, List's main Russian follower

The most outspoken Listian in Russia was beyond any doubt Sergey Witte, railway engineer and administrator, subsequently the minister of finance and the prime minister of Russia. Witte's position might be characterized as liberal and nationalist. The acquaintance with List's "National System" changed his worldview, which was previously Slavophile. At that former stage, Witte regarded capitalism as a danger for social order and the state of the working classes. Witte published his first brochure about List, titled "National Economy and Friedrich List," in 1889, two years before the Russian translation of "National System of Political Economy" appeared. In fact, Witte wrote the brochure to make Russian audiences who could not read German familiar with List's ideas, and, therefore, he followed the German author very closely and in detail. The pages-long citations of List are separated with very short comments which fulfill three main tasks:

1) to show that List's ideas were followed in Bismarck's policy and eventually led to the prosperity of the German nation;
2) to warn the Russian public that everything List wrote about Germany in its relations with England could be equally said after 50 years about Russia in its relations with Germany; and
3) to express his view of the "positive" nationalism and distinguish it from the "egoistic" one[7] (nationalism was not considered as an undoubted evil by List and by Witte).

Thus, the brochure served not as an independent investigation of Witte but as a means to convey List's ideas. Therefore, it is probably interesting to see which aspects of List's book Witte left out and did not mention. Being not an academic economist, Witte, nevertheless, underlined the main logic of List's work: the concepts of stages, the notion of productive forces and the implementation of a policy that leads to the achievement of the highest stage through protection of infant industries. This logical sequence was reproduced very closely by Witte. The principal methodological opposition between Smith's theory of exchange values and List's theory of productive forces was also presented very persuasively. One could think that Witte was a professional theorist, not an engineer and applied economist. The omitted chapters dealt with the relation of manufacturing industries to agriculture, trade, navigation, natural productive forces and progress in general. They were parts of the "triumphant song of commodity production" that Struve mentioned in his book (Struve [1894] 2015: 124). Apparently, for Witte, these points were self-evident. The same could be said about the last chapters, devoted to tariff policy itself.

Witte was at that time at the very beginning of his skyrocketing career, which brought him to the second post in the country after the Tsar. He was a high-ranked railroad administrator and no more. Being the minister of finance from 1892 to 1903, Witte pursued an active and largely successful policy based on industry development and railroad construction, supported by the government and using foreign capital (attracted by a strong rouble convertible into gold). We could suppose that Friedrich List would have approved of the policy of his follower. Witte's use of protectionist measures was not extremist. He even lowered somewhat the protectionist tariff introduced by his predecessor Vyshnegradsky. His most "Listian" measures of economic policy were connected to the enormous scope of his railroad-building (including the famous Transsiberian line) with the decisive participation of the state (two-thirds of Russian railroads were transferred into state ownership). He opened new sources of capital (including foreign ones) for industrial enterprises, and created a system of technological and commercial education in Russia. It must be mentioned that under the rule of Witte the Russian Ministry of Finance was responsible for the development of transport, education, commercial credit and other things. For all these activities the super-ministry had a large budget, a substantial portion of which consisted of revenues from alcohol sales. Witte made this important source of income a government monopoly.

Witte accepted nearly all the facets of List's system except one of most important ones – political liberalism and republicanism. In one of his notes sent to the Tsar, Witte wrote about constitution in general being "the greatest lie of our time" and completely inapplicable to Russia with its multiethnicity (Bogomazov, Blagikh 2010: 286). In fact, he believed in the combination of absolute monarchy and enlightened bureaucracy, which could guarantee a considerable individual freedom. But over the course of time Witte remained a staunch monarchist and wrote the Royal Manifest of 1905, which was actually the first Russian Constitution.

Being the minister of finance, Sergey Witte was also responsible for the economic education of the Tsar's brother Grand Duke Mikhail, the heir to the Russian throne before the birth of Prince Alexey.[8] Witte's lectures on economics were delivered in 1900–1902. Almost at the same time, Carl Menger was educating Kronprinz Rudolph – the heir to the Austrian throne. The comparison of these two royal teachers is interesting: Menger was an academic scholar who made his name with a theoretical treaty. Witte was the acting minister of finance, a professional engineer with no education in social sciences (Menger graduated from the law faculty). We can probably make some conclusions about the relative importance of academic social sciences in both countries. The subjects that Witte had to explain to the Grand Duke were economic theory and state finance (*Volkswirtschaft und Staatswirtschaft*). But they were taught more from a practical than a theoretical point of view and abounded in references to contemporary Russian practice. According to some sources, Witte was not the immediate author of the course, which was written by his secretary Guriev, professor Ivanyukov and professor Brezhsky. But he delivered all the lectures himself and definitely had full responsibility for their content.

There was no room for such Listian favourite themes as productive forces and, certainly, democratic institutions in Witte's course. But lecture XVIII, which deals with foreign trade, corresponding theory and protectionist policy, contains the immediate discussion of List's work and Bismarck's policy. List is discussed in the context of one-sidedness of mercantilism and physiocracy. Then the time comes to discuss Smith's arguments for free-trade, which are strong theoretical theses but *inapplicable to concrete countries.* Smith's theory served the interests of England because it persuaded less-developed countries of the benefits of free trade. But in general Smith's ideas about the benefits of free trade were untimely. List introduced the theory of the national development of each country consisting of stages, with protectionist trade policy being important for achieving the highest stage of commercial-industrialism. List, according to Witte, established the connection between protectionism and nationalism, which was historically proved by the German and Italian states. Bismarck was considered by Witte as a true follower of List except on one point – he spread protectionism also to agriculture, which went against List's standpoint. The Russian protectionist policy introduced under Alexander III by Bunge and Vyshnegradsky was highly praised. In the same course of lectures Witte clearly expressed his view of the wise policy concerning foreign capital. He mentioned that Russia had always suffered from the lack of its own funds due to a number of historical events. What made the country raise its head was attracted foreign capital. In lecture XIII, Witte claimed that Russia, as a country facing economic backwardness, should plant and develop its own manufacturing industry through protectionist policies, and accelerate this process using the capitals of countries that were historically ahead of Russia (Witte 1912: 139).

The second edition of Witte's brochure about List, with a changed name, "On The Question of Nationalism. National Economy and Friedrich List" was published in 1912 (20 years after the first edition). Why at that time and why the changed title? By that time protectionism had asserted itself worldwide and made some nations (first of all, Germany and Russia) relatively stronger. Witte, who looked back at the period when he was actually ruling the country and experienced sharp criticism from various circles, deliberated about healthy and sick nationalism. He characterized List and Bismarck (and implicitly himself) as representatives of healthy nationalism – self-conscious and led by reason. The other current, nationalism led by feelings (for instance revenge) and not by reason, was represented in Witte's brochure by the Turkish Sultan Abdul Hamid but, apparently, he had some influential Russians in mind.

About the same time, in 1892, List's ideas were actively used by the famous Russian scientist Dmitry Mendeleev, who besides his works in fundamental and applied chemistry could be considered one of the leading applied economists in Russia of his time. His ideas were vital for the development of Russian oil-producing and coal mining industries together with the means of transportation accommodated for them. He also proposed industrial development as the principal means of improving Russian agriculture. The protectionist tariff of 1891 was considered by Mendeleev as an adequate policy to promote the national productive forces. As we may see, these ideas fully correspond to List's, and Mendeleev wrote about it explicitly. In his work "The Sound Tariff," which was considered by his contemporaries as "the Bible of Russian protectionism" (Antonov 2008: 266), Mendeleev appeals to follow List and rename the political economy "national economy." The transition from the former to the latter, according to him, will be equal to the transition of algebra and geometry to mechanics (List 2005: 310). As an example of the abstract political economy, Mendeleev refers to "Der isolierte Staat" by Thünen. The jump from individuals to humanity omitting nations is an erroneous way of economic reasoning, especially when trade tariffs are discussed (List 2005: 308). Mendeleev and Witte had similar ideas and collaborated in the work on Russian industrial development, but they had some differences regarding Russian "*obshchina*," which Mendeleev considered survivable.

## 13.5. The perception of List in the context of spreading Marxism

Pyotr (Peter) Struve combined nationalism and liberalism in a manner that resembled Friedrich List. He was one of the important participants of the discussion about the fate of capitalism in Russia, which was the main topic in Russian society in the 1880s and 1890s. After the great reforms of 1861 the agricultural land was divided into two roughly equal parts. The first was given to the nobility as private property and was nominally considered the capitalistic sector. The second was given to the peasants as collective property, where the land could be redistributed by the commune itself. This part was considered as the sector of people's production. The economic results of the people's sector proved to be bad, but for the capitalist sector they were disastrous. A lot of noblemen used their lands as collateral for obtaining loans, which they spent primarily for consumer purposes. The government did not want the nobility, its main political support, to lose its economic roots. So it organized a special bank and adopted some other measures of dubious effectiveness. The agricultural output from this part of Russian lands decreased significantly, which was regarded as a proof of the inferiority and inefficiency of capitalist production. At the same time, the people's part was overpopulated (about 90% of the Russian population were peasants) and poor.

In industry the real capitalist sector developed rapidly and drove the domestic industries of peasant households out of the market, which made their situation even more dangerous. The leading radical advocates of people's production (Vorontsov and Danielson) argued for government financial support for peasants, which could arguably strengthen their position. Struve, at that time one of the first Russian Marxists, published in 1894 the book *Critical Notes on Economic Development of Russia* (the book included six articles published previously in the German press) where he countered the view of the populists and argued for the inevitability and temporary benefits of capitalist development in Russia (having in mind the final transition to socialism). The book ended with an appeal to Russians to acknowledge the lack of culture and go through the school of capitalism. In a sense Struve was a more consistent Marxist than Marx himself, who had changed his view about Russia under the influence of Chernyshevsky and started to believe that this country could avoid the capitalist stage in its development.

The real solution for Russian economic problems, according to Struve, was a rapid industrialization that could attract the agrarian population to cities and create additional demand for agricultural production. Here he found strong support not only in Marx's writings (first of all, "The Communist Manifesto") but also in List's eulogies for industrialization and his idea of transforming an agrarian state into an agro-industrial one. In Russia of that time, the Ministry of Home Affairs was responsible for the support of agriculture whereas the Ministry of Finance (headed by Bunge, Vyshnegradsky and Witte) advocated the interests of industry. So Struve and Witte happened to be on the same side of the debate. The most important thing which Struve found in List's "National System" he expressed as follows: "I don't know any other book that argues so persuasively for historical inevitability and necessity of capitalism in the wide sense of the word" (Struve [1894] 2015: 123). An interesting point was Struve's comparison of the main works of Ricardo, Marx and List. Ricardo's principles, being a deep abstract analysis of the capitalist system as it was present in England at the beginning of the 19th century, struck the reader with their business-like objectivity, dryness and narrowness. The reader was offered neither a broad historical view nor a social-political viewpoint. Marx's "Das Kapital," giving a further theoretical development and deepening of Ricardo's ideas, offered simultaneously a broad historical picture and social-political blemishing of the capitalist system. List's "National System" was "a victorious song of the triumphant commodity production proclaiming its cultural and historical power and the victorious march in all nations" (Struve [1894] 2015: 124). Well, a song, even a victorious one, is not a theory, so this comparison could be considered as rather looking down on List, but we must remember that the main task of Struve in his *Critical Notes* was to prove the inevitability and necessity of capitalism in Russia.

Sergey Bulgakov, first a Marxist and then an orthodox priest, in his "History of Economic and Social Doctrines" estimated List's contribution with remarkable sympathy:

> Nowadays the notion of productive forces and the development of production are so tightly connected with the doctrine of Marx and his school that we forget that Friedrich List was the first who expressed this idea. His notion of productive forces was fuller, richer and more fruitful than the Marxian one. Marx treated them as material exchange values, as products more than forces.
>
> (Bulgakov 2007: 353)

Bulgakov appreciated also List's protectionist ideas, saying that at the present time these ideas of List were so universally accepted that free trade was supported only as specific means in specific circumstances and not as a universal principle of economic policy (Bulgakov 2007: 354).

Another merit of List's, according to Bulgakov, is that he led the political economy out of the deadlock where it was put by Smith's distinction of productive and unproductive labor. Bulgakov lectured in the history of political economy at Moscow Commercial Institute in 1910–1917 after his conversion to idealism and Christian orthodoxy. In the same period he published "The Philosophy of the Economy" and other works, which are more like theological treaties than economic ones. It is understandable that he sympathized with List's approach and his critique of Smith's materialist doctrine. His fragment on Friedrich List finishes as follows: "List is the founder of historical political economy. He consciously and obviously puts the problems of economic life on the historical foundation and this determines his place in the history of political economy" (Bulgakov 2007: 356).

So, summing up, we should state that for Samarin, Chuprov and Bulgakov, List represented the national and anti-cosmopolitan political economy of the historical school; for Struve and Witte, he was a herald of European capitalism; and for Cancrin, a pure protectionist.

## 13.6. Attitudes towards List in Soviet Russia

During the Soviet era, List was treated in two main ways:

1) as a "vulgar economist," representing the ideological position of industrial bourgeoisie and actually eliminating the theoretical tasks of political economy (Karataev 1963: 120); and
2) as a German nationalist in a geopolitical context (Rumyantsev 1973: 358).

The Soviet publications about List could be interesting not only as manifestations of the Soviet reception of List, but as examples of the Soviet quasi-scientific discipline called the "Critique of bourgeois economic thought." Soviet readers were not allowed or supposed to read the works of bourgeois economists themselves; they had to trust professional "critics of bourgeois economic thought" who usually did not offer the content of the criticized theories (this was called "objectivism" and considered a serious ideological failure), but limited their remarks to critical theses which sometimes had little or nothing in common with the works in question. Two main attributes of "bourgeois economic doctrines" assigned by Soviet historians and critics were "vulgar" and "apologetic." Marx, in Volume I of "Das Kapital," presented, as he thought, the essential categories of the political economy of capitalism: value as wholly determined by labor inputs, value of labor force as the value of subsistence means, surplus value as a product of unpaid labor only, the result of deduction of the value of labor force from the whole value of a commodity and so on. These essential categories could be discovered only by a theoretical investigation because they were not encountered in real economic life. There we can find only the transformations of the essential categories: price, wage, profit and so on. So the economists who operate only with the later categories just touch the surface of economic life and handle it from the point of view of economic agents. Accordingly, the evolution of economic thought was represented as going uphill from Petty to Ricardo, elaborating the labor theory of value. Then came "Das Kapital" at the summit. After the essence of economic phenomena was discovered by Marx, any further developments could be considered a vulgarization of political economy.

The term "apologetic" indicated that the economists in question represented the interests of a certain class (bourgeoisie or petit-bourgeoisie), which did not allow them to be truly scientific. A good example of such a literature could be an article in a provincial scientific journal published in the city of Vyatka (later renamed as Kirov) in 1927 (Tanayevsky 1927):

- "Class sympathies of List as *an ideologist of industrial bourgeoisie* could not lead him to a correct evaluation of facts of economic history"; and
- "Using as a foundation of his economic system false conception of productive forces, List could not correctly evaluate economic phenomena, and gave perverted explanations of some economic factors, which contradicted objective situation and *the true essence* of these phenomena" (Tanaevsky 1927: 66).

The article in question is not completely hopeless (in 1927 a certain degree of objectivity was still allowed). The author names some real features of List's theoretical system; for instance, his attempts "to eliminate the theory of value from political economy and solve all essential problems of economic science from the standpoint of his theory of productive forces" (ibid: 70). But at the same time, Comrade Tanayevsky makes serious errors in his analysis. He declares that List understood under productive forces *only* non-material factors (ibid: 73) and incriminates him for "ignoring of primacy of production characteristic for a bourgeois economist" (ibid: 77). It is clear that the author presupposed that his reader could never verify his claims.

Attitudes towards List in Soviet Russia were largely the result of Marx's view of List's ideas. One can easily reveal the connection, having read an article, published in 1971 in the "Issues of CPSU (Communist Party of Soviet Union) History" (Marx 1971). The article is claimed to be a reproduction of Marx's manuscript, sent to the Soviet Institute of Marxism and Leninism by Marx's great-grandson. However, there were missed pages in the manuscript, and it is hard to distinguish words written by Marx himself from those added by Soviet publishers. Nevertheless, the article reflects the reasons for the critical reception of List's ideas in Russia during the heyday of the Soviet regime.

The introduction to the article is especially valuable, as it sets the tone for the subsequent narrative. The Soviet reader discovers that "both Marx and Engels felt it necessary to criticize List's book, which became a manifesto of the perking German bourgeoisie, striving for wealth and domination" (Marx 1971: 3).

Marx criticized List for his ideological, theoretical and ethical position. There is no doubt that the most dangerous, in Marx's opinion, was the ideological delusion, demonstrated in List's book. According to Marx, Friedrich List was none other than a mere bourgeois, dreaming of wealth. At the same time he tried to "justify" his materialistic goal. Marx states that "the German bourgeois begins his creation of wealth with the creation of a sentimentally pompous, hypocritically idealizing political economy." This "new political economy," based on the theory of productive forces (*Produktivkräfte*), allows the German protectionist to acquit government intervention. In fact, List recognized only protective duties, the measure which helped the German bourgeois to reach his goal, namely wealth and domination (Marx 1971: 11).

Further Marx describes the controversy of List's ideas. The only thing that the German bourgeois desires is to get rich; however, this contradicts the German idealism and "his own conscience." Marx concludes that the German bourgeois, represented by List, "tries to prove that instead of nasty, finite exchange values, he strives for a spiritual essence, an infinite productive force" (Ibid). Therefore, Marx discovers that for List the theory of productive forces was just a means to reconcile his materialistic views with the ideology of idealism that prevailed in German society.

According to Marx, the main theoretical mistake made by List, was the confusion of the two concepts: material goods and exchange values. Thus, Marx recommends List to "realize that the transformation of material goods into exchange values is the product of the existing social system, the society of developed private property" (Marx 1971: 14). Eventually, Marx stated that List was not familiar with the ideas of so-called classical school, yet he managed to criticize these ideas. That was another argument about the controversy of List's doctrine presented by Marx.

Then Marx proceeds to List's nationalistic views. According to his point of view, List wants to be an exploiter within the country without being exploited outside the country. Actually, Marx makes fun of List, claiming that the latter "turns into a 'nation' and says: I do not submit myself to the laws of competition, this is contrary to my national dignity; as a nation I am a being towering above the haggling." As for Marx, there is no other nationality for a worker than labor and free slavery; there is no other government for a worker than capital; there is no other air for a worker than factory air (Marx 1971: 15).

Probably the first attempt to evaluate List's work and his personality in a more balanced way in the Soviet era was made by Andrey Anikin, the author of the best Soviet history of economic thought written for younger learners, in a spirit which resembled Robert Heilbroner's "Worldly Philosophers." Since the second edition this popular book has included a chapter on Friedrich List (Anikin 1975: 323–333) with a biography and analysis of his ideas that almost avoids Soviet ideological clichés.

## 13.7. List's comeback in post-Soviet Russia

This general situation changed only under Gorbachev's *perestroika* that introduced the freedom of speech and abolished the theoretical monopoly of dogmatic Marxism. But the time for List's revival did not come at once. Initial favourites of the Russian public were Hayek, Mises and other market fundamentalists. However, in 1992 Witte's brochure "National Economy and Friedrich List" was republished in the leading Russian economic journal *Voprosy Ekonomiki* [The issues of Economics] (no. 2) under the heading "Browsing old editions" with a benevolent introduction supporting both the antimaterialistic aspects of List's productive forces theory and his support of national industry as an alternative to exporting raw materials, which was found by the author (A. Kryukova) to be very important. Kryukova added one more important aspect – List's struggle for the unity of national market without any tariff barriers. This point became important in the pre-reforms Russia of 1991, where some regions wanted to protect their markets against shortages.

When the market reforms went further, the controversies between energy- and raw-material-exporting industries and Russian manufacturing industries became evident. The former sector being the most powerful in Russian politics was adherent to a free-trade policy, joining the World Trade Organization and so on. The latter wanted to support the competitive Russian manufacturing industries by protectionist measures. Then the time came for Friedrich List to reappear on the Russian stage. The editor in chief of the well-known magazine *Expert*, Valery Fadeev, initiated in 2005 the republication of the "National System Of Political Economy" (with Trubnikov's foreword) together with Witte's brochure "On Nationalism. National Economy And Friedrich List" and Dmitry Mendeleev's paper "A Sound Tariff" (List 2005). Fadeev's short introduction to the publication shows that the sympathy of the publisher is wholly on the side of List and his followers. Since this publication, List's ideas have never been out of sight in disputes about Russian economic and foreign trade policy, despite their influence being moderate until now.

## Notes

1 "I was born a republican and recall my youth and the value of human existence in freedom" (letter to his fiancée) – (Wendler 2015: 20). For instance, the magistrate in Reutlingen was elected for one year. Public courts and juries were respected in Reutlingen but not in the Duchy of Württemberg.
2 Probably, the "most scientific" work by Mordvinov is his brochure "Some considerations on the subject of manufactories in Russia and on the tariff" where he

expressed his opinion about the necessity of protectionist measures for Russian industry.

3 Even the order of enumeration of these goods is fully reproduced in List's book (See Zweynert 2008b: 76)

4 "The unforgettable Friedrich List was the first who pointed to mistakes of economists who used the scale of equity and utility applicable to private life to social and national issues" (Zweynert 2008a: 181).

5 In his essay, Vernadsky mentioned even H.H. Gossen who, as we know, was completely forgotten and rediscovered by Jevons only several decades later (Vernadsky 1858).

6 J. Zweynert estimates his position among Russian economists as similar to Schmoller's position in Germany (Zweynert 2008a: 231).

7 This idea was explicitly stated in the second edition of Witte's brochure, published in 1912.

8 In February of 1917 Nicholas II left the power not to his son Alexey, who suffered from a hereditary illness, but to Mikhail, who in turn did not accept it.

# References

Anikin, A. V. (1975). *Yunost' nauki* [The Youth of the Science]. 2nd edition. Moscow: Mysl. [In Russian].

Antonov, M. F. (2008). *Ekonomicheskoye uchenie slavyanofilov* [Economic Doctrine of the Slavophiles]. Moscow: Institut russkoy tsivilizatsii. [In Russian].

Avtonomov, V., Gloveli, G. (2015). The influence of the German historical school on economic theory and economic thought in Russia. *The German Historical School and European Economic Thought*, 185–203. [J. L. Cardoso, M. Psalidopoulos, editors]. New York: Routledge.

Bogomazov G. G., Blagikh I. A. (2010). *Istoria ekonomiki i ekonomicheskoy mysli Rossii* [The History of Russian Economics and Economic Thought]. Moscow: Ekonomika.

Bulgakov, S. N. (2007). *Istoria ekonomicheskikh i sozialnykh uchenyi* [The History of Economic and Social Doctrines]. Moscow: Astrel. [In Russian].

Karataev, N. K. editor. (1963). *Istoria ekonomicheskih uchenij: Uchebnik dlya vuzov* [History of Economic Thought: Textbook for Universities]. Moscow: Izdatel'stvo social'no-ekonomicheskoj literatury. [In Russian].

Marx, K., Lista, F. (1971) "Nazionalnaya sistema politicheskoj economii" [K. Marx on F. List's book "The National System of Political Economy"]. *Voprosy istorii KPSS* [Issues of CPSU (Communist Party of Soviet Union) History], Vol. 12. [In Russian]

List, F. (2005). *Nazionalnaya sistema politicheskoy ekonomii." Graf S. Yu. Witte "Po povodu natsionalizma. Natsional'naya ekonomiya I Friedrich List. D.I.Mendeleev "Tolkovy tarif ili issledovaniye o razvitii [romyshlennosti Rossii v svyazi s eyo obshim tamozhennym tarifom 1891 goda].* Moskva: Evropa. [In Russian].

Pokidchenko, M. G., Kalmychkova, E. N. editors. (2003). *Istoriki ekonomicheskoj mysli. V. V. Svyatlovsky, M. I. Tugan-Baranovsky, V. Y. Zheleznov.* [Historians of Economic Thought. V. V. Svyatlovsky, M. I. Tugan-Baranovsky, V. Y. Zheleznov]. Moscow: Nauka. [In Russian].

Rumyantsev, A. M. (1973). *Ekonomicheskaya Enzyclopedia. Politicheskaya ekonomia* [Economic Encyclopedia. Political Economy]. Moscow: Sovetskaya Enzyclopedia. Vol. 2.

Struve, P. B. ([1894] 2015). *Kriticheskie zametki k voprosu ob ekonomicheskom razvitii Rossii* [Critical Notes on the Economic Development of Russia]. 2nd edition. Moscow: LENAND. [In Russian].

Tanayevsky, V. A. (1927). *Friedrich List i ekonomicheskaya geografiya [Friedrich List and Economic Geography]. Trudy Vyatskogo Nauchno-issledovatelskogo Instituta krayevedeniya, Tom III* [Works of Vyatka Research Institute of Local History, Vol 3]. Vyatka. [In Russian].

Vernadsky, I. V. (1858). *Ocherk istorii politicheskoy ekonomii* [Essay on the History of Political Economy]. Saint-Petersburg: edaktsiya "Ekonomicheskogo ukazatelya". [In Russian].

Wendler,E. (1996). *Die List-Rezeption in Russland//Wendler,E. Die Vereinigung des europäischen Kontinents*. Stuttgart: Schäffer-Poeschel, 473–490.

Wendler, E. (2015). *Friedrich List (1789–1846): A Visionary Economist with Social Responsibility*. Berlin, Heidelberg: Springer-Verlag.

Witte, S. Y. (1912). *Konspekt lekcij o narodnom I gosudarstvennom hozyajstve, chitannyh Ego Imperatorskomu Vysochestvu Velikomu Knyasu Mikhailu Aleksandrovichu v 1900–1902 gg* [A Summary of Lectures on the National and State Economy Read to His Imperial Highness Grand Duke Mikhail Alexandrovich in 1900–1902]. Saint-Petersburg: Brockhaus-Efron. [In Russian].

Zweynert, J. (2008a). Between Reason and Historicity: Russian Academic Economics, 1800–1861. In: Barnett, V. and Zweynert, J. (eds.) *Economics in Russia: Studies in Intellectual History*, 57–74, Burlington: Ashgate.

Zweynert, J. (2008b). *Istoriya ekonomicheskoy mysli v Rossii: 1805–1905* [The History of Economic Thought in Russia: 1805–1905]. L. I. Zedilin, Trans. Moscow: SU HSE. Original work published 2002.

# 14 Friedrich List in China's quest for development

*Mei Junjie*

Friedrich List was a leading 19th-century German political economist who put forward a theory of "national economics" based on the growth of "productive resources". He believed that a nation's competitiveness lay in developing its productive resources rather than boasting its current exchange value. Strongly critical of the *laissez-faire* and cosmopolitan economics of Adam Smith, List opposed the doctrine of universal free trade while systemizing the "infant industry argument" that called for protection in catch-up industrialization. He gave prominence to the nation-state perspective, stressing that a country lagging behind should adopt policies in line with its particular stage of development, instead of following the policies or prescriptions of the leading nation(s). With his theoretical support for laggards in development, Friedrich List has been highly appealing to Chinese economic circles even to this date. An overview of List's influences on the modern evolution of China, while interesting for academic inquiries in economic history, may also demonstrate what this great development strategist can offer to the Chinese in their ongoing transformation.

## 14.1. Initial introduction of List into China

When Friedrich List was born in 1789, China was at the zenith of its imperial prowess and complacent isolation. It is recorded that, as Lord Macartney journeyed to Beijing for business opportunities in 1793, the Chinese Emperor Qianlong addressed the English monarch in these words:

> Our Celestial Dynasty's majestic virtue has penetrated onto distant lands under Heaven, and Kings of all nations have offered their costly tribute by land and sea ... we possess all things. I set no value on objects strange or ingenious, and have no use for your country's manufactures.
>
> (Bozan 1979: 305)

By 1846 when List passed away, the situation for China had become utterly different. With the Treaty of Nanking signed in 1842 following the Opium War, China embarked upon a century-long road of peripheralization and resistance. Very precisely, the lifetime of List coincided with the steady decline of China.

As the door of China was forced open, western economics spread to China, first of all, thanks to a German missionary by the name of Karl Friedrich Gutzlaff (1803–1851), who around 1840 published in Chinese two booklets on political economy and commerce respectively (Trescott 2007: 12, 23). Friedrich List was understandably not introduced to the Chinese, since Gutzlaff believed that only a free market and *laissez-faire* operating in a British-type system would lead to economic and social progress.

The spread of western economic ideas into China did not accelerate until Chinese students returned from their overseas studies. In 1902, *The Wealth of Nations* was published in Chinese, its translator being Yan Fu, a UK-returned scholar who followed Adam Smith in advocating unrestricted international trade (Trescott 2007: 34). Yet, List was among the 20 or so economists mentioned in the preface to the Chinese version, and furthermore, other heavyweight Chinese intellectual leaders were attracted to List's arguments. For example, Liang Qichao, aware of the German historical school and List, resented the free trade imposed on China by western powers and urged China to implement a mercantilist policy (Junduan 2004: 118, 124, 211–212, 220, 307).

Classroom notes taken in 1911 by the Xiong brothers, two students at Peking Imperial Law School, indicate that List and his theory had been addressed in lectures. The anonymous lecturer apparently had sufficient knowledge of List's major viewpoints. In 1914, *Dang Bao*, a marginal newspaper published by some Chinese political activists in Japan, carried an article by Xu Zhongying "On the Relationship between Protection Policy and National Economy". Although the actual identity of the author remains obscure even today, Xu's article gave a fairly detailed introduction to the key aspects of List's doctrine, highlighting the strategic need to make short-term sacrifices for long-term development (Peng 2015: 90–91). Then in 1922, Ma Yinchu, a returned student from America, made a speech in Peking on "Doctrines of Marx and List: which is fit for China?" Ma's conclusion was that China needed List more than Marx, as the country suffered from a very low level of productivity rather than any conflict between capital and labor (Peng 2015: 91–92).

After all this, a full account of List and his theory came into China largely owing to the efforts of the Chinese studying in Germany. In 1925, a biography of List first appeared in China. It was authored by Liu Binglin (1891–1956), who had studied economics at the University of Berlin and the University of London during 1920–1925 (Binglin 1925). In the same year, Wang Kaihua (1893–1976), a PhD candidate at the University of Tübingen, translated *The National System of Political Economy*, which came out in Chinese as *National Economics* in 1927. It is known that Wang graduated from Tübingen in 1926 with his dissertation on *The Theory of List and Its Relevance to China* (Genliang et al. 2015: 87–89).

These two returned scholars from Germany showed a high appreciation of List and his arguments.

## 14.2. Appealing points of List to the Chinese

The Chinese were attracted to Friedrich List primarily because of List's emphasis on tariff protection for catch-up industrialization. As remarked by Wei Chenzu, the Chinese minister at the German legation who wrote a preface to the translated List work:

> China has been deprived of the right to set its tariff rates; on the other hand, the Chinese are becoming Europeanized in their consumption taste. As a result, foreign goods abound in our market, driving domestic industries to further decline. Given our weak productivity and heavy reliance on other countries for various needs, it is highly proper that List's theory should be adopted in China.
>
> (Chunzu 1929: preface)

Those who introduced List into China were fully aware of the role that the Listian strategies had played in German history. It was believed that Germany and America became able to rival Britain in industrial competition largely by drawing upon the propositions of List. List's theory was therefore compared to "a good prescription for the current Chinese disease", deserving "research by patriots and political economists". For these Chinese, as noted by Wang Kaihua in his own preface to the translation:

> If our country hopes to seek wealth and power, industry and commerce must be developed, and to develop them, it is imperative to resist the foreign competition in our market, so that domestic products may prevail. Protective tariff is an effective strategy for curtailing foreign competition and a sharp weapon for nurturing our own business.
>
> (Kaihua 1929: 2)

List was appreciated by the Chinese also for his nationalist inclination. The Chinese economic community viewed western economics broadly in three schools: individualism, represented by Adam Smith; nationalism, represented by List; and socialism, represented by Karl Marx, a position still strongly held today.[1] While each school of economic thought had its distinctive strengths, it was pointed out that the nationalist approach of List was especially applicable to China, since it was recognized that the Chinese state was not functioning effectively just as the Chinese market was not yet consolidated. Specifically, the Chinese conceived of using List's theory to offset the excessive liberalist influence of the Smith theory. As Liu Binglin, the Chinese biographer of List, wrote, "Those Chinese with inadequate knowledge of economics are often misled by works of the British into believing that economic undertakings have no national boundaries", even though economic cosmopolitanism is far from an established existence in the real world (Binglin 1925: 3).

On the whole, Friedrich List had ardent followers in China in the early 20th-century. As assessed by Liu Binglin, "List should be considered No. 1 in terms of his contribution to the development of the German manufacturing"; and "List should also be considered No. 1 among all the German economists during and before his time". The Chinese concluded that, with his outstanding achievements, List "occupies a status actually no lower than that of Adam Smith in the history of economic thoughts". (Binglin 1925: 46, 121)

## 14.3. Influence of List on the Chinese economists

List and his theory were embraced by the Chinese just when China was grappling with the huge peril of colonization following the western intrusion. The replacement of the imperial system by a republic in the early 1910s was no immediate cure for the economic peripheralization and social decay. On the contrary, the setbacks in resurrection and the consequent frustrations nurtured radicalization of the popular sentiments, leading to further chaos and disintegration of the nation. All this went far beyond what List's theory could readily provide for.

However, the key themes of the theory, notably industrialization, tariff protection and state intervention, cut to the very core of the challenges that China faced. Sun Yat-sen, the founding president of the Republic of China, for instance, asserted that "the life-or-death issue for China hereinafter boils down to one thing only, i.e., the development of its industry". He proposed that "to advance industrialization, China should dispel foreign products and protect local products by following the protectionist policies of Germany and America". (Rongli 2008: 29) Economists like Ma Yinchu felt that the strategies of List were among the most useful ones for China, since Chinese industries could never get developed when the national tariff right was not recovered. Without protective tariffs imposed for industrialization, "China would forever remain a supplier of raw materials and a consumer of manufactured goods" (Yinchu 2005: 49).

It is interesting to review in some detail the thoughts of Chinese economists regarding tariff and related development issues, so as to discern the actual influence of List's theory on the Chinese political economic thinking, and some of its adaptations to the Chinese context.

Firstly, Chinese economists focused more on "recovering the tariff right" than on enforcing strict trade protection. Partly due to the "reverse discrimination" against Chinese businesses on Chinese soil, and partly due to their conviction that Chinese businessmen were competitive enough to deal with their foreign counterparts when put on a level field, Chinese academics and industrialists in principle did not call for high import tariffs, and did not even believe them to be that necessary.[2]

Secondly, Chinese economists realized in a balanced way that free trade and protection each had its application scope, with the former fit for advanced industrial powers and the latter fit for industrial latecomers. China, as a latecomer, should, of course, discourage imports and promote exports given the persistent trade deficits, and to promote industrialization, import rates should be set differently on different categories of products, inversely proportional to their extent of manufacturing.[3]

Thirdly, considering the lack of inventive activities at home, Chinese economists knew well that imports were conducive to Chinese industrial improvement and even to social evolution, as already proven by the opening of the "treaty ports", although imperialist oppression was the other side of the story. For the purpose of industrialization, foreign trade should be encouraged, imports of capital goods should be greatly facilitated, and with it, export of primary products should not be restricted, at least not for the time being.[4]

Fourthly, Chinese economists claimed that they were in theory also supporters of free trade and international cooperation, except that the prevailing practice of international trade presented all too sharp a contrast to the free trade doctrine. As argued, with the western powers returning to protectionism, China could only resort to trade protection to survive. But in the long run, emphasis should be put on the growth of productive forces. With this aim in mind, reciprocal trade was deemed a better option than restricted trade, and, by the way, agriculture should not be protected.[5]

Fifthly, Chinese economists noted that, given the incompleteness of the Chinese sovereignty, mass boycott of foreign goods would be a more practical and effective tool to protect the local market and local industries. Indeed, many regarded this non-tariff means as the only feasible weapon for a weak country like China to cope with the unfair competition from the strong.[6]

Sixthly, Chinese economists maintained that trade and economic development demanded, aside from some tariff protection, the removal of various other barriers in finance, transportation, business practices, internal governance, and so on. It was thus emphasized that any development strategy, be it trade protection, government intervention or economic planning, should not go to the extremes, particularly for a populous country like China.[7]

## 14.4. No chance for systematic implementation

The above overview shows that Chinese economists were obviously influenced by List on trade and development issues, as List was mentioned or alluded to in their writings. Their closeness to List in position was surely no coincidence, since quite some Chinese held List in esteem rationally after having made comparisons between the doctrine of Adam Smith and that of List, and between the situations of China and other countries. It is undeniable that China was already well-equipped in the first half of the 20th century with the theoretical sophistication needed for industrial development, just as it is undeniable that the ruling Nationalist government demonstrated an impressive orientation towards modernization.

However, neither the theoretical sophistication of the academia nor the modernization orientation of the government led to solid outcomes in China's economic and social progress. Indeed, the Nationalist government itself collapsed in the Communist takeover in 1949. The reasons for this abrupt turn were basically threefold: 1) the Nationalist government could never tame the armed opposition from other domestic forces, which constituted a perennial and mounting disturbance to national reconstruction; 2) the protracted Japanese invasion broke down fatally the hard-earned initiation of industrialization and modernization; and 3) the overall level of the national wealth and strength was far too low to create any immediate wonder.

What China had achieved by the mid-20th century was a type of "lop-sided development" fairly typical of the early stage performance of countries under "prepheralization pressures", but still appreciable enough. The development is regarded lopsided, because: 1) it was primarily driven by foreign capital that dominated China's key sectors such as steel and iron production, coal mining, power generation, foreign trade, banking, shipping and so on; 2) the development was limited to the enclave of "treaty port" cities, with the vast countryside undergoing painful transformation following the erosion of the traditional economic and social fabric; and 3) the economic growth was based on the export of primary commodities, with light industries, textile in particular, seriously suppressed by the Japanese competition, and the heavy industry making only a modest start. On the whole, Chinese manufacturing remained at a seriously underdeveloped stage.

Both the achievements and difficulties of the Chinese initial development are readily seen from the statistics: in the early 1920s, modern industries and handcraft industries took up respectively 4.9% and 10.8% in the overall industrial and agricultural output, growing to 10.8% and 20.5% respectively in 1936, more or less a pre-war peak year; the import of light industrial products decreased from 54.6% in 1912 to 14.3% in 1936, whereas the import of heavy industrial products increased from 13.7% to 47% during the same period; and the proportion of the urbanized population expanded slowly from 5.1% in 1843 to 10.6% in 1949, further testifying to the sluggish but undeniable advance of the modern Chinese development (Rongqu 1993: 327–329).

## 14.5. Unintended crude practice of Listian strategies

The Communist victory in 1949 altered the whole course of events. The radical regime change meant not only a breakdown of the incrementally progressing modernization, but also a total discarding of the theoretical sophistication and development experience so far accumulated. It is therefore no surprise that the new leadership was basically ignorant, and perhaps disdainful, of List's theory or indeed any other theories labeled "bourgeois", even though a new translation of *The National System of Political Economy* appeared in 1961. But ironically, due to the overall "delinking" from the capitalist world, the new regime quite unwittingly followed the Listian strategies of trade protection and state intervention for its catch-up industrialization, though often carried to extremes.

If the previous approach to development harbored any risk of peripheralization, the Communists put an end to all this. In the meantime, their effective organization of society gave observers an impression of a thorough clean-up in the national outlook. However, a radical revolution, though probably good at sweeping old barriers and creating new preconditions for modernization, cannot in itself ensure sustained modern economic growth. Development is understandably a comprehensive project of socioeconomic reengineering that demands more than what can be offered by class struggles, administrative orders or even sacrifices of the masses.

The Maoist system of mobilization, the deprivation of the peasants, the technical assistance from the Soviet bloc and so on, could make up for some gaps in development, even leading to impressive performance in areas like irrigation improvement, railway construction, industrial expansion, healthcare extension and more. Yet, they could hardly lift industrialization and modernization to any substantially higher level. In fact, disasters were caused in economic and human terms when the leadership, with its power unchecked, engaged in wishful thinking as well as incessant infighting. This demonstrates, among other things, that the loss of sound development strategies represented by List's theory could claim high prices.

For a fair assessment of the post-1949 performance, it should be acknowledged that China's economy experienced massive accumulation and remarkable growth led by a prioritized development of the heavy industries that formed the backbone of the national economy. Breakthroughs were made in a handful of selected defense and industrial projects, and the basic welfare of the people was to some extent improved on the basis of egalitarianism. But given the nature of the command (rather than planned) economy, the development witnessed huge fluctuations.

Furthermore, those leverages, effective in pushing forward development within the socialist framework, proved obstructive to sustained economic growth and dynamic social progress in the long run. Some salient problems were: repeated political campaigns abused social resources; political domination of the economy stifled entrepreneurial activities; removal of the market mechanism hampered social self-organization and economic self-balancing; a bloated sector of heavy industries crowded out the consumption of the people; political blunders in economic restructuring led to tragic famines; isolation from the developed world meant a lack of stimuli for progress; and underdevelopment of the agricultural sector hampered the growth of the domestic market. These problems, while common in the Stalinist model, became particularly acute in China.

## 14.6. Time to embrace List's far-sighted aspirations

List once wrote that, no matter where and when, the welfare of a nation is directly proportional to the intelligence, morality and diligence of the people, with which wealth increases or decreases. He went on to stress that the industriousness, thriftiness, inventiveness and enterprise of individuals will never lead to any major achievements if divorced from liberty in the domestic politics, proper public institutions and laws, sound state administration and foreign policies, as well as the special support from the national solidarity and power. These words from List are sufficient reasons to explain why China embarked upon "reform and opening-up" shortly after the end of the Maoist era in the late 1970s. Deng Xiaoping and his associates provided to the Chinese people a liberal market, a basic order, administrative support and sensible diplomacy, thus reversing the previous faulty policies and creating a space for people to tap their intelligence, industriousness and entrepreneurship for individual and national prosperity.

Over the past several decades of transformation, the Chinese people successfully resolved such typical Stalinist problems as short supply of consumer goods, rigidity of the planned economic system, cut-off from the developed economies, lack of autonomy for the enterprises, dearth of infrastructural facilities, suffocation of the social vitality and so on. However, new tensions have now risen related to establishing the rule of law, implementing constitutional rights, expanding political participation, curtailing rent-seeking by interest groups, liberalizing the monopolized sectors, rebalancing the resources between the state and society, deepening the domestic market, transforming the crude pattern of economic growth, preventing the ballooning of public debts, reducing industrial overcapacity and overdependence on export, modernizing the financial sector, closing the gap in wealth distribution, promoting the efficiency of agriculture, protecting the environment and so on. How successfully China overcomes these problems will determine how well it can avoid the much feared "middle-income trap".

There are heated discussions in China regarding the possibility of getting stranded in the "middle-income trap", as economic growth is slowing down and impediments have accumulated. It is interesting to see if the theory of List can in any way inspire the Chinese to break the bottleneck in their further development. List's emphasis on the development of productive resources rather than on the exchange value, his caution regarding excessive financial liberalization, his call for a balanced development of comprehensive sectors of the economy, his warning against an overzealous government in stimulating or regulating the economy and so on, all seem to be relevant to China today. In particular, the neo-Listian recommendations put forward by Professor Dieter Senghaas for a "far-reaching de-feudalization (or de-oligarchization)", "a nationally integrated economy", "a broad domestic market", a "broad distribution of export receipts", a "broad-based domestic economic development process", "a shift towards decentralized administrative structures and increased political participation", "a decisive institutional innovation" and so on (Senghaas 1985: 165, 174, 163, 154, 202), are especially pertinent to the current Chinese case if China is to evolve into a developed society instead of a "partial power".

Clearly, List is by no means fading away on the Chinese stage. In 1997, the Chinese version of *The Natural System of Political Economy* came out amidst China's heightened efforts to join the World Trade Organization. And right at this moment, we are arranging for the translation and publication in Chinese of the List biography by Professor Eugen Wendler. Of course, when China at this stage renews its interest in List, it is advisable that a long-term perspective be adopted. As well understood, List had both short-term and long-term aspirations, which are rightly incarnated by his remark that "freedom is the daughter of industry and wealth", or simply put, "To Freedom via Prosperity". It is especially worthwhile for the Chinese today to remember that List stressed that, although some government action was essential to stimulate the economy, an overzealous government might do more harm than good. "It is bad policy to regulate everything and to promote everything by employing social resource, where things might better regulate themselves and can be better promoted by private exertions". If tariff protection is at the heart of List's more short-term pursuit, then free trade, international coalition, individual freedom, the rule of law and so on constitute his long-term aspirations. It is high time that a rising China embraced the long-term aspirations of this far-sighted German economist and visionary.

## Notes

1 See, for example, Shaowen (2000).
2 For example, Ma Yinchu and He Bingxian. See Rongli (2008: 43, 138).
3 For example, Qi Shufen and Wu Yugan. See Shufen (1925: 100), and Yugan (1930: 520).
4 For example, Zhu Jin and Pei-Kang Chang. See Pei-Kang Chang (1949: 195–236).
5 For example, Song Zexing and Hong Yisheng. See Rongli (2008: 167–185).
6 For example, Ma Yinchu and Wu Yugan. Yinchu (2005: 24, 49); and Yugan (1930: 591).
7 For example, Mu Ouchu and Chu Baoyi. See Ouchu (2011: 213–214), and Baoyi (1945: 56–65).

## References

Baoyi, C. (1945), *Industrialization and China's International Trade*, Chongqing: The Commercial Press.
Binglin, L. (1925), *The Economic Theory and Biography of List*, Shanghai: The Commercial Press.
Bozan, J. (ed.) (1979), *An Outline History of China*, Vol. 3, Beijing: People's Publishing House.

Chang, P.K. (1949), *Agriculture and Industrialization: An Inquiry into the Adjustments that Take Place as an Agricultural Country Is Industrialized*, Cambridge: Harvard University Press, reprinted by Beijing: China CITIC Press, 2012.

Chunzu, W. (1929), "Preface", in Kaihua, W. (ed.), translation of Friedrich List's work, *The National Economics*, Shanghai: The Commercial Press.

Genliang, J. et al. (2015), *New Listian Economics in China*, Beijing: Renmin University Press.

Junduan, Z. (2004), *Research on Liang Qichao's Economic Thoughts*, Beijing: Chinese Academy of Social Sciences Press.

Kaihua, W. (1929), *The National Economics*, translation of Friedrich List's work, Shanghai: The Commercial Press.

Ouchu, M. (2011), *Collected Writings of Mu Ouchu*, Shanghai: Shanghai Classics Publishing House.

Peng, Y. (2015), "The Spread of List's Economic Theory in China During the Republican Era", *Study and Exploration*, No.1, pp. 89–97.

Rongli, L. (2008), *Research on the Foreign Trade Thoughts in the Period of the Republic of China*, Wuhan: Wuhan University Press.

Rongqu, L. (1993), *A New World Perspective on the Modernizing Process in China*, Beijing: The Peking University Press.

Senghaas, D. (1985), *The European Experience: A Historical Critique of Development Theory*, Leamington Spa: Berg Publishers Ltd.

Shaowen, Z. (2000), *Classic Economics and Modern Economics*, Beijing: The Peking University Press.

Shufen, Q. (1925), *China under Economic Aggression*, Shanghai: Guanghua Press. reprinted by Beijing: Sanlian Bookstore, 1954.

Trescott, P.B. (2007), *The History of the Introduction of Western Economic Ideas into China, 1850–1950*, Hong Kong: The Chinese University Press.

Yinchu, M. (2005), *Selected Speeches and Papers by Ma Yinchu*, Beijing: The Peking University Press.

Yugan, W. (1930), *An Overview of China's International Trade*, Shanghai: The Commercial Press.

# 15 Industrial development strategies in Asia

## The influence of Friedrich List on industrial evolution in Japan, South Korea and China

*Alexander Gerybadze*

### 15.1. Introduction

This chapter explores the influence of Friedrich List on development economics and on trade policy in three Asian countries. While his writings and his work had a strong impact on industrialization processes in Germany, as well as in North America and in Europe, his influence on economic development and industrial policy in Asia remains rather sketchy. It is our intent to analyze the sequential growth experiences of three countries in East Asia, namely, Japan, South Korea and China, and to study documents that may show how List's ideas have influenced people in academia as well as in politics in those countries.

Very few countries in the world have succeeded in realizing long-lasting and sustainable growth processes, which were strong enough to transform their economies from a backward stage to an advanced industrial system. During the twentieth century, only a small number of East Asian countries have realized such a consistent growth pattern, while many other temporarily successful nations have lost steam in later periods, or were lost in the "middle-income trap".[1] Those few Asian countries that have become successful in the long-run were playing the "catch-up game", and they have learned from other, more advanced nations how to implement industrial development strategies and how to build dynamic capabilities.

Two countries that were characterized by a rather backward agrarian society at the beginning of the nineteenth century and that were able to transform into an advanced industrial power before World War I were the United States and Germany. The growth and transformation processes in both countries were built on a sequence of establishing modern institutions and on the interplay between private entrepreneurship and a strong state. In both countries we have also observed contentious debates and the political struggle between free-traders and protectionists. Friedrich List was one of the most outspoken proponents of business revival and the role of a strong state in Germany. During his lifetime, he had experiences in academia, in business, in public administration, in lobbying, as well as in journalism.

Particularly his experiences with early and unsuccessful attempts at new industry formation in Germany during the years 1810–1815, and his active role in establishing the General German Association of Trade and Industry in 1819, had a lasting influence on his support of protectionist trade policies, and on his refusal of liberal free-traders. Industry in continental Europe was not able to develop in a regime characterized by low external tariffs, particularly in the trade relationship with Britain's dominating manufacturing industries. While British manufacturing goods were flooding the markets on the continent, high domestic trade barriers between Prussia and the various German states further complicated early industrialization efforts, particularly between 1820 and 1870.

Certainly, Friedrich List was not the first to develop ideas of industrial catch-up processes and on protectionist trade policies. Many of his economic ideas on economic development and trade policy were shaped by economists from the United States (Alexander Hamilton), from England (Daniel Raymond) and from Ireland (Mathew Carey). List became actively involved in the debate on free trade and early industry formation while he lived in Pennsylvania between 1826 and 1830. Most of his economic ideas were sharpened during this period of active participation in the rise of the "American system" of early catch-up growth. Alexander Hamilton probably had the strongest influence on List through his "Report on Manufactures" already published in 1791. Hamilton's agenda for the up and coming American economy included core elements of fiscal as well as industrial policy, and these were later taken up by economic development planners in many countries. In particular, Hamilton's development agenda emphasized the following elements:

- The formation of a productive industrial system and the development of a large enough home market for manufacturing goods;
- the balanced development and interaction between the agricultural system and the manufacturing sector;
- protecting duties with a stimulating effect on industry formation in the catch-up country;
- a government pursuing an active and dirigist economic and financial policy;
- the formation of a central bank and a modern banking system;
- the promotion of inventions and the development of new machinery and, last but not least,
- strong investment processes for the build-up of the transportation infrastructure.[2]

List was strongly influenced by the early growth experience in Pennsylvania and in several other New England states, and he developed Hamilton's ideas further. During his stay in the U.S., he became strongly involved in the debate between free traders and the promoters of an active government and of early industry protection.

## 15.2. Friedrich List's theory of economic development and growth

Friedrich List had learned from experiences in Germany as well as in America and was convinced that state intervention and protectionism is needed at least during the early stages of economic development. After his return to Germany in 1833, List refined the ideas of Alexander Hamilton and his followers further. He became active in promoting strong industry associations, the build-up of the national rail infrastructure and the process of national integration of the independent German states. He was convinced of the formation of a large integrated home market and the development of a strong indigenous manufacturing sector.

> Manufactures ... are the nurses of arts, sciences and skills, the sources of power and wealth. A merely agricultural people remains always poor; ... and a poor people having not much to sell, and less with which to buy, can never possess a flourishing commerce, because commerce consists in buying and selling.[3]
>
> (List, Outlines, letter 2)

The process of transformation from an agrarian society into a more advanced economy with a strong manufacturing sector, however, needs to be managed in an intelligent way, combining the productive forces and the linkages between both sectors (agriculture and manufacturing). Development of agriculture is needed to feed increasing numbers of labourers in new urban locations. The manufacturing sector, on the other hand, produces agricultural machinery and fertilizers for an increasingly productive farm sector and for food production. This reciprocal relationship between agriculture and manufacturing played a strong role during early development in Europe, and this idea of inter-sectoral co-development was strongly emphasized in the writings of Alexander Hamilton (1791) and Daniel Raymond (1820).

> As power secures wealth, and wealth increases power, so are power and wealth, in equal parts, benefited by a harmonious state of agriculture, commerce and manufactures within the limits of the country.
>
> (List, Outlines, letter 2)

This strong interaction between manufacturing development and productivity increases in agriculture was also emphasized by development planners in Asian countries, as will be shown in the following sections on Japan, South Korea and China.

Based on the experiences in continental Europe and in the United Stated, Friedrich List became a strong promoter of protective tariffs. A less advanced country that wants to develop new industries needs to shield off entrepreneurial new companies from foreign competition, at least temporarily. For safeguarding and nurturing a growing manufacturing sector within the limits of the

country, protective tariffs need to be established in order to secure the formation of indigenous firms able to survive competition from dominant large
corporations located in the lead country. In the case of Germany and the U.S.,
new firms had to be shielded off from the competition of the much more
advanced and mechanized British rivals. A free trade regime in the trade
relationship with Britain was primarily supporting the advanced firms from
Britain, and left no breathing space for newly established firms in continental
Europe or in the U.S. Furthermore, this problem was aggravated in the case of
Germany, because a free trade regime with Britain was combined with high
remaining domestic trade barriers for internal trade between the still fragmen-
ted territorial states. British manufacturers flooded the markets on the continent, while German manufacturing companies still had to overcome severe
trade restrictions even if they were selling to other German customers. Similar
problems were reported in China after signing the Treaty of Nanjing, and
Friedrich List was commenting on this dual problem of external free trade and
internal trade barriers in later writings.[4]

Friedrich List was not arguing against free trade per se. In his debate with
Adam Smith and other promoters of free trade, List distinguished between
the vision of a potential future world and the existing world characterized
by large disparities between countries. Free trade would be advantageous
only for advanced countries of similar economic power. Free trade, by
contrast, would lead to unfair competition in the existing world, where
few advanced nations are competing with many underdeveloped countries.
An underdeveloped nation, so went his argument, would never be able to
build-up industry and create lasting wealth without passing through a
period of protective policy and state intervention.

> These gentlemen, with cosmopolitical principles on their lips, design to
> persuade all other powers to cede their political power in order to
> render English productive and political power omnipotent ... A new
> people with a new form of government and new ideas of general
> welfare and freedom has arisen. This people has learned ... to distin-
> guish the true from the false, visionary systems from clear perceptions,
> cosmopolitical from political principles, sayings from doings. ... Cos-
> mopolitical institutions like those of free trade are not yet ripe for being
> introduced into practice.
>
> (List, Outlines, letter 3)

List became famous as a strong promoter of protecting duties during the early
formation of an industry. The original idea came from Mathew Carey (1760–
1839), the owner of a publishing company and the founder of the Society for
the Promotion of Material Industry at Philadelphia.[5] Friedrich List was
introduced to the members of this society by General Lafayette in 1825,
even though he didn't have personal contact with Carey.[6] The experiences
and debates within this industry society had a strong influence on List's view

of early industry protection. Carey's as well as List's arguments on infant industry protection and the temporary shielding off from free trade were later taken up by development economists, and have certainly influenced development strategies in Asia, as will be shown later.

List also argued strongly in favour of a strong, dirigist state. Early development strategies in most of today's advanced countries were triggered off by state intervention and through active involvement of the ruling class on industry formation processes. A less-developed nation like Germany or the U.S., according to List's observation, will be characterized by the powerplay between importers and new manufacturing firms. Traders and importers are in favour of low tariffs and free trade, while up and coming new manufacturing firms need to be protected through tariffs at least during their early growth phase. Free trade and market liberalism will result, according to List, in the predominance of the former group, and in the persistent dependence on imports.

> It is bad policy to regulate everything and to promote everything, by employing social powers, where things may better regulate themselves and can be better promoted by private exertions; but it is no less bad policy to let those things alone which can only be promoted by interfering social power. ... An absence of liberal institutions may be extremely injurious to a full development of the productive powers of a nation, some classes may find their reckoning in this bad state of things. The nation may suffer from an absence of manufacturing industry, but some people may flourish in selling [foreign-made AG] manufactures.
>
> (List, Outlines, letter 6, p. 85ff.).

After his return to Germany, List became actively involved in the formation of the German Manufacturers Association (the "Handels- und Gewerbeverein"). His ideas and writings were very influential in the later formation of a unified German nation and on Bismarck's policy. Strong centralized political and social institutions and the new role of the historical school in Germany were partly developed using central ideas of Friedrich List. In later periods, some of these ideas and role models were taken up in Asia, primarily during the Meiji restoration in Japan, but indirectly also in other Asian counties like South Korea and China.

## 15.3. Industrial development in Japan

Japan strongly influenced industrial development in other Asian countries during the first half of the twentieth century, through her role as an imperial and colonial power, particularly between 1920 and 1945. Later, the process of rebuilding Japan's economy after World War II served as a role model for an active industrial policy. The radical transformation of Japan and the country's industrial modernization processes were implemented in four consecutive phases. During the Meiji restoration period between 1860 and 1880, modern political, economic and social institutions were established, often based on Western ideas. Strong investment to build greater presence in primary and secondary sectors led to the establishment of manufacturing industries. Japan tried to learn as much as possible from the catch-up growth experience of Germany, the United States and other Western nations. The second period involved the interwar years between 1920 and 1941. This imperialist period was characterized by a rapid uprising of Japan's industrial as well as military systems. During this period Japan established strong industrial sectors in machinery, transportation, shipbuilding and aircraft production, often linked to military production. Through the formation of the Zaibatsu structure, Japan followed an active cartel policy strongly influenced through Germany's cartel-managed export-subsidy regime of the period 1890–2014.[7] During this period, Japan followed expansionist policies throughout Asia. Korea and Taiwan became colonies, and Japan had an early influence on institution-building, with a lasting impact also on later industrial policies in those two countries.

The postwar period may be subdivided into two additional phases of industrial development: the early development processes of growth and reconstruction primarily between 1950 and 1975, followed by the period of rapid transformation of high-tech industries and research and development primarily between 1975 and 1995. We will concentrate on these two phases of development until 1995, and will not be concerned with the more recent phase of consolidation (the years after 1995 and following the Asian crisis).

During early modernization before World War II, Friedrich List and many other German economists and political scientists had considerable influence on Japan's economic development agenda, and on industry formation as well as on export policies. As a result of the American occupation and U.S. development aid, American economists and political administrators became more dominant during the early 1950s. However, Japan remained cautious in following their recommendations, and political administrators made sure that a strong national system could be re-established in spite of moderate opening up to the Western world. Friedrich List seemed to be watching from behind the curtain. Many elements of Japan's industrial development agenda between 1960 and 1980, like the emphasis on manufacturing, on infant industry protection and on export promotion, have a close correspondence to List's early writings and his toolbox of economic emulation and development.

### 15.3.1 List's early influence on Japan

During the early phase of the Meiji restoration (1868–1880), economic theories from England, the U.S. and France strongly influenced economic thinking in Japan. In many cases, liberal ideas became adopted as a sort of fashion of the day. However, Japan needed to establish social, political and economic institutions in order to develop internal capabilities for being able to compete with the predominant colonial powers. As a result, more protectionist ideas of foreign economists were seen as more appropriate for Japan during the 1880s. Giichi Wakayama translated the textbook of Carey (1876) and published an essay on the role of protective tariffs.[8] The United States as well as Germany served as role model for the development of latecomer nations, which effectively applied protectionist policies. The formation of manufacturing and institution-building in Prussia and the catch-up process after the formation of the unified German nation in 1870 attracted the interest of policy-makers and academic scholars in Japan. The German Historical School had an increasing influence on economic and political thinking throughout the 1880s. At the political and administrative level, the structure of the central state in Prussia served as a role model for institution-building in Japan, based on the writings of Lorenz von Stein and Hermann Rösler. Hirobumi Ito had studied under von Stein in Germany, and his scholars were becoming very influential in Japan. German principles of law as well as social and cultural practices and the educational system were assimilated in Japan, as a result of Ito's work. Japan's modern constitution was written by Hirobumi Ito and Kowashi Inoue, and contained many elements of the Prussian constitution. Several German scholars were invited to spend some time in Japan. Hermann Rösler served as advisor to the Japanese government.[9]

Economic ideas based on the German Historical School became disseminated in Japan at the end of the nineteenth century. Inejiro Tajiri had originally studied at Yale, but was strongly influenced by William Sumner, the American representative of the German historical school. Tajiri had considerable influence on several younger Japanese scholars, and later also served as the vice minister of finance in Tokyo. His scholar Tsunejiro Nakagawa published the first textbook summarizing economic principles of the German Historical School in 1886. The work of Wilhelm Roscher was translated into Japanese and several German economists and political scientists were invited as guest lecturers and advisors to the Japanese government.[10]

The debate between protectionism and free trade and the writings of Friedrich List on infant industry protection and on catch-up growth became more widely known through the writings of Sadamasu Oshima. Oshima translated List's "National System of Political Economy" twice into Japanese (1886 and 1895) and was known as the "Friedrich List of Japan". Oshima argued that protective tariffs and infant industry protection are inevitable for successful economic development of a backward country like Japan (Taiyoji 1970). The role of a strong central state, and strategies of industry nurturing through temporary protectionism, the basic ideas of Friedrich List, became guiding principles for Japan's modernization throughout the twentieth century.

### 15.3.2 Japan's industrial development between 1950 and 1975

In the following, we concentrate on the early catch-up phase during which Japan became a strong exporter for products primarily available in other

Western countries. This process covered the post-war period until about 1975. After this early period, decisive efforts of technological innovation, the establishment of new industries and continuous upgrading were being undertaken (primarily between 1975 and 1995). We will first analyse the early catch-up phase, and will then describe Schumpeterian-type growth processes in Section 15.3.3.[11]

After the first reconstruction period following World War II (1945–1953), the Japanese government implemented strong national policies and realized a remarkable growth process. The period between 1953 and 1975 was characterized by the advancement of a strong and competitive Japanese industry combined with the "visible hand" of an active government, quite similar to earlier ideas promoted by Friedrich List. There is a specific mechanism and regulatory framework called administrative guidance,[12] through which Japanese government agencies can exert a strong influence on managerial decisions in private firms. The Ministry of International Trade and Industry (MITI) played a strong and active role for industry restructuring, particularly during the period 1960 to 1975.[13] At regular intervals, MITI formulated long-term visions and strategies in close collaboration with industry. In 1963, MITI developed an influential long-term vision for the industrial structure and for targeted international trade programmes.

Two selection criteria were emphasized for industry targeting: (1) the income-elasticity criterion and (2) the productivity-increase criterion. The first focused on world markets with very high potential demand growth, in which Japanese firms were able to penetrate world export markets. The second criterion (productivity-increase) emphasized products and markets where Japanese firms were able to exploit learning-curve effects in order to compete with improved mass-produced products. This selective and targeted approach allowed Japanese firms to leap-frog and penetrate international export markets. The industrial development strategy until about 1970 was primarily emphasizing growth in industries already established elsewhere in the world: automobiles, chemicals, radio and TV, machine-tools as well as cameras and optical instruments. Most of these industries may be considered medium-tech by today's standards. This strategy was built on imitation and continuous improvement. By offering products with an improved price-performance ratio, Japanese firms were able to conquer world export markets. At the same time, key industries were being protected, at least during an early formative phase. Japan was observing a sort of "explosive growth" throughout this early post-war period. GDP was growing at an average rate of 9.4% between 1953 to 1965, and was just slightly reduced during the following ten years. Manufacturing output grew by 13.6% per year.[14]

### 15.3.3 Technology-based industrial development 1975–1995

The next phase of Japan's growth and industrialization followed Schumpeterian economic principles, but many elements had already been foreseen by

Friedrich List in his stage models. List emphasized the productive power of national systems and key elements such as scientific work, education and infrastructure, which can effectively be shaped by far-sighted policies. The increasing role of systematic scientific work, the international transfer of capabilities through the import of specialists, and List's emphasis on "capital of mind" were seen as central for a country's later growth phases.[15] After completing the first post-war growth phase, Japanese industry and the government followed an active upgrading policy. Already in 1970, the Industrial Structure Council developed the "Vision of MITI Policies in the 1970's", and emphasized a shift towards a knowledge-intensive industrial structure, with strong emphasis on research and development (R&D), inward technology transfer and human capital. Following this new strategy, Japanese companies strongly invested in the formation of new industries, particularly in advanced high-tech fields.[16]

Between 1975 and 1990, Japanese corporations strongly diversified into future lines of business. This was complemented by successive R&D programmes and collaborative consortia. Through this process, remarkable industrial capabilities became established in microelectronics, in computers and telecommunication. The structure of industry continuously moved from medium-tech to high-tech activities. The growth of the R&D enterprise was much stronger than in many of the formerly advanced Western countries.

Japan's industrial policy was thus implemented through active learning and the strengthening of absorptive capacities. It involved inward technology transfer and reverse engineering in early periods, and the formation of strong Japanese R&D and intellectual property in later phases. A typical knowledge-enhancing process involved the continuous upgrade of patent ownership. In a first phase, foreign inventors dominated applications for patents in Japan. Later, Japanese firms and researchers became stronger and stronger in patent applications at the Japanese patent office. In a third phase, Japanese firms and inventors attained a greater share of patent applications in strategic areas at the U.S. and European patent offices.[17] This process of continuous improvement in patent ownership was later also replicated by other Asian countries.

Another important feature of Japanese technology upgrading involves the strong interaction between R&D investment and advanced manufacturing. This allows the redesign of an entire production system and thinking in integrated value chains. This "system approach" in innovation has been a major characteristic underlying Japanese success in the automobile industry, in consumer electronics and in a number of other industries.[18]

Even though Friedrich List didn't foresee the role of R&D and of patents at his time, the process of strengthening of absorptive capacities, major advancements in science and "mental capital" realized in Japan during the period between 1975 and 1995 corresponds closely to his descriptions of leapfrogging in Germany and the United States during the nineteenth century.

Manufacturing policy was copied from the example of Germany, which in the late nineteenth and early twentieth centuries provided Meiji Japan with a contemporaneous case study of successful industrialization. From Japan, ideas spread to the Japanese colonies of Korea and Taiwan, and also to China, whose modern development started about two decades behind that of Japan.

(Studwell 2013, 66)

## 15.4. Industrial development in South Korea

South Korea has followed similar policies of industrial development like Japan and realized a comparable sequence of transformation from a low-income country to an advanced high-tech nation within just 30 years. To a certain extent, the development strategies of South Korea and Taiwan are comparable. Both countries were occupied by Japan until 1945 and have later implemented quite ambitious national development policies, partly supported by U.S. development agencies. Both countries were actively trying to learn from Japan's industrialization strategy, and often followed a similar pattern of industry formation.[19] The debate about the East Asian miracle in 1996 has highlighted the comparative growth experience of South Korea and Taiwan. The industrial structure of Korea, with the strong emphasis on large corporations and conglomerates, is somewhat closer to the situation in Japan, while Taiwan has a more differentiated structure of small- and medium-sized family businesses. In the following, we will concentrate on industrial development patterns of South Korea.[20]

### 15.4.1 Early processes of industrialization in South Korea

The first phase of industrial development (up to the early 1960s) involved a period of import substitution, a restructuring of agriculture and the food sector, and a shift towards light industry. More targeted and top-down industrial development was initiated after the military coup by General Park Chung Hee in 1961. His regime implemented a dedicated programme of industry development, with strong emphasis on heavy industries and investment goods as well as on export promotion. General Park was strongly influenced by experiences gained during the Japanese occupation. He emphasized large structures and vertical lines of authority, having been exposed to the huge industrialization drive in Korea and Chinese Manchuria.[21] He was also interested in the histories of rising powers and was knowledgeable about Germany's early industrialization process. During his presidency, he published several books and emphasized "coordination and supervisory guidance, by the state, of mammoth economic strength".[22] This perspective closely corresponds to the concept of administrative guidance used by industrial policy in Japan. He also emphasized the role of industrial leadership and investment in very large infrastructure and manufacturing plants, for which he needed the support of strong business investors.

During the period 1962 to 1979, the South Korean central government followed an active top-down policy of building targeted industries quite similar to earlier Japanese efforts: steel and metalworking, shipbuilding, petrochemicals and automobiles. The emphasis was laid on the formation of large industrial conglomerates, the chaebols, that were somewhat similar to the Japanese Keiretsu structure, and quite in contrast to the small- and medium-sized enterprise-based strategy followed in Taiwan.

The South Korean economy has realized a remarkable growth process over a period of 30 years. The compound average growth rate was almost 9% for the three decades after 1962.[23] GDP per capita was just at a level of 110 $ in 1962, and Korea ranked at position 99 in the world. Forty years later, GDP per capita has attained a level of 26 000 $. South Korea thus represents a remarkable case of a country that has moved from a low-income status to an advanced industrialized nation. In terms of GDP, Korea now ranks at position 13 in the world.[24] The main difference from the growth experience of many other countries that became caught in the middle-income trap, however, is probably that South Korea has managed to implement a process of upgrading since the early 1980s. This provided a major boost to the economy and resulted in the continuous advancement of the national innovation system.

### 15.4.2 *The Schumpeterian growth experience in Korea (1982–2000)*

Korea has gone through quite similar stages of developing the economy and national innovation system as Japan, maybe with a time lag of 15–20 years. While Japan started in the 1970s to invest in more high-technology oriented and capital-intensive industries, this upgrading process was initiated in South Korea during the mid-1980s. The period of the 1970s was still dominated by a big push into heavy and chemical industries (HCI). This includes targeted industries such as steel, petrochemicals, machinery, automobiles and shipbuilding. Economies-of-scale and big structures were supported through import protection, credit allocation, subsidies and the granting of privileges to specific corporations.[25] Giant conglomerates (the chaebol firms) represented the cornerstone of the economy. After having established strengths in traditional sectors like machinery, in shipbuilding, steel and automobiles, these large Korean corporations diversified into high-tech industries like semiconductors, electronics and telecommunications. This process was primarily business driven, but was quite often also initiated through top-down government initiatives. Within quite a short period, and based on smart investment strategies, Korean companies were able to outperform their rivals from Japan and North America. There are excellent case studies on this process in specific fields such as memory semiconductors, flat panel displays, cellular mobile communication and so on.[26] Business firms as well as public institutions went through a process of targeted technology upgrading, initially through emphasizing inward technology transfer. Later, they strongly invested in R&D and indigenous technology, in quite a comparable way as has been described for Japan's uprising in the period 1975 to 1995.

Complementing the diversification strategies of large corporations, the Korean government implemented an ambitious plan for developing the science and technology infrastructure. Since the 1990s, several world class public research centres and universities were established. While R&D expenditures were still far below the OECD average throughout the 1960s and 1970s, an ambitious target was set to increase R&D spending per GDP. National R&D expenditures as a percentage of GDP were later increased from 2.3% in 2000 to 4.4% in 2012.[27] Government funding of research was growing tremendously, and the country invested more and more in basic research, after having been transformed from a catch-up country to a high-tech nation moving closer to the technological frontier.[28]

While Korea's actual strategy closely follows the national innovation system paradigm and Schumpeter's ideas in particular,[29] the earlier policies of industry formation and export promotion were definitely influenced by Friedrich List and his disciples. Many of the ideas of infant industry protection and catch-up development closely followed the earlier recommendations of Alexander Hamilton, Friedrich List and Mathew Carey summarized in Section 15.2. The influence of List may be traced back to Japanese as well as Korean scholars who had studied in Germany. As Robert Wade mentioned in the foreword of the second edition of his book on industrial policy in Asia:

> In Korea List's ideas carried weight. A German disciple advised the Korean government in the late nineteenth century in connection with the government's efforts to stave off Japanese colonialism. In Seoul, in 1979, bookshops around the universities had whole shelves of pirated copies of List's books.[30]
>
> (Wade 2004)

For a more detailed account of List's reception in Korea see Wendler (2004, 285ff.). Rhie Joosung had originally studied in Germany and published a monograph in German on "Friedrich List's Critique on Adam Smith" (Seoul 2000), as well as a number of books and articles in Korean and English. He translated List's "National System of Political Economy" into Korean (published in 1983). Additional articles on List and his concepts of infant industries and protectionism were published in the proceedings of the Symposium of the Korean-German Association for Economics held in Seoul. This event was the only symposium outside of Germany commemorating Friedrich List's 200th birthday. The articles by Ahn (1990) and Besters (1990) in this monograph highlight the strong role of List's ideas on industrial development and trade policy in South Korea.[31]

## 15.5. Industrial development in China

Even though Friedrich List may not have had much direct influence on industrial development in China during the last decades, we may detect a "temporary flirting relationship" between List and academic scholars in China every now and then. Friedrich List was well aware of economic development and trade policy in China, even though he never visited Asia. He had written on the disastrous impact of applying free trade rules to China's external trade with the colonial powers, while Chinese producers inside China had to deal with persisting internal trade barriers. The problems encountered for China were exactly the same that Friedrich List had observed before the formation of the German Zollverein, the trade union established to overcome significant trade barriers that had existed between the independent German states.

The strongest influence of List's ideas came through Chinese academic scholars who had studied for some time in Germany and who were interested in learning about Germany's early industrialization process as well as about Listian economics. Wang Kaihna, with a PhD from Göttingen University, translated List's "National System of Political Economy" into Chinese (published in 1929). Lin Binglin had studied economics in Berlin during the early 1920s and wrote an influential biography on Friedrich List that was published in 1930. Primarily the ideas of catch-up growth and protective tariffs were receiving attention among economists as well as political scientists. Ma Yinchu was a strong supporter of List in China, and he felt that his ideas of manufacturing development and trade protection were particularly suited for China's development strategy. Sun Yatsen, the founding president of the Republican China, was a strong promoter of similar ideas. In his political programme during the 1920s and early 1930s he clearly emphasized industrial development, a strong central government and tariff protection. In this sense, he followed the ideas of Friedrich List and Alexander Hamilton.[32]

In this section on industrial policy and economic development in China, we will concentrate on the period after 1978, and we will describe successive stages of China's remarkable catch-up growth. China has certainly replicated economic development patterns observed in other Asian countries like Japan, South Korea, Taiwan and Singapore. We will focus on the influence of the industrialization strategies of Japan and Korea, which were used as a sort of blueprint for China's economic development agenda. The ideas of Friedrich List were indirectly imported through studying growth processes and by learning from political and administrative experiences in these other Asian countries.

### 15.5.1 Market-based reforms under Deng Xiaoping

Since the beginning of the transformation process from a communist system towards a state-controlled market governance system, initiated during the late 1970s, China has learnt a lot from earlier development strategies in other

Asian countries. There are many similarities, especially with respect to industrial development and trade policies implemented in Japan and South Korea, but also in Taiwan and Singapore. Deng Xiaoping initially implemented a deregulation process within the agricultural sector in 1978. This early experiment resulted in a considerable increase in productivity in this sector. Based on these experiences in agriculture, further deregulation processes were later implemented in the manufacturing sector. Both the primary and the secondary sector developed a self-reinforcing process of growth and productivity increase during the 1980s. This emphasis on strong complementarities between the agricultural sector and manufacturing has also been a striking feature of Japan's development process during the 1950s. Similar processes of co-evolution between agriculture and manufacturing were replicated in South Korea about ten years later. Alexander Hamilton had already written in 1771 "that the aggregate prosperity of manufacturers and the aggregate prosperity of agriculture are intimately interconnected". Friedrich List, in studying early growth processes in Germany and in the United States, called this the "harmonious state of agriculture and manufactures". This synergy effect between agriculture and manufacturing represents a key success factor for the development agenda in China, which had experienced terrible starvation periods during the "great leap forward".[33]

The next phase of development in China involved several reforms of the manufacturing sector, combined with strong growth of export, particularly during the period 1985 to 2000. Similar industries were developed during this period that had been a target of earlier development strategies in Japan and Korea: textiles and clothing, chemistry, steel, automobiles and machinery. China attracted foreign multinationals from other Asian countries as well as from the U.S. and Europe that were primarily interested in low-cost locations. Special economic zones were important hub locations during the early phase of industrialization. Later on, the manufacturing system was strengthened involving four types of entities simultaneously. Large state-owned enterprises (SOE) that still dominate economic sectors of national strategic importance were complemented by joint ventures between foreign enterprises and domestic firms. Newly-established Chinese medium-sized firms were up and coming, enhanced through several regulatory and financial reforms, and, in addition, subsidiaries of foreign companies were seen as an important vehicle to improve the efficiency of the manufacturing sector in China.[34]

Through the tightly-controlled formation of all four elements, Chinese planners were closely watching processes of inward technology transfer and the continuous strengthening of home-grown large firms as well as small- and medium-sized enterprises (SMEs). This targeted and sector-specific process of inviting foreign multinationals while nurturing ever-stronger domestic corporations was also characteristic of Japan's industrial development strategy. In a similar way, Korea was developing large chaebol corporations into strong national, and later global, players. This emphasis on home-grown corporations that can later transform into strong multinational players is also something that distinguishes China and other Asian nations from development strategies observed in countries that primarily rely on foreign-based multinationals.

Even though Friedrich List never really played a strong role during these first two phases of post-communist industrial development, there was some revival of Listian ideas around the turn of the new century. During the time when China became involved in negotiations for membership in the World Trade Organization (WTO), economists and planners were strongly debating the pros and cons of joining this transnational organization. While central government was emphasizing the advantage of stronger participation in the world trading system, some Chinese scholars were promoting stronger indigenous growth of the up and coming Chinese industry, and thus argued against free trade. Friedrich List's critique of Adam Smith and the argument of infant-industry protection became a big issue, and several influential economists were arguing in favour of new forms of protectionism. Even though China eventually joined the WTO in 2004, many important mechanisms that are not in line with WTO rules such as local content requirements, non-access of foreign firms to specific industries and so on, still remain in place.

### 15.5.2 The next phase of upgrading in China after 2000

Since about 2000, a new phase of industrial development has become implemented in China. The new industrial upgrading process is very similar to strategies implemented in Japan during the 1980s and in Korea during the 1990s. From being a manufacturing base for low- or medium-tech products, China strongly attempts to transform into a more advanced export and production system. The National Medium- and Long-Term Plan of 2006 emphasizes the restructuring of the R&D system, stronger endogenous capabilities as well as the growth of selected high-tech industries for the period 2006 to 2020. National R&D expenditures were stepped up from a level of 0.9% of GDP in the year 2000 to about 2.0% in 2012. China has now reached a level that Japan had attained in 1975 and Korea by the year 1990.

Similar to these Asian "benchmark countries", China places a strong emphasis on R&D in the business sector: three quarters of national R&D expenditures are performed by business enterprises, and business R&D expenditures were growing at a remarkable rate of 26% per annum during the period 2000 to 2010.[35] At the same time, China is now also strengthening the public research system and has strongly emphasized scientific publications and the role of intellectual property generated in China ("indigenous innovation"). Similar to the development observed in Japan and Korea between 1985 and 2000, China is now trying to overcome the former status of licensee and the dependence on inward knowledge-transfer. The country attempts to overcome the strong dominance of foreign multinationals from advanced nations. While foreign applicants still accounted for three quarters of patents granted by the Chinese Patent Office (SIPO) in 2002, their share was reduced to 37% in 2010.[36]

China's economic development strategy has resulted in a remarkable 30-year growth process, hardly ever realized by any other country in the world before. Only a few Asian countries have realized similar growth rates over a period of 25 years, but had to adapt to somewhat lower levels of growth since about 1997. In most cases, such persistent growth processes were attained partly through dirigistic policies and through temporary protection envisaged by earlier writings of Friedrich List. Even though China has more recently accepted growth rates in the range of 6 to 7% per year, some of the policies implemented may be seen as a role model for other emerging countries.[37]

## 15.6. Summary conclusions

In this article, we have tried to describe the formation of ideas about successful development of industries and nation states. List's conviction was that free trade in a world with great disparities between nation states can lead to increasing segregation between rich and poor countries.[38] Most advanced countries, according to List, had gone through an early period of accumulation and institution-building before they were strong enough to successfully compete in highly competitive world markets. The three Asian countries analyzed (Japan, South Korea and China) are excellent examples of latecomer nations that have implemented a long-lasting and remarkable growth process. Japan and South Korea have become advanced countries with high levels of GDP per capital. China has followed comparable development strategies even though the country is still in a middle-income stage.

We have shown how Japan has learnt from American and German growth experiences during the initial industrialization process in both countries. Some of the ideas were influenced by Friedrich List and other economists of the German historical school. Economic development has involved continuous learning, institution-building and the adaption of ideas to the particular Asian context. Strategies of industry formation and of government–industry interaction were then transferred to South Korea and other "Asian Tiger countries" during the 1970s and 1980s. Later on, China learnt from experiences in Japan, Korea and Taiwan and has applied quite similar policies. During this process, Listian ideas became applied and revived, either explicitly or in an unconscious or tacit form. We have tried to trace back whether Asian scholars and political decision-makers were aware of the origin of these ideas and of List's main contributions and arguments.

Neo-Schumpeterian economics and the national systems of innovation (NIS) paradigm have received wide-spread attention in all three countries in Asia. The most prominent authors within this line of innovation research have explicitly pointed out the early influence of Friedrich List's work:

The first systematic and theoretically based attempt to focus upon national systems of innovation goes back to Friedrich List. ... List makes a distinction between Adam Smith's "cosmopolitan" approach which puts the focus upon exchange and allocation and his own national perspective focusing on the development of productive forces. ... The only element of List's quite complex and rich ... analysis still left in modern economics is his argument for protection of "infant industries". His analysis went much further, however, indicating the need for governmental responsibility for education and training and for developing the infrastructure supporting industrial development. Actually, he sketched some of the most important elements of the national system of innovation.

(Lundvall 1993, 16)

Even though List concentrated on the "National System of Political Economy", his early writings already contained important elements of more refined "National Systems of Innovation" in a nutshell. The integrated and modern NIS paradigm was developed much later by Nelson (1993), Lundvall (1993) and Freeman 1987). Even though all three authors highlight his early contribution, Friedrich List should receive much greater attention, particular in up and coming countries in Asia and in other parts of the world.

## Notes

1 Development policies in South America and Africa were often characterized by early successes during the 1960s and 70s, but have often failed to realize sustainable long-term growth. Typical examples are Argentina, Brazil, Ghana and Nigeria, to name just a few.
2 Alexander Hamilton, Report on Manufactures (1791).
3 List, Outlines of American Political Economy, Letter 2, 1827.
4 See our description in the section on economic development in China in Section 15.5.
5 See Carey (1822) and Carey (1833).
6 For an interesting description of Carey's ideas and his influence on Friedrich List see Liebig (2004, 192ff.).
7 See Studwell (2013, 72) for a comparison of the Zaibatsu structure and Germany's cartel policies. For a description of the role of big industries in the large continental powers see Trebilcock 1982).
8 Wakayama (1871) adapted the ideas of Henry Charles Carey, the son of Mathew Carey, and argued for a more protectionist Japanese foreign trade policy.
9 Between 1878 and 1893, Hermann Rösler acted as a legal advisor to Japanese government. See Taiyoji (1970).
10 Karl Rathgen acted as advisor in Japan between 1882 and 1890, as well as Georg Michaelis between 1885 and 1889. See Taiyoji (1970).
11 This classification corresponds to the view of my Korean colleagues Bogang Jun and Tai-Yoo Kim (2015), who differentiate between the expansionary reproduction system (with innovation) and the basic reproduction system (without innovation). See our description of Korea's industrial development in Section 15.4.

12 Administrative guidance (gyōsei shidō) is a typical mechanism through which government agencies exert (more informal than formal) influence on managerial actions. It is sometimes called the "lifted eyebrow" through which administrators try to attain compliance. If necessary, it will be backed up by credible threats of retaliation against the noncompliant party. See Lepou (1978) and Weinstein (1995) for a description of administrative guidance in Japan.

13 For a detailed analysis of MITI's policy during the early period see Johnson (1982), Vogel (1980) and MITI (1980, 1983). In later periods, with a strengthened and more self-conscious Japanese industry, MITI (and today the METI) has become somewhat less influential.

14 See Maddison (1969, 50f), and the empirical studies by Ohkawa et al. (1957; Ohkawa, Shinohara and Umemura 1965).

15 See Soete, Verspagen and Weel (2010) and Wendler (1989).

16 See Odagiri and Goto (1993), Goto and Wakasugi (1988), and Freeman (1987, Chapter 2) for an excellent survey on the formation of the Japanese national innovation system.

17 See Freeman (1987, 39ff.) on this reversal of technology flow and the increased presence of Japanese inventors in international patenting.

18 See Jones (1985) for the case of the Japanese automobile industry, and Sciberras (1981) on consumer electronics as well as Peck and Goto (1981).

19 In Japanese studies on economic development in Asia, this sequence of industrial investment strategies has been interpreted as the "Flying geese model". This "Flying geese model" was originally developed by the Japanese economist Akamatsu. See Akamatsu (1961) and Reinert (2007, 141).

20 An excellent study of Taiwan's industrial development strategy was published by Wade (2004).

21 See Studwell (2013, 75). Park served as a lieutenant in the Japanese colonial military and oversaw part of this industrialization drive.

22 Park (1962), Our Nation's Path: Ideology for Social Reconstruction, Seoul, cited from the second edition Park (1970, 218).

23 See Wade (2004) who emphasizes that Korea's long-term growth performance was even stronger than for Japan, which was growing at 7% in the quarter century after 1960. See Schlossstein (2009) for a study on South Korea´s innovation-led growth.

24 World Bank (2015). The gross domestic product of Korea has reached a level of 1,400 billion U.S. dollars.

25 See Amsden (1989), Wade (2004) and Timmer (1999, 127).

26 See Hobday (1997) for an interesting account of the development strategy of the Korean and Tiwanese electronics industry.

27 OECD, Main Science and Technology Indicators 2014/2.

28 Between 2000 and 2012, basic research expenditures as per cent of GDP increased from 0.3% to 0.8% (OECD, MSTI 2014/2, Table 6).

29 See Lee's study of Neo-Schumpeterian industrial policy followed by Korea (Lee 2013).

30 Wade (2004, xlvi). Wade also mentions that List was totally forgotten in the U.S.: "When I tried to borrow List's book from the MIT library in 1993, I had to wait several days for a copy to be brought in from a remote warehouse for rarely borrowed books. My copy had last been borrowed in 1966" (ibid).

31 For a more detailed description of Friedrich List's influence on development economics in Korea see Jun, Gerybadze and Kim (2016), Jun and Kim (2015) and Kim and Heshmati (2013).

32 For a more detailed analysis of List's influence on Chinese scholars and political decision makers see Mei Junjie's contribution in this volume as well as Wendler (2004).
33 See also Studwell (2013), Wade (2004) and Naughton (2007).
34 See also EFI (2012, 105) for an analysis of China's industrial development strategy.
35 See OECD MSTI, Volume 2014/2 and the analysis in EFI (2012, 105).
36 See EFI (2012, Table 11) and SIPO (2010).
37 This has led to a debate on a new form of "Beijing consensus" seen by some countries as an alternative to the "Washington consensus" that has dominated development economics during the last decades. See Halper (2010).
38 See List (1841) and the surveys on List's ideas on development economics in Senghaas (2014) and Reinert (2007).

# References

Ahn, D.S. (1990), Der neue Protectionismus und der Erziehungsgedanke von Friedrich List, *Zeitschrift für Wirtschaftswissenschaften*, Seoul, 124–140.

Akamatsu, K. (1961), A Theory of Unbalanced Growth in the World Economy, *Weltwirtschaftliches Archiv*, No. 86, 196–217.

Amsden, A. (1989), *Asia's Next Giant: South Korea and Late Industrialization*. Oxford and New York: Oxford University Press.

Besters, H. (1990), 'Handel und Protectionismus – Die Bedeutung zwischen alten und neuen Industriestaaten', *Zeitschrift für Wirtschaftswissenschaften*, Seoul, 141–157.

Carey, M. (1822), *Essays on Political Economy; Or the Most Certain Means of Promoting the Wealth, Power, Resources and Happiness of Nations: Applied Particularly to the United States*. Philadelphia, PA: H.C. Carey & I. Lea.

Carey, M. (1833), *Displaying the Rise and Progress of the Tariff System of the United States: The Various Efforts Made from the Year 1819, to Establish the Protecting System; Its Final Triumph in the Tariff of 1824*. Philadelphia, PA: Thomas B. Town.

Carey, M. (1876), *Commerce, Christianity and Civilization vs. British Free Trade. Letters in Reply to the London Times*. Philadelphia, PA: Collins.

EFI. (2012), *Research, Innovation and Technological Performance in Germany, Report of the Expert Commission of Research and Innovation to the German Federal Government, Chapter B5 on Innovation in China*. Berlin: EFI.

Freeman, C. (1987), *Technology Policy and Economic Performance: Lessons from Japan*. London: Pinter.

Goto, A. and Wakasugi, R. (1988), Technology Policy, in: Komiya, M., Okuno, M., Suzumura, K. (Eds.), *Industrial Policy of Japan*, 183–204, Tokyo: Academic Press, Inc.

Halper, S. (2010), *The Beijing Consensus. How China's Authoritarian Model will Dominate the Twenty-First Century*. New York: Basic Books.

Hamilton, A. (1791), *Report on the Subject of Manufactures, Reprinted in Taussig, F. (Ed.), State Papers and Speeches on the Tariff*. Cambridge, MA: Harvard University Press.

Hobday, M. (1997), *Innovation in East Asia: The Challenge to Japan*. Cheltenham, UK: Edward Elgar.

Johnson, C. (1982), *MITI and the Japanese Miracle: The Growth of Industrial Policy, 1925–1975*. Palo Alto, CA.: Stanford University Press.

Jones, D.T. (1985), Vehicles, in: Freeman, C. (Ed.), *Technological Trends and Employment, Vol. 4: Engineering and Vehicles*. Aldershot: Gower.

Jun, B., Gerybadze, A. and Kim, T.Y. (2016), The Legacy of Friedrich List: The Expansive Reproduction System and the Korean History of Industrialization, Paper presented at the International Schumpeter Society (ISS), Montreal, July 2013.

Jun, B. and Kim, T.Y. (2015), *A Neo-Schumpeterian Perspective on the Analytical Macroeconomic Framework: The Expanded Reproduction System*. Maastricht: UNU-MERIT.

Kim, L. (1993), National Systems of Industrial Innovation: Dynamics of Capability Building in Korea, in: Nelson, R.R. (Ed.), *National Innovation Systems: A Comparative Analysis*. New York, 357–383.

Kim, L. (1999), Building Technological Capability for Industrialization: Analytical Frameworks and Korea's Experience', *Industrial and Corporate Change*, No. 8 (1), 111–136.

Kim, T.Y. and Heshmati, A. (2013), *Economic Growth: The New Perspectives for Theory and Practice*. Berlin: Springer.

Lee, K. (2013), *Schumpeterian Analysis of Economic Catch-up. Knowledge, Path-Creation and the Middle-Income Trap*. Cambridge, UK: Cambridge University Press.

Lepou, J.M. (1978), Administrative Guidance in Japan, *The Fletcher Forum*, vol. 2, 139–157.

Liebig, M. (1998), Friedrich List and the American System of Political Economy, *EIR* 25, No. 12, 25–29.

Liebig, M. (2004), *Friedrich List and the "American System" of Economics, Commentary to the New Edition of List on "Outlines of American Political Economy"*. Wiesbaden, 155–257.

Lim, Y. (1995), 'Industrial Policy for Technological Learning: A Hypothesis and Korean Evidence', ISS Working Paper Series, Vol. 201, The Hague: Institute of Social Studies ((ISS, June 1995)).

List, F. (1827), *Outlines of American Political Economy*. First published by Samuel Parker, Philadelphia, Penn., newly edited and published by Michael Liebig (2004), Wiesbaden: Dr. Böttinger Verlag.

List, F. (1841), *Das Nationale System der Politischen Ökonomie*. Stuttgart-Tübingen: Cotta Verlag. English Translation: *The National System of Political Economy*, London: Longman 1885.

Lundvall, B.A. (1993), *National Systems of Innovation. Towards a Theory of Innovation and Interactive Learning*. London: Pinter.

Maddison, A. (1969), *Economic Growth in Japan and the USSR*. New York: Norton.

MITI. (1980), *The Vision of MITI Policies in the1980s, Report of the Industrial Structures Council*. Tokyo: Ministry of International Trade and Industry (MITI).

MITI. (1983), *Features of the Industrial Policy of Japan, Japan Reporting*. Tokyo: MITI Information Office.

Naughton, B. (2007), *The Chinese Economy. Transitions and Growth*. Cambridge, MA: MIT Press.

Nelson, R. R. (Ed.). (1993), *National Innovation Systems: A Comparative Analysis*, New York.

Odagiri, H., Goto, A. (1993), The Japanese System of Innovation: Past, Present, and Future, in: Nelson, R.R. (Ed.), *National Innovation Systems: A Comparative Analysis*, 76–114, New York and Oxford: Oxford University Press

OECD. (2014), *Main Science and Technology Indicators.* Volume 2014, Issue 2, Paris: OECD Publishing.

Ohkawa, K., Shinohara, M., Umemura, M. (Eds.). (1965), *Estimates of Long-term Economic Statistics of Japan since 1868.* 13 Volumes, Tokyo: Toyo Keizei Shinposha, 1965 onwards.

Ohkawa, K. and Associates (1957), *The Growth Rate of the Japanese Economy since 1878.* Tokyo: Kinokuniya.

Park, C.H. (1962), *Our Nations's Path*, Seoul: Dong-a Publishing Co.

Park, C.H. (1970), *The Country, The Revolution and I.* Seoul: Hollym Corporations.

Park, T.G. (2004), Discourse on Economic Development in 1950 and its Origin, *Comparative Korean Studies*, No. 12 (1), 97–135.

Peck, M.J., Goto, A. (1981), Technology and Economic Growth: The Case of Japan, *Research Policy*, No. 10 (3), 222–243.

Raymond, D. (1820), *Thoughts on Political Economy.* Baltimore: Fielding Lucas.

Reinert, E. (2007), *How Rich Countries got Rich - and Why Poor Countries Stay Poor.* London: Constable & Robinson.

Rhie, J. (2000), *Friedrich List's Kritik an Adam Smith.* Seoul: Sungshinjoza Universitätsverlag.

Schlossstein, D.F. (2009), *Institutional Change in Upstream Innovation Governance: The Case of Korea.* Frankfurt/Main: Peter Lang.

Sciberras, E. (1981), 'Technical Innovation and International Competitiveness in the Television Industry, *Omega*, 585–596.

Senghaas, D. (2014), Friedrich List: Rückblick für die Zukunft, *Reutlinger Geschichtsblätter*, Neue Folge 53, 85–97.

SIPO (2010), *Annual Report, State Intellectual Property Office of the People's Republic of China.* Beijing: SIPO.

Soete, L, Verspagen, B. and Weel, B. (2010), Systems of Innovation, in: Hall, B., Rosenberg, N. (Eds.), *Handbook of the Economics of Innovation*, Vol. 2, 1159–1180, Amsterdam: Elsevier.

Studwell, J. (2013), *How Asia Works. Success and Failure in the World's Most Dynamic Region.* London: Pacific Books.

Taiyoji, J. (1970), 'Die geistigen Grundlagen der industriellen Entwicklung in Japan', in: Ikeda, K., Kato, Y., Taiyoji, J. (Eds.), *Die industrielle Entwicklung in Japan unter besonderer Berücksichtigung seiner Wirtschafts- und Finanzpolitik*, Berlin: Duncker & Humblot, 167–228.

Timmer, M. (1999), *The Dynamics of Asian Manufacturing. A Comparative Perspective 1963–1993.* Eindhoven: Eindhoven Center for Innovation Studies.

Trebilcock, C. (1982), *The Industrialisation of the Continental Powers, 1780–1914.* London: Longman

Vogel, E.F. (1980), *Japan as No. 1.* Tokyo: Tuttle.

Wade, R., (2004), *Governing the Market: Economic Theory and the Role of Government in East Asian Industrialization*, 2nd Edition, Princeton, NJ: Princeton University Press.

Wakayama, G. (1871), *Reflections on Protective Tariffs*, Tokyo. (In Japanese)

Weinstein, D.E. (1995), Evaluating Administrative Guidance and Cartels in Japan (1957–1988), *Journal of the Japanese and International Economies*, No. 9, 200–223.

Wendler, E. (1989), *Friedrich List. Politische Wirkungsgeschichte des Vordenkers der europäischen Integration.* München: Oldenbourg.

Wendler, E. (2004), *Durch Wohlstand zur Freiheit. Neues zum Leben und Werk von Friedrich List.* Baden-Baden: Nomos.

World Bank. (2015), *Gross Domestic Product by Country 2014, and GDP per Capita by Country.* Washington, DC: World Development Indicators Database, July.

# Index

Printed in the United States
by Baker & Taylor Publisher Services